To our dear Friend

Bob Jones

The Book of Mormon
contains the Secret of a
happy Life

These Scriptures are
Eternal & many Friendships
are meant to Endure.
May you find Joy & Happiness
the rest of your days and enjoy
Health & Happiness for years to
come with your Sweetheart Carol —
Your Eternal Friends
ETERNAL

Nick & Paula

July 2004

AS ONE CRYING FROM THE DUST

BOOK OF MORMON MESSAGES FOR TODAY

AS ONE CRYING FROM THE DUST

BRENT L. TOP

BOOKCRAFT
SALT LAKE CITY, UTAH

Library of Congress Catalog Card Number 99-73576
ISBN 1-57008-681-8

First Printing, 1999

Printed in the United States of America

Behold, the Lord hath shown unto me great and marvelous things concerning that which must shortly come, at that day when these things shall come forth among you.

Behold, I speak unto you as if ye were present, and yet ye are not. But behold, Jesus Christ hath shown you unto me, and I know your doing.

—*Mormon 8:34–35*

CONTENTS

PREFACE

Several years ago I was a coordinator for the Church Educational System in northern Virginia. In addition to supervising seminary instruction, I regularly taught institute classes at various colleges and universities in that area. During one academic year the curriculum I chose to teach was the Book of Mormon. I had taught the Book of Mormon before, but that particular year was different. To say it was merely different or unique would be a gross understatement. It was one of the most remarkable years of my life—one of the most rewarding and growing teaching experiences of my career. My life was profoundly changed in many respects because of that year of deep personal study of the Book of Mormon in preparation for teaching my classes.

On many occasions I would come home from my Book of Mormon class and excitedly tell my wife about the new insights I had gained into particular passages. In many respects it was almost like I was reading the Book of Mormon for the very first time. "I know that wasn't there the last time I read this book," I would often joke with my students when we would discover some "new" doctrinal gem in the scriptures. I came to realize what was so different this time as I approached the Book of

Mormon, different not only in my teaching but also in my personal study. As I listened to the October 1986 general conference, the opening words of Elder Henry B. Eyring, then a counselor in the Presiding Bishopric, struck a particularly familiar chord with me:

> At the close of the last general conference, President Benson said this: "I bless you with increased *understanding* of the Book of Mormon. I promise you that from this moment forward, if we will daily sup from its pages and abide by its precepts, God will pour out upon each child of Zion and the Church a blessing hitherto unknown" (in Conference Report, Apr. 1986, p. 100; or *Ensign*, May 1986, p. 78).
>
> I bear my testimony that I have been blessed as He promised, and I have seen new blessings come to people I love. I am grateful that God honors the promises he makes through his prophet. (In Conference Report, October 1986, p. 94.)

"That's it!" I said to my wife. "Now I know why I have been feeling the way I have recently about the Book of Mormon." I recognized, as Elder Eyring had stated, that I was the beneficiary of a prophetic priesthood blessing. My understanding of the Book of Mormon had indeed increased. My love for that book had greatly grown, and blessings had indeed flowed into my life and into our family. It could not have been any more real than if President Ezra Taft Benson had laid his hands personally upon my head and uttered that magnificent promise just to me alone.

In the many years since that event, I have witnessed many times and still witness blessings in my life not only as a result of *increased understanding* of the Book of Mormon but also from the power that comes through it. President Benson so testified:

> It is not just that the Book of Mormon teaches us truth, though it indeed does that. It is not just that the Book of Mormon bears testimony of Christ, though it indeed does that, too. But there is something more. There is a power in the book which will begin to flow into your lives the moment you begin a serious study of the book. You will find greater power to resist

temptation. You will find the power to avoid deception. You will find the power to stay on the strait and narrow path. The scriptures are called "the words of life" (see D&C 84:85), and nowhere is that more true than it is of the Book of Mormon. When you begin to hunger and thirst after those words, you will find life in greater and greater abundance. (*A Witness and a Warning* [Salt Lake City: Deseret Book, 1988], pp. 21–22.)

My life has been blessed immeasurably by the Book of Mormon, by both the instruction that comes from the doctrines and the spiritual transformation that comes by the Spirit that attends it.

The purpose of this book is not to be a commentary or doctrinal exposition but rather to focus on those timeless themes that the Book of Mormon contains. Those themes, laced with pure doctrine and testimony and illustrated with examples of application, can help us with our own unique challenges. The prophets have testified that the Book of Mormon was written for us and our day. "We must make the Book of Mormon a center focus of study [because] it was written for our day," President Benson testified:

The Nephites never had the book; neither did the Lamanites of ancient times. It was meant for us. Mormon wrote near the end of the Nephite civilization. Under the inspiration of God, who sees all things from the beginning, he abridged centuries of records, choosing the stories, speeches, and events *that would be most helpful to us.*

Each of the major writers of the Book of Mormon testified that he wrote for future generations. . . .

Mormon himself said, "Yea, I speak unto you, ye remnant of the house of Israel" (Mormon 7:1). And Moroni, the last of the inspired writers, actually saw our day and time. "Behold," he said, "the Lord hath shown unto me great and marvelous things concerning that which must shortly come, at that day when these things shall come forth among you.

Behold I speak unto you as if ye were present, and yet ye are not. But behold, Jesus Christ hath shown you unto me, and I know your doing" (Mormon 8:34–35).

If they saw our day and chose those things which would be of greatest worth to us, is not that how we should study the Book of Mormon? We should constantly ask ourselves, "Why did the Lord inspire Mormon (or Moroni or Alma) to include that in his record? What lesson can I learn from that to help me live in this day and age?"

And there is example after example of how that question will be answered. . . .

. . . Can anyone doubt that this book was meant for us and that in it we find great power, great comfort, and great protection? (In Conference Report, October 1986, pp. 5, 6; emphasis added.)

The prophet Isaiah prophesied that the Book of Mormon would speak to the peoples of the last days "out of the ground" and the message of that book would be like a "familiar spirit" that whispers to us "out of the dust" (see Isaiah 29:4). Truly the Book of Mormon is filled with "voices from the dust"—testimonies and messages from the past, written for our day. Nephi, like Mormon after him, knew that his record, containing his prophecies, teachings, and testimony, was to be preserved for those who would read it many centuries in the future. "And now, my beloved brethren, all those who are of the house of Israel, and all ye ends of the earth, I speak unto you as the voice of one crying from the dust," he wrote as he closed his record. "Farewell until that great day shall come." (2 Nephi 33:13.) Moroni likewise closed his record with a similar witness and yet another reminder that the "voices from the dust" are for our blessing and benefit today. We will be condemned if we do not listen and respond to these words that "whisper out of the dust."

And I exhort you to remember these things; for the time speedily cometh that ye shall know that I lie not, for ye shall see me at the bar of God; and the Lord God will say unto you: Did I not declare my words unto you, which were written by this man, like as one crying from the dead, yea, even as one speaking out of the dust? (Moroni 10:27.)

It is a lifetime pursuit to hear and hearken to all those "voices from the dust" contained in the Book of Mormon— messages of real people directed to us today. Nephi "liken[ed] all scriptures" unto his family, "that it might be for our profit and learning" (see 1 Nephi 19:23). That is precisely what I have tried to do in this book—"liken the scriptures" to our own needs and circumstances. In the end it is my objective to show how the timeless themes of the Book of Mormon are truly relevant today and can and do and will give us greater power to resist today's many temptations, greater comfort amidst today's many trials and troubles, and greater strength to keep the commandments of God.

I am the first to admit that not all of the relevant themes and important applications that could be gleaned from the Book of Mormon are included in this work. I have merely tried to include some of my favorites—those that have blessed my life most profoundly and personally. No one can glean all that the Book of Mormon has to offer. The more I study that great book, the more I find "new" lessons to liken to myself and the more I discover its doctrines are deeper and broader and clearer than I ever could imagine. It is a new adventure for me each time I read and study this great book. I rediscover relevant messages for my life, profound doctrines that enlighten my mind anew, and I experience again the thrill of the "power of the word." It need never grow old to us. It must never become irrelevant to us. It must always be studied, pondered, and applied. As Elder Neal A. Maxwell so eloquently stated:

> The Book of Mormon will be with us "as long as the earth shall stand." We need all that time to explore it, for the book is like a vast mansion with gardens, towers, courtyards, and wings. There are rooms yet to be entered, with flaming fireplaces waiting to warm us. The rooms glimpsed so far contain further furnishings and rich detail yet to be savored, but decor dating from Eden is evident. There are panels inlaid with incredible insights, particularly insights about the great question. Yet we as Church members sometimes behave like hurried tourists, scarcely venturing beyond

the entry hall. *(The Neal A. Maxwell Quote Book*, ed. Cory H. Maxwell [Salt Lake City: Bookcraft, 1997], p. 33.)

It is impossible to "outgrow" the Book of Mormon. It is impossible to have discovered all of its "secret treasures."

It is my hope that the words that follow instruct, inspire, and testify. But more than that, that they serve as a catalyst for even greater study of the Book of Mormon, which in turn will bring new insights and renewed strength that only the Spirit of the Lord can give. I pray that this book, in some small measure, will contribute to all that read it a renewed "adventure" with the inexhaustible Book of Mormon. And from that adventure it is my deepest desire that each of us, reader and author alike, will learn that we lift the condemnation—that spiritual darkness that has been upon us for neglecting the Book of Mormon—not just by reading it more but also by living its teachings more completely (see D&C 84:55–57).

Although I have a fervent testimony of the Book of Mormon and feel that the words I have written in this book are true and reflect my love for the restored gospel, I do not speak for The Church of Jesus Christ of Latter-day Saints. This book has been a private endeavor—a labor of love for the Book of Mormon—and although I am indebted to the insight and help of many others, I alone am responsible for the conclusions drawn from the scriptural evidence cited. No one should construe this book to be an official publication of either the Church or Brigham Young University. With that disclaimer, however, I earnestly hope that my feeble efforts will build faith, increase understanding of and appreciation for the timeless relevance of the Book of Mormon, and most of all that it may invite the reader "to seek this Jesus of whom the prophets and apostles have written" (Ether 12:41).

And they did press forward through the mist of darkness, clinging to the rod of iron, even until they did come forth and partake of the fruit of the tree.
—1 NEPHI 8:24

CHAPTER 1

HOLD TO THE ROD

Only a few times in my lifetime have I really feared for my life. Each time it had to do with driving in hazardous conditions with limited visibility. One particular episode is still fresh in my memory—indelibly engraven upon my mind because of the sheer terror I felt.

Utah's Wasatch Front is notorious for cold-air inversions in the winter that trap fog in the valleys. A few years ago this phenomenon was especially bad and we had nearly six straight weeks of heavy fog in the valleys. One winter night, as my wife and I were driving home from an appointment, we encountered a fog bank like no other I had ever experienced, though I had driven in fog many times—even fairly dense fog. As we entered the fog it was as if the lights went out. We could only see our headlights bouncing off the fog. We could not discern headlights in front or back of us and couldn't even make out street lights or stop lights. The visibility was reduced to a few feet, and at times we could see only a few inches in front of us. Even on a main road we had traveled hundreds of times before, we were totally disoriented and had no idea where we were.

I was afraid to stop the car, for fear we would be struck from behind; and anyway there was no safe place to pull over. We were torn between the fear of plowing into the back of a car in front of us and the fear that we would drive off the road into the river that ran alongside the highway. At one point I tried sticking my head out the window in hopes of seeing better. Of course, that didn't work. The only thing that seemed to help us at all was to open the two front doors slightly and look at the lines on the road. I watched for the striped center line between glances in front for danger. Wendy watched the line at the edge of the road from her passenger seat, letting me know how close I was to the edge. All we could do was to keep going, however slowly, keeping the car centered between the two lines.

We didn't know exactly how far we had yet to drive, and we had no idea if or when the fog bank would lift. We did know, however, that if we could just stay on the road we would find our way home. So though we were terrified, we kept going at our excruciatingly slow pace. Yet we felt hope and some degree of safety as we kept our gaze on the painted lines in the road.

I have driven in all kinds of weather conditions, including icy roads, snow blizzards, even amidst the torrential rains and raging winds of a hurricane. But I have never been more afraid than I was when I felt totally lost and vulnerable in that fog bank. I think I gained from that a greater understanding of what Lehi and Nephi must have meant when they used the term "mists of darkness" in their descriptions of Lehi's dream of the tree of life. Perhaps that kind of darkness, like my experience with the fog, is not just the absence of light but rather a frightening, oppressive, and disorienting kind of darkness that not only may cause a person to lose his way but also exposes one to many other unseen and unforeseen dangers. Thank goodness for those guiding lines down the center and along the edge of the road.

Both Lehi and Nephi saw in their respective visions several things, each spiritually significant in its own right. There were the "dark and dreary wilderness" (1 Nephi 8:4) and the "large and spacious field" (1 Nephi 8:9)—representing our sojourn in mortality. The center of their attention was a tree, whose fruit, Lehi said, "was desirable to make one happy" (1 Nephi 8:10). He had never encountered such a delightful and desirable fruit. It not only tasted good—"it was most sweet, above all that I ever before tasted"—but it was also remarkable in appearance: "the fruit thereof was white, to exceed all the whiteness that I had ever seen" (1 Nephi 8:11). Nephi later tells us that the tree is the "love of God, which sheddeth itself abroad in the hearts of the children of men" and is "the most desirable above all things" (1 Nephi 11:22) and the "most joyous to the soul" (1 Nephi 11:23). There is a "strait and narrow path" (1 Nephi 8:20) that leads to the ultimate goal of eternal life, which Christ offers us.

However, standing in the way of the tree of life were several "hazards," as it were, described by Lehi and interpreted by Nephi. There was a river of filthy waters that ran alongside and dangerously close to the pathway leading to the tree. Nephi learned that this river was the "depths of hell" (1 Nephi 12:16)—an "awful gulf, which separated the wicked from the tree of life" (1 Nephi 15:28). In addition, Lehi described "a mist of darkness; yea, even an exceedingly great mist of darkness, insomuch that they who had commenced in the path did lose their way, that they wandered off and were lost" (1 Nephi 8:23).

As if these "hazards" were not enough, Lehi saw another "hazard"—not as obviously hazardous as the others, but dangerous nonetheless. In a "great and spacious building" were numerous people, both old and young, in the finest of apparel. Lehi observed that these people "were in the attitude of mocking and pointing their fingers" at those who sought to partake of the fruit of the tree of life (1 Nephi 8:26–27). This kind of ridicule and mocking certainly doesn't seem as scary as a blinding mist of darkness or a raging river of filthy waters. It was, however, a "hazard" of distraction and sidetracking. Those who paid more attention to the sideshows in the "great and spacious building" than to the "tree of life" lost their focus, as well as their grip on the "rod of iron." Lehi observed that these "were ashamed, because of those that were scoffing at them; and they fell away into forbidden paths and were lost" (1 Nephi 8:28; see also vss. 31–34). Nephi tells us that the "great and spacious building" and the mocking inhabitants thereof represent the "pride of the world," the "vain imaginations and the pride of the children of men" (1 Nephi 11:35–36; 12:18). Pride, vanity, and trusting in the arm of flesh pose a different kind of threat—distraction and diversion.

In some ways Lehi and Nephi's visions seem to describe a "spiritual obstacle course," with various "hazards," as well as important "helps" all along the way. The desired end of the course is the "fruit of the tree of life"—exaltation and a fulness of joy. This allegorical dream or vision provides us with valuable instruction in safely navigating the obstacle course of life—a course in "spiritual survival."

When I think of an obstacle course I am reminded of the medieval "gauntlet." It is from this "trial by ordeal," practiced in the Middle Ages, that we get the commonly used phrase "running the gauntlet." During that period of time, some convicted criminals were given the option to run the gauntlet rather than be immediately executed. The gauntlet, run between two lines of spectators, some armed with clubs, contained all kinds of life-threatening hazards. One wrong step or move could result in the runner being crushed, cut in halves, or dropped into a pit of ferocious, flesh-eating creatures. If, however, he successfully navigated this deadly obstacle course, he was absolved of his crimes and granted his freedom.

Both cheering and jeering came from the spectators of this "trial by ordeal." Some desired the person to successfully run the gauntlet and would offer encouragement, shout warnings, and seek to guide him to safety. On the other hand some spectators thirsted for blood and violence and would do anything and everything to get the runner to make a fatal mistake—jeering, beating, throwing things (which added another "hazard"), giving false directions—anything that would cause him to become distracted and lose concentration. The runner, of course, was totally on his own. His ultimate success—life and liberty—or his ultimate failure, dismemberment and death, depended solely on his own efforts.

While it is possible to see parallels between "running the gauntlet" and our spiritual obstacle course, as it were, described in the Book of Mormon, there is one major difference. Despite all the "hazards"—the mists of darkness, the awful gulf, the raging river, the strange roads, and the scoffings from the spacious building—we are not left alone to find our own way to the tree of life. The Lord has mercifully provided not only directions, but also an iron rod that leads directly through all the obstacles to our desired destination—the fruit, more desirable than all other things, that fills the soul with joy. The path is marked. The way is provided. We are not alone.

THE IRON ROD IS THE WORD OF GOD

From the time I was in Primary I have loved singing that familiar Latter-day Saint hymn "The Iron Rod," a Book of Mormon anthem.

> To Nephi, seer of olden time,
> A vision came from God,
> Wherein the holy word sublime
> Was shown an iron rod.
>
> While on our journey here below,
> Beneath temptation's pow'r,
> Through mists of darkness we must go,
> In peril ev'ry hour.
>
> And when temptation's pow'r is nigh,
> Our pathway clouded o'er,
> Upon the rod we can rely,
> And heaven's aid implore.
>
> Hold to the rod, the iron rod;
> 'Tis strong, and bright, and true.
> The iron rod is the word of God;
> 'Twill safely guide us through.
> (*Hymns*, no. 274.)

Whether Primary children can read Nephi's words or not, they all know that "the iron rod is the word of God." But ask the question, "What is the word of God?" and you may get several answers—such as scriptures, words of the prophets, answers to prayers, and promptings of the Holy Ghost. Each of these is, indeed, the word of God and each is vital to our "spiritual survival" in the "hazards" of mortality. And each points us to something that is essential if we are to partake of the fruit that "was desirable to make one happy" (1 Nephi 8:10).

The scriptures, as the "word of God," teach us doctrine, inspire us; but even more important, they testify of Christ. "Search the scriptures," the Savior declared, "for in them ye think ye have eternal life: and they are they which testify of me" (John 5:39). The title page of the Book of Mormon itself declares that one purpose of the book is the "convincing of the Jew and Gentile that Jesus is the Christ."

The words of the living prophets invite us to come to Christ and partake of His salvation. As His "special witnesses" they teach and testify of His doctrines and divinity. As John the Baptist did in the days of the Savior, their mission is to direct us to Christ. We cannot receive Him without receiving them (see D&C 84:35–38). The Holy Ghost is a testator, witnessing of the Father and the Son. The Holy Ghost teaches us "all things what [we] should do" (see 2 Nephi 32:3–5). His words to us are the "words of Christ" (see 2 Nephi 31:13; 32:2–3). The rod of iron represents the words of God, as found in each of these sources. The fulness of the gospel of Jesus Christ is also called "the word of God" (see JST John 1:1).

John, the beloved Apostle of the Lord Jesus Christ, begins his Gospel—his testimonial record—with, "In the beginning was the Word, and the Word was with God, and the Word was God" (John 1:1). Later in the same chapter, John identifies the Word of God. "And the Word was made flesh, and dwelt among us, (and we beheld his glory, the glory as of the only begotten of the Father,) full of grace and truth" (John 1:14). The Joseph Smith Translation of this chapter adds this insight: "For in the beginning was the Word, even the Son, who is made flesh, and sent unto us by the will of the Father. And as many as believe on his name shall receive of his fullness. And of his fullness have all we received, even immortality and eternal life, through his grace." (JST John 1:16.) In the book of Revelation, John described a symbolic vision of Christ's ultimate triumph over evil:

> And I saw heaven opened, and behold a white horse; and he that sat upon him is called Faithful and True, and in righteousness he doth judge and make war;
>
> His eyes as a flame of fire; and he had on his head many crowns; and a name written, that no man knew, but himself.
>
> And he is clothed with a vesture dipped in blood; and his name is called The Word of God.
>
> And the armies which were in heaven followed him upon white horses, clothed in fine linen, white and clean.
>
> And out of his mouth proceedeth the word of God, and with it he will smite the nations; and he will rule them with the word of his mouth; and he treadeth the winepress in the fierceness and wrath of Almighty God.
>
> And he hath on a vesture, and on his thigh a name written, KING OF KINGS, AND LORD OF LORDS. (JST Revelation 19:11–16.)

As I study the relevant scriptures I am inclined to believe that Lehi and Nephi are teaching us that the rod of iron is in very deed The Word of God, even Jesus Christ. Others may see in the word of God (meaning basically the gospel concepts) the deliberate symbolic strength of iron that will unfailingly support us on the often difficult road to Christ. The difference of interpretation perhaps matters little, since either way the intent is the same—to bring us to Christ. The words of God, the scriptures, the prophets, the Spirit, the fulness of the gospel—all lead us to Him, and He gives us the fruit of the tree of life.

What a difference it should make to us to know that amidst all the "mists of darkness" in the world and the scoffing and mockings from the "great and spacious building" we are not left to find our way alone! The Savior—The Word of God—is not merely the white line on the side of the road that we must keep our eye on when in a spiritual fog bank. He is not merely point-ing directions and shouting encouragement from the shade of the tree of life. As the iron rod, Jesus is truly not only our desired end but also our very protection—the very means whereby we are saved. He is "The Way." From the vision received by Lehi and Nephi we learn that all that is required of us in order to partake of the fruit of the tree is to be "pressing forward . . . clinging to the rod of iron" (1 Nephi 8:24). We can lose our way only if we let go of the rod.

CLINGING TO THE ROD OF IRON: RELYING WHOLLY ON THE MERITS OF CHRIST

Lehi saw the faithful "pressing forward" to the tree of life, secured by continual "clinging to the rod of iron." It is not, however, just in Lehi's vision or Nephi's interpretations that we see this important principle taught and illustrated. All through-out the Book of Mormon we are taught that the joyous, desir-able fruit of eternal life is obtained only by continual faith and faithfulness—clinging to the rod and trusting in the Savior's atoning sacrifice. "Whoso would hearken unto the word of God; and would hold fast unto it," Nephi taught, "they would never perish; neither could the temptations and the fiery darts of the adversary overpower them unto blindness, to lead them away to destruction" (1 Nephi 15:24). Only Christ can give us that kind of power and protection. Clinging to the iron rod, "pressing for-ward," is described by Nephi as "relying wholly upon the merits of him who is mighty to save" (2 Nephi 31:19; see also Moroni 6:4).

> Wherefore, ye must press forward with a steadfastness in Christ, having a perfect brightness of hope, and a love of God and of all men. Wherefore, if ye shall press forward, feasting upon the word of Christ, and endure to the end, behold, thus saith the Father: Ye shall have eternal life.
> And now, behold, my beloved brethren, this is the way; and there is none other way nor name given under heaven whereby man can be saved in the kingdom of God. (2 Nephi 31:20–21.)

The Book of Mormon was written for our day. The mists of darkness seen by Lehi and Nephi surround us continually, threatening each of us with a total loss of spiritual direction. The "hazards" of today's society come in a variety of ways. Sometimes the most dangerous are not as obvious or as visible as a dense fog bank. Amidst these dangers it is imperative that we cling to the rod of iron. We do that today by "relying wholly upon the merits of him who is mighty to save" (2 Nephi 31:19) to help us resist temptations, endure tribulation, overcome inadequacies, and become and remain clean from the sins of the world.

Resisting Temptation

"The more I see of life," stated President Harold B. Lee, "the more I am convinced that we must impress you young people with the awfulness of sin rather than content ourselves with merely teaching the way of repentance" (*Decisions for Successful Living* [Salt Lake City: Deseret Book Co., 1973], p. 88). While it is true that there are great and glorious blessings associated with repentance, we cannot neglect the even greater blessings that flow from resisting temptations and continuing in righteousness. The atonement of Jesus Christ not only provides the *end* of our salvation but also the *means*. It is true as well with repentance and righteousness. Not only does Christ's atoning blood cleanse us from our sins, upon conditions of faith and repentance, but so too does faith in the Lord Jesus Christ provide us with the means—the strength and inspiration to resist the "fiery darts of the adversary" (1 Nephi 15:24). Referring to the Nephites, Alma taught his son Helaman:

Teach them an everlasting hatred against sin and iniquity.
    Preach unto them repentance, and faith on the Lord Jesus Christ; teach them to humble themselves and to be meek and lowly in heart; teach them to withstand every temptation of the devil, with their faith on the Lord Jesus Christ.
    Teach them to never be weary of good works, but to be meek and lowly in heart; for such shall find rest to their souls.

O, remember, my son, and learn wisdom in thy youth; yea, learn in thy youth to keep the commandments of God. (Alma 37:32–35.)

Many times we set up "rules" or "guidelines" to help our children resist temptation, such as, "Don't be out late," or "Don't date until you're sixteen!" or "Don't go any place where the Spirit can't go!" Such rules can be helpful safety precautions in and of themselves, but they are not the surest means whereby one gains strength to resist temptation. More powerful than any "rule" or catchy saying is faith in the saving power of Christ. If I want to help my own children resist temptation, the best thing I can do is to help instill in them greater faith in the Lord—greater love for the Savior, greater understanding of and appreciation for the Atonement. The same works for me as it does for them. The "shield of faith" is the "armor of God" that will provide us with a spiritual protective coating that repels the myriad spiritual "fiery darts" we face today.

The prophet Alma powerfully taught us the way by which faith to resist temptations can be cultivated in our own lives:

And now, my brethren, I wish from the inmost part of my heart, yea, with great anxiety even unto pain, that ye would hearken unto my words, and cast off your sins, and not procrastinate the day of your repentance;

But that ye would humble yourselves before the Lord, and call on his holy name, and watch and pray continually, that ye may not be tempted above that which ye can bear, and thus be led by the Holy Spirit, becoming humble, meek, submissive, patient, full of love and all long-suffering;

Having faith on the Lord; having a hope that ye shall receive eternal life; having the love of God always in your hearts, that ye may be lifted up at the last day and enter into his rest (Alma 13:27–29).

When we have in our hearts that kind of faith in and that kind of love for the Lord Jesus Christ—a faith cultivated by prayer, study, and obedience—we will have strength to resist temptations and escape Satan's grasp. In this way, holding on to the "rod of iron" allows us to be safely secure even while temptations in the world, like the "mists of darkness," encompass us.

Enduring Tribulations

As a natural course of our mortal existence each of us faces challenges that have the potential to cause our grip on the iron rod to become loosened. These "hazards" are different from the temptations of Satan that are so prevalent in life. They may not, by themselves, destroy us, but they can cause us to let go of the very rod that keeps us safe. When we let go or carelessly loosen our grip, we become far more susceptible to the other "hazards" Lehi and Nephi saw—the "awful gulf," the "great and spacious building," and the "strange roads." These challenges, characterized in the scriptures as "mighty winds" and "shafts in the whirlwind" (see Helaman 5:12), are the physical and emotional trials and tribulations that test our faith and tutor us in the "school of hard knocks."

The atonement of Jesus Christ not only will swallow up the adversities and afflictions that come to mortals by reason of the fall of Adam but will also provide the means whereby we are able to faithfully endure them. His is the "pleasing word of God" which "healeth the wounded soul" (Jacob 2:8). He can be the source of our strength to endure and our comfort in times of need. However, we must "press forward with a steadfastness in Christ." It requires just as much fortitude and faith to cling to the "iron rod" amidst pain and problems as it does when encompassed about by temptations.

We gain increased strength to endure when we understand that, despite our periodic feelings that no one can comprehend the depths of our sufferings, Jesus understands and can lift those burdens because, in some unfathomable way, He bore them long before we did. Alma testified:

And he shall go forth, suffering pains and afflictions and temptations of every kind; and this that the word might be fulfilled which saith he will take upon him the pains and the sicknesses of his people.

And he will take upon him death, that he may loose the bands of death which bind his people; and he will take upon him their infirmities, that his bowels may be filled with mercy, according to the flesh, that he may know how to succor his people according to their infirmities. (Alma 7:11–12.)

"Though he slay me, yet will I trust in him," Job declared (Job 13:15). If we will cling to the iron rod with Job-like faith we need not despair or feel forsaken. We are only lost to such despondency and hopelessness if we let go, for the Savior will not let go of us. "Life has its share of some fear and some failure," Elder Jeffrey R. Holland explained. "Sometimes things fall short, don't quite measure up."

Sometimes in both personal and public life, we are seemingly left without strength to go on. Sometimes people fail us, or economies and circumstance fail us, and life with its hardship and heartache can leave us feeling very alone.

But when such difficult moments come to us, I testify that there is one thing which will never, ever fail us. One thing alone will stand the test of all time, of all tribulation, all trouble, and all transgression. One thing only never faileth—and that is the pure love of Christ. . . .

Only the pure love of Christ will see us through. It is Christ's love which suffereth long, and is kind. It is Christ's love which is not puffed up nor easily provoked. Only his pure love enables him—and us—to bear all things, believe all things, hope all things, and endure all things. (Moroni 7:45.) . . .

I testify that having loved us who are in the world, Christ loves us to the end. His pure love never fails us. Not now. Not ever. Not ever. ("'He Loved Them unto the End,'" *Ensign,* November 1989, p. 26.)

Overcoming Inadequacies

We encounter, almost daily, what Lehi and Nephi saw in vision. It may not appear to us to be quite the same as they described their experience, but the principle is still the same. All around us are people—some we know and many we don't—"in the attitude of mocking" and scoffing at those who seek to cling to the iron rod. The content of their mockings is as diverse as the people of the world and the myriad philosophies they espouse. The danger to us is that, in our quest to partake of the fruit of the tree of life, we can become sidetracked or distracted. Even a momentary lapse could cause us to let go of the safety of the iron rod. Often those worldly scoffings come—whether internally or externally—in the form of thoughts or statements such as these:

— You're not smart enough or talented enough or spiritual enough to be successful!
— You'll never make it! You might as well give up and give in now!
— I have nothing to offer to the kingdom. I'm just a nobody!
— Nobody likes you! You're such a "goody-goody"!
— I'm so afraid to fail! I'll probably just mess things up!

Feelings of inadequacy and unworthiness come to all of us to some degree or another and at some time or other. Often such feelings come when we are striving most earnestly to "press forward" in the kingdom of God. It is easy to feel beaten down emotionally, give up, and then be drawn to those in that "great and spacious building" and ultimately accept its lies. The Book of Mormon prophets knew that these "hazards" would be real among the Latter-day Saints in the last days, so they taught and testified to us of the lifting, encouraging power of the Atonement. Nephi is a prime example. He not only taught us how to deal with the vexing feelings of inadequacy and personal worthlessness, but also he lived it. Even as great a spiritual giant as we see him to be, he didn't always feel that way. More than anyone else he recognized his weaknesses and limitations, but he wouldn't give in to them.

> Nevertheless, notwithstanding the great goodness of the Lord, in showing me his great and marvelous works, my heart exclaimeth: O wretched man that I am! Yea, my heart sorroweth because of my flesh; my soul grieveth because of mine iniquities.
>
> I am encompassed about, because of the temptations and the sins which do so easily beset me.
>
> And when I desire to rejoice, my heart groaneth because of my sins; nevertheless, *I know in whom I have trusted.*
>
> My God hath been my support. . . .
>
> He hath filled me with his love, even unto the consuming of my flesh. . . .
>
> O then, if I have seen so great things, if the Lord in his condescension unto the children of men hath visited men in so much mercy, why should my heart weep and my soul linger in the valley of sorrow, and my flesh waste away, and my strength slacken, because of mine afflictions? . . .
>
> Rejoice, O my heart, and cry unto the Lord, and say: O Lord, I will praise thee forever; yea, my soul will rejoice in thee, my God, and the rock of my salvation. . . .
>
> O Lord, I have trusted in thee, and I will trust in thee forever. I will not put my trust in the arm of flesh; for I know that cursed is he that putteth his trust in the arm of flesh. (2 Nephi 4:17–20, 21, 26, 30, 34; emphasis added.)

Similarly, Enoch felt feelings of total inadequacy upon his call to preach repentance unto a wicked and hardened people. "I . . . am but a lad," Enoch protested, "and all the people hate me; for I am slow of speech; wherefore am I thy servant?" (Moses 6:31.) The Lord promised Enoch that despite his limitations and weaknesses, if he would keep the commandments and open his mouth as the Lord commanded, he would be blessed beyond measure. "Behold my Spirit is upon you, wherefore all thy words will I justify," God promised (Moses 6:34). Despite his mortal frailties Enoch did a remarkable work in teaching his people, performed wondrous miracles, and established Zion—the City of Holiness (Moses 7:19). This did not result because of his physical strength or any extraordinary abilities, but because of the Lord. We too have that kind of assurance of spiritual magnification beyond our mere mortal means, if we will follow the Lord's admonition to Enoch—"walk with me" (Moses 6:34).

When we care more about what the Lord thinks and less about what the mockers in the "great and spacious building" say, we cling to the iron rod. When we put our trust in His strengths instead of focusing so much on our own weaknesses, we "press forward." Only when we rely "wholly upon the merits of him who is mighty to save" will we be protected—securely attached to the iron rod—from the insults and taunts of the world. "He who in the first estate was thrust down delights in having us put ourselves down," wrote Elder Neal A. Maxwell. "Self-contempt is of Satan; there is none of it in heaven." (*Notwithstanding My Weakness* [Salt Lake City: Deseret Book, 1981], p. 10.)

A walk through any major bookstore today will show the success that the mocking and scoffing from those in the "great and spacious building" has had on the emotional well-being of mankind. The self-help section is filled with stacks and stacks of books—all written to help modern man overcome all kinds of inadequacies, weaknesses, and emotional baggage. I am certainly not saying that such books are bad or even unhelpful, for they are not. But the plethora of such books shows how modern society is under assault, not only by temptations but also by all kinds of worldly philosophies and "alternate voices" selling their man-made solutions. The Book of Mormon, written for our day, foresaw such a dilemma and provides us with a spiritual solution. Holding to the rod not only keeps us safe from the "mists of darkness" of temptations but also provides us with the very means whereby we can overcome feelings of inadequacy and personal weakness. "And if men come unto me," the Lord revealed to Moroni, "I will show unto them their weakness. I give unto men weakness that they may be humble; and my grace is sufficient for all men that humble themselves before me; for if they humble themselves before me, and have faith in me, then will I make weak things become strong unto them." (Ether 12:27.)

More powerful than any kind of system of self-help is the Savior of the world. Clinging to the "rod of iron," which is "the word of God," relying wholly upon the atonement of Christ—this allows His grace to strengthen and help us in ways that we simply do not have power to do for ourselves. Holding to the rod allows the Savior to insulate us from the constant refrains of spiritual scoffing and emotional "put-downs" we face in our world today. "In a day when the winds are blowing and the waves beating upon our ship, how do we navigate our course safely into the peaceful harbor?" asked Robert L. Millet.

> What must we do to have our Savior pilot us through tempestuous seas? Amidst the babble of voices—enticing voices which threaten to lead us into forbidden paths or which beckon us to labor in secondary causes—how do the Saints of the Most High know the Way, live the Truth, and gain that Life which is abundant? . . .
>
> . . . We must learn to trust him more, in the arm of flesh less. We must learn to rely on him more, and on man-made solutions less. We must learn to surrender our burdens to him more. We must learn and work to our limits and then be willing to seek that grace or enabling power which will make up the difference, that sacred power which indeed makes all the difference! (*Life in Christ* [Salt Lake City: Bookcraft, 1990], p. 108.)

Becoming Clean Through the Blood of the Lamb

While watching the summer Olympics on television, I was amused to see that many of the male swimmers had the head completely shaven. At first I thought it was just some sort of fad, but I learned differently as the television commentators discussed this phenomenon. They explained that these swimmers not only had shaved their heads but also their arms, legs, and chests. "How weird," I thought. "What good would that do?"

The answer was that there was indeed an important purpose in their shaving their bodies. It was to give them a competitive edge. Even the relatively small amounts of hair on the body would serve as a resistance against the water and could slow the swimmer down—even if it was only for a fraction of a second. By the shaving they were eliminating something that might possibly prevent them from winning the race. To these highly trained athletes there was no such thing as "just a little thing." Anything that could thwart them in their quest for the gold medal must be discarded.

Just as with swimmers, designers of automobiles, airplanes, and ocean liners always seek to eliminate undesired resistance. Resistance, whatever the source, reduces efficiency at best and can actually prove dangerous or life-threatening at worst. The same principle applies in the spiritual field. Extra resistance or unnecessary weight slows our progress. The additional "drag" of sin can weigh us down, cause us to lose the strength needed to "press forward," and may actually cause us to lose our grip on the iron rod. President Thomas S. Monson, illustrating how the burden of sin can weigh us down, brought to our attention a comparison of sins to barnacles that attach themselves to the hulls of ships.

> Ship captains . . . know that as their ships travel the seas, a curious salt water shellfish called a barnacle fastens itself to the hull and stays there for the rest of its life, surrounding itself with a rock-like shell. As more and more barnacles attach themselves, they increase the ship's drag, slow its progress, decrease its efficiency.
>
> Periodically, the ship must go into dry dock, where with great effort the barnacles are chiseled or scraped off. It's a difficult, expensive process that ties up the ship for days. . . .
>
> Sins are like those barnacles. Hardly anyone goes through life without picking up some. They increase the drag, slow our progress, decrease our efficiency. Unrepented, building up one on another, they can eventually sink us. ("Harbor of Forgiveness," *Church News,* 30 January 1988, p. 16; as quoted by

Thomas S. Monson in "You Make a Difference," *Ensign*, May 1988, p. 42.)

As we "press forward" in our quest to partake of the fruit of the tree of life, each of us will pick up his share of the barnacles of sin. This extra baggage adds even more spiritual resistance against us, threatening our safety and our ultimate arrival at the desired destination, the tree of life. We cannot let go of the iron rod to personally pick off all of the barnacles, but by our continually clinging to the rod we are exercising the means the Savior provides whereby we can be cleansed while we are yet continuing our journey. By our "relying wholly upon him who is mighty to save," the spiritual resistance caused by sins can be eliminated. Truly, Jesus—the Word of God—is not only the *end* of our spiritual cleansing but also the very *means*. As Amulek taught:

> And behold, this is the whole meaning of the law, every whit pointing to that great and last sacrifice; and that great and last sacrifice will be the Son of God, yea, infinite and eternal.
> And thus, he shall bring salvation to all those who shall believe on his name; this being the intent of this last sacrifice, to bring about the bowels of mercy, which overpowereth justice, and bringeth about means unto men that they may have faith unto repentance. (Alma 34:15.)

We inevitably encounter many "hazards" as we journey through life, seeking to do God's will and serve Him in faithfulness. As Nephi and Lehi saw, the "mists of darkness" encompass us round about like the most dense fog bank possible. At every possible turn there are other "hazards" that can destroy us. The means is provided, however, that can safely secure us against such danger. It is much more than merely staring at the lines in the road while encompassed in fog. It is the iron rod—the word of God. It is more than reading scriptures, saying prayers, or going to church, as important as each of these is, that will protect us against the evils of the world. "The iron rod is the word of God; 'Twill safely guide us through."

Yea, we see that whosoever will may lay hold upon the word of God, which is quick and powerful, which shall divide asunder all the cunning and the snares and the wiles of the devil, and lead the man of Christ in a strait and narrow course across that everlasting gulf of misery which is prepared to engulf the wicked—

And land their souls, yea, their immortal souls, at the right hand of God in the kingdom of heaven, to sit down with Abraham, and Isaac, and with Jacob, and with all our holy fathers, to go no more out. (Helaman 3:29–30.)

If ye will not harden your hearts, and ask me in faith,
believing that ye shall receive, with diligence in
keeping my commandments, surely these things
shall be made known unto you.
—1 Nephi 15:11

CHAPTER 2

HAVE YOU INQUIRED OF THE LORD?

During a sacrament meeting a while back, one of my teenage children got up in the middle of the meeting to leave the chapel. "Where are you going?" I whispered.

"Home!" came the emphatic and not-so-quiet response.

"Why?" I probed. "Are you sick?"

"No," came the response. "I just want to go home. I'm bored!"

Well, that wasn't good enough for me. Boredom is not justification for skipping meetings or leaving church early. If it were, I could have had far more time on my hands through the years. I tried as delicately yet firmly as I could, as a father, to get that message across to my daughter, recognizing that I had to do this well since all of the other children were watching closely to see how I would handle the situation.

"Just sit down, the meeting won't last much longer," I said, trying to "buy time" and avoid a scene in the chapel. "You can't go home now. We will go home together as a family." I thought that would let her know that I wasn't about to let her go home on grounds of boredom. When she ignored what I said and continued trying to leave the meeting, I became a little more firm. "Sit down," I said, taking her by the arm and guiding her back to her seat. "You are not going home now!" I thought that would solve the problem once and for all, but I was wrong. As she pulled away she said something that left me speechless—stunned and saddened.

"I'm going home!" she insisted. "I don't believe any of this stuff, anyway!"

When we got home that day there really wasn't much said. I think everyone felt a little uncomfortable and at a loss what to say and do. In the days and weeks that followed, however, our daughter would make comments or ask questions that opened the door for discussion concerning her unbelief. It soon became apparent that most of her doubts were the result of ideas and questions that some of her friends had put in her head. Some of these friends didn't have an understanding of gospel principles, nor did they share in our values and standards of behavior. As a result their "philosophies" were often nothing more than rationalizations for unacceptable behavior. Whenever my daughter asked what she thought was a "hard question" about the Church or a gospel principle, I gave her an answer from the scriptures and from gospel teachings. "You have been taught this all of your life," I would remind her. "You know the answers to these questions."

The longer we talked, the more I realized that this matter was not about my expounding doctrine, exposing the fallacy of her notions, or knocking down her "straw man" theories and ideas. It was not about my *giving her answers*. It was all about her *finding her own answers*. I could provide information and guide her in the right direction, but only she could find the answers. I couldn't do it for her, nor should I try.

When the immediate "parental panic" of this experience subsided a little, I was able to think more clearly and see how my daughter's doubts and questions were part of a spiritual metamorphosis that most of us go through in some way and at some time or another. I was reminded of experiences in my own life, as well as in the lives of others I knew and loved, who came to find the answers that now provide a sure foundation for life.

While we were living out of the country for a while, my children were enrolled in a private English-speaking school with students of many nationalities, races, and religious beliefs. Unbeknown to my wife and me, our teenage son's belief system was being challenged by some of his classmates, and one class and teacher in particular. It may have been the first time in his young life that he had ever faced any serious questioning of his beliefs. Some of the young people in the school were children of clergy or missionaries of other faiths. As a result they often challenged my son, as one of the handful of Mormons in the school, with many of the typical anti-Mormon questions and arguments. My other children more or less ignored these challenges, but my son was bothered by them and could not ignore or totally dismiss the questions. In the school library there was a rather impressive section of anti-Mormon books and pamphlets. The more my son was challenged, the more he read the anti-Mormon propaganda, which resulted in even more questions. The more he questioned, the more he desired to know the answers.

If I had known at the time what he was being exposed to I probably would have been stricken with "parental panic" and feared for his spiritual safety. Fortunately, however, I was somewhat in the dark and could only offer help rather than get in the way of his quest. He was assigned in his religion class to make a presentation on Mormonism (since he was the only LDS student in the class). This became the vehicle to take him on his quest for answers to the questions and issues that hounded him. Without telling me that he had struggled with his own doubts and questions, he asked me to help with his presentation by referring him to good LDS sources that would be able to answer the traditional anti-Mormon attacks. From his preparation for the presentation he not only found answers to the challenging questions his non-believing friends would throw at him, but he also found answers to his own questions. From his questions came not only answers but also, more important, faith and testimony.

As I reflected on his experience and the growth that came to him as a result of this "crisis of faith" I was able relax a little concerning my daughter's doubts. It didn't mean she was on the "high road to apostasy" or that she was repudiating her parents' teachings. It did mean, however, that she was at a crossroads in her life—reaching beyond the spiritual comforts of her home to find answers to her questions and to build on her own foundation. With that in mind I assured her that there is nothing inherently wrong with having doubts or asking tough questions. Often it is part of the process of growth. There is, however, a difference between *faithless cynicism* and *faithful questioning*. The one is stagnant and yields no answers and spiritual growth, whereas the other is dynamic and leads one to find the right answers—leads one to the very Source of Truth Himself.

FAITHFUL QUESTIONING

When it comes to the gospel, all too often we equate questions or doubts with faithlessness at best, and something akin to apostasy at worst. Such should not be the case. We would expect an investigator to approach the gospel brim full of questions, doubts, and even a healthy dose of skepticism. We expect that and teach the questioner how to get beyond that point. But when it comes to a lifelong member of the Church, particularly if that person is our own child, we usually view such doubts and questions with alarm. We tend to think something is seriously wrong with the questioner. In reality it is neither the questions nor the doubts that should be feared, but rather what one does with them. "Doubt, unless transmuted into inquiry, has no value or worth in the world," Elder John A. Widtsoe wrote. "A lasting doubt implies an unwillingness on the part of the individual to seek the solution of his problem, or a fear to face the truth." (*Evidences and Reconciliations* [Salt Lake City: Bookcraft, 1987], p. 31.)

The Book of Mormon gives us a classic example of the difference between faithful inquiry and lasting doubt. We often think of Laman and Lemuel as doubters and murmurers—and rightfully so. But we hardly ever think of Nephi as having his own struggle with doubts and questions. In Nephi, we tend to look at the *end product* of his spiritual strength and firm testimony, but we often overlook the *process* by which those traits came.

Undoubtedly, with all his dad's visions and prophesying about the destruction of Jerusalem Nephi must have wondered what was going on. He must have asked why it was necessary to leave the comforts of his home, the familiarity of his land, language, and culture to live in a dangerous desert for an unknown period of time until the family arrived at some yet-unknown destination. Like any teenager facing the trauma of moving away from friends and family he might never again see, Nephi may have experienced emotions of sadness and confusion. Out in the desert "I did cry unto the Lord," Nephi tells us: "and behold he did visit me, and did soften my heart that I did believe all the words which had been spoken by my father; wherefore, I did not rebel against him like unto my brothers" (1 Nephi 2:16). How could his heart be softened if it hadn't been somewhat hardened by questions and concerns?

The difference between Nephi and his brethren is clearly stated and demonstrated over and over again. Nephi had questions and doubts, but went to the Lord for answers. Laman and Lemuel would not. When they murmured against Lehi as "a visionary man" and complained that they could not understand the meaning of their father's visions and prophecies, Nephi challenged them with a simple yet profound question: "Have ye inquired of the Lord?" (1 Nephi 15:8.) It was a straightforward question—no hidden agendas, no tricks or traps. It came from a pure heart who had found answers to his own questions by doing the very thing he asked of his brothers. Laman and Lemuel's response to Nephi's question perhaps explains better than other means the difference between faithful questioning and faithless cynicism. "We have not," they answered, "for the Lord maketh no such thing known unto us" (1 Nephi 15:9). At which, Nephi could only ask: "How is it that ye will perish, because of the hardness of your hearts?" (1 Nephi 15:10.)

As can be seen in the different approaches to doubts and questions, the real issue is not the doubts but what is to be done about them. I need not become paralyzed with "parental panic" when a child shocks me with the statement, "I do not believe any of that stuff." There need not be despair with the appearance of doubt. I only become alarmed when a daughter makes no effort to find out for herself the truthfulness of gospel principles. My job is not to answer all her questions but to ask, as Nephi did, "Have you inquired of the Lord?" and then teach how one comes to know the truth.

"Doubt is not wrong unless it becomes an end of life. It rises to high dignity when it becomes an active search for, and practice of truth," Elder Widtsoe wrote. "Doubt which immediately leads to honest inquiry, and thereby removes itself, is wholesome. But that doubt which feeds and grows upon itself, and, with stubborn indolence, breeds more doubt, is evil." He further counseled:

> The strong man is not afraid to say, "I do not know"; the weak man simpers and answers, "I doubt." Doubt, unless transmuted into inquiry, has no value or worth in the world. . . . To take pride in being a doubter, without earnestly seeking to remove the doubt, is to reveal shallowness of thought and purpose.
>
> Perhaps you are questioning the correctness of a gospel principle. Call it doubt if you prefer. Proceed to take it out of the region of doubt by examination and practice. Soon it will be understood, or left with the many things not yet within the reach of man. But remember: failure to understand one principle does not vitiate other principles. When proved false, one doctrine may cast distrust upon other doctrines, but the others must be tested for their own correctness.
>
> Doubt of the right kind—that is, honest questioning—leads to faith. Such doubt impels men to inquiry which always opens the door to truth. . . .
>
> On the other hand, the stagnant doubter, one content with himself, unwilling to make the effort, to pay the price of discovery, inevitably reaches unbelief and miry darkness. His doubts

grow like poisonous mushrooms in the dim shadows of his mental and spiritual chambers. At last, blind like the mole in his burrow, he usually substitutes ridicule for reason, and indolence for labor. The simplest truth is worth the sum of all such doubts. He joins the unhappy army of doubters who, weakened by their doubts, have at all periods of human history allowed others, men of faith, to move the world into increasing light. (*Evidences and Reconciliations*, pp. 32–33.)

EXPERIMENTING UPON THE WORD:
HOW TO OBTAIN KNOWLEDGE OF SPIRITUAL THINGS

A scientist discovers truth through an objective scientific method of observation, theorizing, and experimentation. Coming to know the spiritual truths of the gospel and the mind and will of the Lord also requires experimentation. Yet just as revelation differs from reason, the scientific method and the spiritual method of inquiry also differ. While they share some things in common, there are fundamental differences that cannot be ignored. Each has its own set of rules for discovery of truth. And ignorance or direct violation of those rules will compromise the experiment and yield faulty or false results that hence cannot be trusted. In contrast to the scientific method that requires a degree of detachment on the part of the researcher, the spiritual method requires direct and personal involvement in the experiment. One cannot come to know God and His truths by detached observation.

With hardened hearts, Laman and Lemuel personified this kind of detachment. They murmured against their father's prophecies, refusing to believe that God could reveal such things to man. They *would not* believe, and therefore, *did not* even try to dispel their doubts through personal involvement in spiritual inquiry. Nephi, on the other hand, approached his quest with spiritual hunger. "For it came to pass after I had *desired* to know the things that my father had seen," Nephi recorded, "and *believing* that the Lord was able to make them known unto me, as I sat *pondering* in mine heart I was caught away in the Spirit of the Lord" (1 Nephi 11:1; emphasis added).

To the Zoramites who desired to develop faith in God, Alma illustrated and amplified this process of inquiry when he admonished them to "awake and arouse your faculties, even to an experiment upon my words" (Alma 32:27). Alma's suggested experiment follows much the same pattern that Nephi had followed in his own quest—desire, belief, pondering. But he adds (v. 37) an additional element—*nourish*. These elements comprise the divinely designated process—the "rules" of faithful questioning, the "imperatives" of spiritual inquiry—*desire, belief, pondering,* and *nourishment.* Just as it was for Nephi and Alma, so it is for us today in our own quest for knowledge of spiritual things.

Desire

"Even if you can no more than desire to believe," Alma taught the Zoramites concerning this experiment, "let this desire work in you, even until you believe in a manner that ye can give place for a portion of my words" (Alma 32:27). Desire is the first step for almost everything in life. A great talent or skill cannot be acquired and fully developed devoid of some degree of desire. Often athletic events are won as much by desire as by skill. "They wanted it more than we did" is a phrase that reflects this "will to win." Even in the more significant struggles of life, desire makes a difference—oftentimes all the difference. A struggling marriage cannot be repaired unless both partners desire to save it. An addict—whether his problem be alcohol, drugs, or some other addiction—must first desire to be liberated. A distraught person who threatens or attempts suicide cannot be permanently helped until the desire to live is stronger than the desire to die.

The story (perhaps apocryphal) is often told of the Greek philosopher who was approached by a pupil desiring the key to acquiring great knowledge. Suddenly the old sage pushed the young student's head under water and held it there until the youth was desperately seeking to extricate himself. When the old tutor finally let go of the young man's head, the latter angrily asked, "Why did you do that?" The great philosopher then proceeded to teach the young student the very lesson he had so earnestly sought. "When you desire knowledge as much as you desired air when your head was under water, you will not need to ask me. You will gain the knowledge that you seek."

The greater the desire for something, the greater the price one is willing to pay for it. The greater the desire, the greater is the effort to acquire what is desired. For this reason, having genuine desire to gain a testimony and know the truths of the gospel not only is the first step but also it actually facilitates all the other steps. "Desire must precede all else in the winning of a testimony," Elder John A. Widtsoe wrote. "The desire to know the truth of the gospel must be insistent, constant, overwhelming, burning. It must be a driving force. A 'devil-may-care' attitude will not do. Otherwise, the seeker will not pay the required price for the testimony." (*Evidences and Reconciliations*, p. 16.)

The great spiritual giants of both the past and the present all started their journey to knowledge, wisdom, and spirituality with the same first step—desire.

> I, Nephi, being exceedingly young . . . and also having great desires to know of the mysteries of God . . . (1 Nephi 2:16).

> I, Abraham, . . . sought for the blessings of the fathers . . . desiring also to be one who possessed great knowledge, and to be a greater follower of righteousness, and to possess a greater knowledge (Abraham 1:1–2).

> If any person needed wisdom from God, I did; for how to act I did not know, and unless I could get more wisdom than I then had, I would never know. . . .
> At length I came to the conclusion that I must either remain in darkness and confusion, or else I must do as James directs, that is, ask of God. I at length came to the determination to "ask of God," concluding that if he gave wisdom to them that lacked wisdom, and would give liberally, and not upbraid, I might venture. (Joseph Smith—History 1:12–13.)

Even if it is merely the earliest inklings of desire to know, this spiritual sojourn of eternal importance always begins with that first step.

Believe That You Will Receive

Akin to desire is belief that God will reveal truth to you. Having a believing heart is as essential to the process of spiritual inquiry as the mind is. Nephi was able not only to see what his father had seen in vision, but also to receive further heavenly instruction. His desire to know coupled with his belief that God could and would indeed reveal truth to him yielded the desired results. "And blessed art thou, Nephi, because thou believest in the Son of the most high God; wherefore, thou shalt behold the things which thou hast desired" (1 Nephi 11:6).

In contrast, Laman and Lemuel *would not believe*. And as a result *they could not know*. They were like a scientist or researcher who determines the conclusions before the experiment is conducted and results are analyzed. Such unbelieving people will not honestly evaluate the evidence and will dismiss all findings contrary to their own preconceptions, even in the presence of overwhelming evidence of truth. A researcher guilty of such a sham would characterize the worst of intellectual dishonesty—a total defiance of established rules of inquiry. His conclusions would be thrown out and his future "research" would be viewed with suspicion.

The same principles apply in the spiritual realm. One cannot thumb his nose at the very process of spiritual inquiry and the divinely established "rules" for revelation and yet be trusted to come up with the right answers. "Ironically, many refuse to examine gospel truths simply because of *how* God reveals them," Elder Neal A. Maxwell profoundly observed. "These very methods swell skepticism among many. . . . Many in the world hold back from making the 'leap of faith' because they have already jumped to some other conclusions." ("The Inexhaustible Gospel," in *Brigham Young University 1991–92 Devotional and Fireside Speeches* [Provo, Utah: University Publications, 1992], p. 144.) The prophet Amulek knew something of this "pseudo-spiritual-inquiry" from his own experience. "I did harden my heart," he recalled, "for I was called many times and I would not hear; therefore I knew concerning these things, yet I would not know" (Alma 10:6).

The Book of Mormon teaches and testifies that the truth can penetrate any heart that is not so badly scar-tissued by willful unbelief that it leaves one "past feeling" (see 1 Nephi 17:45). "If ye will not harden your hearts, and ask in faith, believing that ye shall receive," Nephi promised his brothers, "surely these things shall be made known unto you" (1 Nephi 15:11). To the faith-seeking Zoramites, Alma taught:

> Now we will compare the word unto a seed. Now, if ye give place, that a seed may be planted in your heart, behold if it be a true seed, or a good seed, *if ye do not cast it out by your unbelief, that ye will resist the Spirit of the Lord*, behold, it will begin to swell within your breasts; and when you feel these swelling motions, ye will begin to say within yourselves—It must needs be that this is a good seed, or that the word is good, for it beginneth to enlarge my soul; yea, it beginneth to enlighten my understanding, yea, it beginneth to be delicious to me. (Alma 32:28; emphasis added.)

There is a promise attached to this principle. The Book of Mormon has its own "guarantee"—the promise made in the last chapter of Moroni. That guarantee—like other warranties—is voided through fraud or purposeful disregard of the conditions attached to it. "Real intent," Moroni tells us, must be the guiding influence of one's search for truth. You can even ask if things are "not true," but you must believe that God can and will give you an answer. But that is not all—then you must be willing to honestly acknowledge and accept what He teaches you.

> And when ye shall receive these things, I would exhort you that you would ask God, the Eternal Father, in the name of Christ, if these things are not true; and if ye shall ask with a sincere heart, with real intent, having faith in Christ, he will manifest the truth of it unto you by the power of the Holy Ghost.

And by the power of the Holy Ghost ye may know the truth of all things. (Moroni 10:4–5.)

Read, Ponder, and Pray

Moroni reminds us that desire to know and a believing heart must also be accompanied by efforts on our part—intellectual and spiritual efforts. Someone once told me, "In order to get *inspiration* you must first get *information*." In other words, obtaining a knowledge of the truth requires both the head and the heart.

Amidst the many discussions that my wife and I had with our daughter concerning her questions about doctrine and doubts about the truthfulness of the Church, I asked her where she was getting the information that was forming her opinions. "From my friends," was her answer. "We talk about this stuff a lot!" That was what I had supposed, so I posed some questions to her.

"Have you tried to find answers to your questions in the scriptures? Have you looked up anything in any Church books or read about these issues in Church magazines?"

"Have you talked with anybody else to get their feelings and ideas on these concerns—like your Young Women leaders, the bishop, or your seminary teacher?"

"Have you posed these questions to your temple-married big sister and your returned-missionary big brother, whom you love, respect, and really look up to?"

"Have you prayed about this?"

The answer to all of these questions was, of course, "No." I tried to explain to her that *where* you get your information is sometimes as important as *what* information is received. I didn't want her to think that I was totally dismissing anything and everything her friends said, but I wanted her to see that some sources are better than others. "If you want to get the information you will need to pass your biology test, do you get it in your English class?" I asked. It may have seemed a dumb question, because the answer was so obvious, but it caused her to think. "Would you go to Saddam Hussein to get the 'truth' about

America?" I queried. "Of course not!" came her response. "He hates America!" At that point I wanted to say, "Gotcha!" but that would have done more harm than good. So I tried to teach the principle with examples she could relate to.

Just as a journalist must obtain verifiable information from the most reliable sources for the news story to be factual and trustworthy, so too must we in our spiritual quest for knowledge. Some sources are better than others. There are secondary sources and primary sources even in spiritual inquiry. Each can provide important information. In order to sift through all kinds of bias, you must gather as much information as you can. Secondary sources are "second-hand"—the opinions, feelings, experiences, teachings of someone else—like parents, teachers, friends, Church leaders, and even critics (to some extent). They are not bad sources of information, but they are not the most important or most reliable. The primary sources include the scriptures and the teachings of the prophets. The ultimate primary source is the Lord Himself. Once you have obtained *information*—from secondary sources, such as friends, teachers, even parents, and primary sources, such as the scriptures and teachings of the Church—you then approach the Lord in prayer ready to receive *inspiration*. I concluded with some personal counsel: "You have lots of sources of information available to you. You don't have to rely on your friends' ideas or even my testimony alone. Just make sure you give the Lord equal time."

To the anti-Christ Korihor, Alma demonstrated this hierarchy of spiritual sources. He spoke of the testimonies of others, the words of the scriptures and the prophets—even the earth itself was evidence of God's truth (see Alma 30:36–44). But the ultimate source, the best primary source, was to be had even beyond these witnesses. "Do ye not suppose that I know of these things myself?" Alma declared. "I testify unto you that I do know that these things whereof I have spoken are true. And how do ye suppose that I know of their surety? Behold, I say unto you they are made known unto me by the Holy Spirit of God. Behold, I have fasted and prayed many days that I might know these things of myself. And now I do know of myself that they are true; for the Lord God hath made them manifest unto me by his Holy Spirit; and this is the spirit of revelation which is in me." (Alma 5:45–46.)

The sons of King Mosiah, and Alma the son of Alma the Nephite prophet-high priest, certainly had been taught the gospel all of their lives. Yet even they had a rebellious period of doubt. From being doubters and dissidents they were transformed into mighty men of faith and conviction—"they had waxed strong in the knowledge of the truth." The process of their conversion included both intellectual and spiritual effort— information and inspiration. "For they were men of a sound understanding and they had searched the scriptures diligently, that they might know the word of God. But this is not all; they had given themselves to much prayer, and fasting; therefore they had the spirit of prophecy, and the spirit of revelation, and when they taught, they taught with power and authority of God." (Alma 17:2–3.)

Continual Nourishment

Even after one has exercised his desire for knowledge of the truth, believing that God will reveal it to him, and has studied, pondered, and prayed for guidance, the "experiment" must continue. Even after the "experiment" produces, as Alma described, an enlargement of the soul and an increased enlightenment of the mind, there is yet work to be done because "it hath not grown up to a perfect knowledge" (Alma 32:29). You can't stop now. You must continue with what has thus far been done, but also add an additional element—continual nourishment of the seedling of testimony. You must "nourish it with great care," Alma admonished, "that it may get root, that it may grow up, and bring forth fruit unto us."

> And now behold, if ye nourish it with much care it will get root, and grow up, and bring forth fruit.
>
> But if ye neglect the tree, and take no thought for its nourishment, behold it will not get any root; and when the heat of

the sun cometh and scorcheth it, because it hath no root it withers away, and ye pluck it up and cast it out. . . .

And thus, if ye will not nourish the word, looking forward with an eye of faith to the fruit thereof, ye can never pluck of the fruit of the tree of life.

But if ye will nourish the word, yea, nourish the tree as it beginneth to grow, by your faith with great diligence, and with patience, looking forward to the fruit thereof, it shall take root; and behold it shall be a tree springing up unto everlasting life.

And because of your diligence and your faith and your patience with the word in nourishing it, that it may take root in you, behold, by and by ye shall pluck the fruit thereof, which is most precious, which is sweet above all that is sweet, and which is white above all that is white, yea, and pure above all that is pure; and ye shall feast upon this fruit even until ye are filled, that ye hunger not, neither shall ye thirst.

Then, my brethren, ye shall reap the rewards of your faith, and your diligence, and patience, and long-suffering, waiting for the tree to bring forth fruit unto you. (Alma 32:37–38, 40–43.)

A few words that Alma uses in his description of the "experiment" have special significance to me—*continue, diligence, patience*. Being an avid gardener, I have a deep appreciation for what Alma is teaching. From the practical experience of gardening, I understand better the spiritual process Alma is describing. Each year I can hardly wait for the snow to melt in early spring so that I can start planting my vegetable garden. Even before the seeds can be planted there is much work to be done to get the soil ready. When I can finally plant the seeds, I anxiously wait for the first signs of sprouting. Sometimes it takes longer than I expected and, as hard as it is for me to wait, I must be patient and not give up. More than once I have replanted the carrots in my impatience. Only later did I discover that if I had just patiently waited for the first planting to sprout I would have had a much better crop.

While I wait for my plants to grow, and as I count the days until I can partake of the literal "fruit of my labors," many gardening chores need my constant attention—tasks like weeding, watering, fertilizing, thinning. It's a continual process. If I slack off or give up, the weeds take over in almost no time at all. If I forget to water—even for a short time—during the blistering heat of the summer, the plants will die quickly. If I let up even for a while, I can lose my entire garden (except maybe zucchini, which I can't kill even when I want to!). There will be neither sweet corn nor fresh tomatoes, no juicy watermelons, green beans, or red potatoes. All of my efforts would also be totally wasted. To be able to harvest all of those delicious treats I must *continue* my efforts with all *diligence* and *patience.* A bounteous harvest, spiritually as well as agriculturally, doesn't come easily or quickly.

"If any man will do [God's] will, he shall know of the doctrine," the Savior taught, "whether it be of God, or whether I speak of myself" (John 7:17). Without obedience to God-given principles one cannot know of the truthfulness of those principles. The "rules" of spiritual inquiry require right behavior as well as right thinking. While the world may say, "I will live that principle *when* I know it is right," the Lord would have us say, "I will live that principle *so that* I can know it is right!" Thus King Benjamin taught his people that *behavior* must accompany *belief* if one is to possess knowledge of God and His ways. "And again, believe that ye must repent of your sins and forsake them," he declared, "and humble yourselves before God; and ask in sincerity of heart that he would forgive you; and now, if you believe all these things see that you do them" (Mosiah 4:10). He added: "And behold I say unto you that if ye do this ye shall always rejoice, and be filled with the love of God, and always retain a remission of your sins; and ye shall grow in the knowledge of the glory of him that created you, or in the knowledge of that which is just and true" (Mosiah 4:12; see also Alma 26:21–22; Ether 4:13).

After all of the work and weeding and watering, no gardener would knowingly spray a toxic herbicide on his garden as a substitute for fertilizer. Yet, spiritually speaking, that is what is done when one thinks he can come to know the things of God while willfully living a life that is at odds with the "rules" of spiritual inquiry the Lord has established. "I don't seem to get answers to my prayers," a young person who was guilty of immorality said to his bishop. "I don't even know whether God exists." He will never get the spiritual knowledge he seeks when he is, as it were, spraying "Round-Up" on the spiritual seeds in his heart. Faith, repentance, and diligence in keeping the commandments are the real fertilizers of testimony. Alma declared to the questioning critic Zeezrom:

> It is given unto many to know the mysteries of God; nevertheless they are laid under a strict command that they shall not impart only according to the portion of his word which he doth grant unto the children of men, according to the heed and diligence which they give unto him.
>
> And therefore, he that will harden his heart, the same receiveth the lesser portion of the word; and he that will not harden his heart, to him is given the greater portion of the word, until it is given unto him to know the mysteries of God until he know them in full.
>
> And they that will harden their hearts, to them is given the lesser portion of the word, until they know nothing concerning his mysteries; and then they are taken captive by the devil, and led by his will down to destruction. Now this is what is meant by the chains of hell. (Alma 12:9–11.)

Coupled with continued efforts of diligence and obedience is the difficult principle of patience. When we want something that is important to us it is most difficult to wait. But like gardens, testimony and spiritual understanding take time to become fully developed and recognized as such. "Clearly, without patience we will learn less in life," Elder Neal A. Maxwell explained. "We will see less; we will feel less; we will hear less. Ironically, 'rush' and 'more' usually mean 'less.' The pressure of 'now,' time and time again, goes against the grain of the gospel with its eternalism." ("Patience," *1979 Devotional Speeches of the Year* [Provo, Utah: Brigham Young University Press, 1980], p. 217.) If I eat them before they are ready, I certainly can't make a valid evaluation of the quality of the tomatoes I planted or the sweet corn I grew. So it is with the "fruits" of the gospel.

When I was young, I prayed for a witness of the truths of the gospel. I guess I wanted to have a Joseph Smith-like experience—complete with visions and visitations of heavenly beings. As the weeks and months wore on without any remarkable experiences, I questioned both the process and the end product. I wasn't willing to be patient—I wanted my witness right now! And though I wouldn't admit it at the time, I wanted it on my terms! Years later, however, I received the witness that I desired. But it did not come when or how I had expected it. I learned, as President David O. McKay had experienced in his own life, that a knowledge of the truthfulness of the gospel most often comes "as a natural consequence of doing one's duty." So it is with gardens. We can carefully and continually cultivate, weed, and water the plants, but ultimately we have to stand back and watch and wait. Spiritually speaking, after all we can do—desire, believe, study, ponder, pray, fast, obey, serve, and repent—we must still patiently, and in faith, wait upon the Lord. Only by doing this can we partake of that divinely delicious fruit—knowledge of God and the truthfulness of His gospel.

"I COULD NOT BE SHAKEN"— THE "FRUITS" OF PERSONAL TESTIMONY

Why do I want my daughter to overcome her doubts and come to know the truths of the gospel? What does it matter? Why do I need a testimony? What value does it have in today's world? Each of these questions is perhaps best answered by examples from the Book of Mormon.

Sherem was known as an anti-Christ because he declared to the Nephites "that there should be no Christ" and he sought to "overthrow the doctrine of Christ" (Jacob 7:2). With his great learning and "perfect knowledge of the language," his powers of persuasion and flattery, and the power he had received from the devil himself, Sherem had great success in leading away the hearts of many people (see Jacob 7:3–4). Possessing natural arrogance and bolstered by his success among the people, Sherem took it upon himself to "reason" with Jacob—the prophet-president of the Nephite Church. "And he had hope to shake me from the faith," Jacob recorded, "notwithstanding the many revelations and the many things which I had seen concerning these things" (Jacob 7:5).

Jacob wasn't as concerned about his own faith as he was of that of his people. He therefore confounded Sherem with reason, with the scriptures, and most of all because "the Lord God poured in his Spirit into my soul" (Jacob 7:8). Why wasn't he threatened by Sherem's flattery and powers of persuasion and all of the "philosophies" that seemed so reasonable? "I had heard the voice of the Lord speaking unto me," Jacob declared, "wherefore, I could not be shaken" (Jacob 7:5). Sherem's assault on the faith of Jacob had no effect because Jacob was protected by and firmly founded upon his testimony of the truthfulness of the gospel and his spiritual understanding of the "doctrine of Christ."

In a similar way, when Enos heard the voice of God in his own heart he was strengthened spiritually and his faith fortified. "And there came a voice unto me, saying, Enos, thy sins are forgiven thee, and thou shalt be blessed. . . . thy faith hath made thee whole," he recalled. "And after I, Enos, had heard these words my faith began to be unshaken in the Lord." (Enos 1:5, 8, 11.) The knowledge Enos had obtained served as a strength throughout his life and as a guide in his ministry among the people.

Hearing the "voice of the Lord," having a spiritual knowledge of the truthfulness of the gospel, doesn't mean that one knows all things or has answers to all questions. It does, however, give comfort and confidence even when we don't know all the answers to the "tough questions" or know how to adequately respond to criticisms. Nephi's answer to the question posed by an angel of the Lord illustrates the power of knowing without knowing everything. "Knowest thou the condescension of God?" the angel asked. "And I said unto him: I know that he loveth his children; nevertheless, I do not know the meaning of all things." (1 Nephi 11:16–17.) Nephi humbly acknowledged that he didn't know everything, but he did know the love of God. What Nephi knew was far more important than what he didn't know. The same is true for us. With a testimony of the gospel we can still be confident in the face of questions for which we may not have answers. It becomes our rock foundation for us. Without that solid base everything else falls apart amidst doubt and criticism.

Several years ago I saw this principle in action as full-time missionaries were presenting a lesson to a friend of mine. With each concept presented by the elders, my friend would challenge their assumptions with contentious questions and arguments. He would seek to tear apart their reasoning with his training in logic and philosophy. This friend had been a national debate champion in college and it certainly manifested itself in his "discussion" with the missionaries. Finally, after a torturous hour of trying to make it through the lesson, the junior companion from a small town in Idaho spoke up. "I am not very good with words," he started out. "I can't hold a candle to you when it comes to debating. I don't even know the meaning of the big words you've been using. I can't answer all of the questions you have raised. I don't know very much, but I do know that the Book of Mormon is true and that this Church is the true church on earth. I know that with all my heart and there is nothing you can say that can change that!"

With that statement there was silence. For over an hour my friend had tied these young elders in knots with his knowledge and debating skill, but now he had nothing to say. What the young junior companion didn't know, in comparison to the worldly knowledge of my friend, paled in comparison to that which he *did* know. Because of that firm foundation he may have been flustered and frustrated, but he, like Jacob of old, was not shaken.

Each of us today will face challenges to our faith from many critics and unbelievers. We may also encounter a personal "crisis of faith" through adversity and affliction in our private lives. There may even be troubling issues of doctrine or history that threaten the very underpinnings of our faith, leaving us uneasy and without rational explanations. It is comforting to know that we need not know all things if we will but know the right thing—the truthfulness of the gospel, the divinity of Jesus Christ, and that the Church is, indeed, "the only true and living church upon the face of the whole earth" (D&C 1:30).

I do not believe it is merely coincidence that the first several questions of the temple recommend interview deal with our personal conviction of the fundamental teachings of the gospel—the reality of God, the transforming power of the Atonement, the truthfulness of the Restoration, and the authoritative and inspired ministry of living prophets. This is the knowledge that is foundational to all other things and that will protect us in times of doubt and difficulties. "I am satisfied, I know it's so," President Gordon B. Hinckley testified, "that whenever a man has a true witness in his heart of the living reality of the Lord Jesus Christ all else will come together as it should. . . . That is the root from which all virtue springs among those who call themselves Latter-day Saints." (*Teachings of Gordon B. Hinckley* [Salt Lake City: Deseret Book, 1997], p. 648.)

We are being spiritually assaulted today by means of the same tactics and philosophies utilized anciently by Sherem, Nehor, Zeezrom, and Korihor. To remain unfazed and unshaken we must be like Nephi, Jacob, Enos, having a personal knowledge and conviction of the truth. We are living in the days of and experiencing the very fulfillment of President Heber C. Kimball's prophecy of the last days.

> To meet the difficulties that are coming, it will be necessary for you to have a knowledge of the truth of this work for yourselves. The difficulties will be of such a character that the man or woman who does not possess this personal knowledge or witness will fall. . . .
>
>   . . . The time will come when no man nor woman will be able to endure on borrowed light. Each will have to be guided by the light within himself. If you do not have it, how can you stand? (As quoted in Orson F. Whitney, *Life of Heber C. Kimball* [1888; reprint, Salt Lake City: Bookcraft, 1967], p. 450.)

"Have ye inquired of the Lord?" Nephi asked his brothers. That question is as relevant to my daughter, my family, and myself as it was anciently for Lehi's family. Only from seeking truth as Nephi did and "experimenting" upon the word of God as Alma taught can we stand upon a firm, rock-solid foundation in a world of shifting values and quicksands of cynicism. Only with a testimony burning in our hearts can we remain "unshaken" like Jacob in the face of anti-Christs—whatever their modern disguises. The words of Helaman to his sons, Lehi and Nephi, are needed just as much today by my own doubting daughter, as well as by each of us in our own lives.

And now, my sons, remember, remember that it is upon the rock of our Redeemer, who is Christ, the Son of God, that ye must build your foundation; that when the devil shall send forth his mighty winds, yea, his shafts in the whirlwind, yea, when all his hail and his mighty storm shall beat upon you, it shall have no power over you to drag you down to the gulf of misery and endless wo, because of the rock upon which ye are built, which is a sure foundation, a foundation whereon if men build they cannot fall (Helaman 5:12).

Behold, I say unto you that ye must pray always and not faint;
that ye must not perform any thing unto the Lord save in the
first place ye shall pray unto the Father in the name of Christ, that
he will consecrate thy performance unto thee, that thy performance
may be for the welfare of thy soul.
—2 NEPHI 32:9

CHAPTER 3

CRY UNTO THE LORD

When I was about twelve or thirteen years of age I had an experience that was at first frightening but became, as I later thought about it, a profound lesson that has guided me in the years since. My father and I were pheasant hunting near our home in southeastern Idaho. Dad had always been a stickler when it came to gun safety. I had been taught and trained over and over again how to care for a gun and how to hunt safely. I guess what I hadn't been trained in was what to do when others around me were not so careful in their hunting practices.

When we had decided upon the field we were going to walk through in our quest for the ever-elusive (at least for us) ringneck, we had pulled over to the side of the road and parked the car. We took our shotguns out of the trunk, loaded our guns, and grabbed several additional shotshells to put in our jacket pockets. About the time we closed the trunk, locked the car doors, and were ready to start into the field, we heard several gunshots from the field on the other side of the road. Almost instantaneously a big, beautiful rooster pheasant flew over our heads. Before I could even react, shot pellets from the guns of the hunters in the opposite field began peppering us and bouncing off the car.

I was more stunned than hurt. Fortunately, the pellets did not penetrate our skin, but only stung a little. My immediate thought was, "You idiots! Don't you know that you never, never, never shoot across a road!" (My father had taught me that safety rule hundreds of times!)

In the instant I was mentally castigating "those dumb hunters" in the other field, my father had pulled me down to the ground and covered me up with his own body. I was as stunned by his quick action as I was by the initial shots. At first I was embarrassed—when you are a tough teenage boy you don't want your dad hugging you, let alone lying on top of you! When all the initial excitement was over and after a few moments of grumbling our displeasure with the hunters who had disregarded our safety, I realized what my father had done. He was protecting me because he loved me and was more concerned about my safety than his own. Even though I never said anything to him about it, I couldn't get it out of my mind. Even now, many years later, I get emotional when thinking about his split-second decision to protect me. He acted out of reflex, but the reflex was based on his love and concern for the safety of his son.

I got a glimpse that day of how much my Heavenly Father must also love me. His love is infinitely greater for me than even that of my earthly parents. His desire for my spiritual safety and protection from the evils of the world far surpasses even my dad's risking his own safety to protect me from physical harm.

We live today in a dangerous world—both physically and spiritually. Often we tend to focus on the physical dangers that can be seen. These can maim and kill the body. There are, however, other dangers in the world, dangers not always easily seen by the eye or discerned by the mind. These cannot only affect the body but also can injure the mind, wound the heart, and pierce the soul. These spiritual dangers are lethal, destroying lives and homes here and now and sometimes destroying souls eternally. How grateful I am that my Heavenly Father, like my earthly father, loves me enough to protect me. He has given us the means whereby we can be shielded from these "fiery darts of the adversary."

To His Nephite disciples the resurrected Christ spoke of the spiritual dangers they would face and the means whereby they could be protected. "Behold, verily, verily, I say unto you, ye must watch and pray always lest ye enter into tempation," Jesus taught, "for Satan desireth to have you, that he may sift you as wheat. Therefore ye must always pray unto the Father in my name." (3 Nephi 18:18–19.) Satan desires to destroy you! What a frightening thought! "Therefore, ye must always pray." What a loving and protective warning!

The Prophet Joseph Smith experienced on many occasions the power of Satan and his devilish desires to destroy. After the loss of the 116 pages of the Book of Mormon manuscript the Prophet was reminded by the Lord that Satan sought to destroy him and the work of God. With this warning also came divine counsel which, if followed, would bring safety and heavenly protection. The counsel is as vital to us today, if not more so, as it was to the young prophet in 1828. "Pray always, that you may come off conqueror," the Savior promised, "yea, that you may conquer Satan, and that you may escape the hands of the servants of Satan that do uphold his work" (D&C 10:5).

"WATCHFUL UNTO PRAYER CONTINUALLY"— IT'S A MATTER OF LIFE OR DEATH

"One can pray and yet not really pray," Elder Neal A. Maxwell insightfully observed. "Prayers can be routinized and made very superficial. When this happens, there is very little communication and very little growth. Yet, given the times in which we live, improving our prayers should be one of our deepest desires if we are genuinely serious about growing spiritually." (*All These Things Shall Give Thee Experience* [Salt Lake City: Deseret Book, 1980], p. 91.)

The roadblock to greater spirituality posed by "praying without really praying" is all too prevalent in the world today, even in the lives of those who profess to know the power of prayer and how to pray. It is certainly a challenge that we struggle with in our own family. Sometimes when one of our children has offered the family prayer or the blessing on the food at mealtime, I have to take a quick peek to see if someone is really praying or if it is just a tape recording. It might as well be a tape recording, because it is exactly the same each time—same sequence, same wording, same tone of voice. If anyone says anything different, everyone notices.

As parents we tend to think our children's prayers are too short and not thoughtful enough. On the other hand, our children tend to think *our* prayers are too long. "Don't call on Mom for family prayer," my children used often to lament. "We'll be late for school again!" I have discovered, however, that the length of the prayer does not necessarily translate into fervency or faith. "Vain repetitions" can be found in long prayers as well as in short, "automatic" prayers. The emphasis should not be solely on the word *repetition,* but also on *vain,* for even if words or phrases are not repeated over and over again, a prayer can be "vain"—without meaning, empty, fruitless. And the repetition of some phrases doesn't constitute "vain repetitions" when the repeated words come from deep within the soul and are heart-felt expressions of faith.

While I sometimes get after my children for praying without thinking, I have sometimes found myself falling into the very same trap of offering the same prayer in the same way time after time. While I may be able to identify exactly what each child will say in his or her prayers, they too can pretty well predict what I am going to say. I have often sarcastically joked with our family when one of the children offers one of those "pre-recorded" or "automatic" prayers, as it were, "Boy, that prayer will really have the power to protect us today!" or "Wow, that one really got Heavenly Father's attention!" On a more serious side, I have wondered how differently I would approach prayer, whether it be personal or family, if I knew that that prayer would be my last uttered words and expressions in mortality. How would we approach prayer if it was a matter of life or death to us? I came to find out in a very personal and traumatic way the difference between "saying prayers" and what the Book of Mormon characterizes as "crying unto the Lord" in "mighty prayer."

Several years ago while our family lived in northern Virginia, our two-year-old daughter had a serious accident that struck terror into our hearts. She was outside with her older sisters and their friends dancing and playing. When the other kids were not paying much attention to her, she climbed up on top of our big station wagon (which our kids had lovingly dubbed "Latter-day Saint Limo"). She was dancing and jumping on the roof of the car when she lost her footing and fell head-first off the car onto the concrete driveway. She was knocked unconscious and her seven-year-old sister picked her up and carried her, like a rag doll, to her mommy.

As our little girl convulsed and drifted in and out of consciousness we were scared to death, not knowing whether she was seriously injured. Not wanting to take any chances, we rushed her to our pediatrician's office. After examining our daughter, the doctor told us it could be a very serious head injury, and she wanted our daughter to be flown by medical helicopter to the trauma center several miles away.

Amidst all the noise and comings and goings of the doctor's office I laid my hands on my daughter's head and gave her a priesthood blessing, promising her that she would recover fully from her injuries. A moment later the doctor told us the helicopter was on another mission and we must transport our daughter to the trauma center by ambulance. My wife, Wendy, accompanied Emma Jane in the ambulance with its medical crew. Our doctor called the trauma center and arranged for a neurosurgeon to await their arrival. There was no room in the ambulance for me, so I was left alone to drive our car behind the ambulance.

It was only about fifteen miles to the Fairfax County Trauma Center, but it seemed like hundreds. As I followed behind the ambulance I felt totally helpless. All I could do was cry and pray. My prayers during those next several minutes, however, were much different than our family prayer that morning or the blessing on the food at lunch. I was not just "saying prayers." I was truly "crying unto the Lord," pleading with Him to bless my daughter, to bless the doctors, to bless my wife. Never before had I so fervently pleaded with God. Never before had I felt so much love for my children, as I fearfully faced the prospect of losing one. I continued to plead with God in silent prayer at the hospital as the doctors examined Janey and ran all kinds of tests. My prayers ending that day were truly a matter of life or death.

After a miraculous recovery from a serious concussion, Janey returned home to a happy reunion with her brother and sisters. Our fervent prayers for her recovery were replaced with heartfelt prayers of thanksgiving and love.

From this experience I came to better understand why the Book of Mormon never uses the phrase "saying prayers" but rather speaks repeatedly of "mighty prayer." Because of the dangers we and our families face each day of our lives—dangers that can destroy spiritually as well as physically—we need "mighty prayer," not just "saying prayers." It is indeed a matter of spiritual life or death! It is one of the means our Heavenly Father, in His infinite love for us, has provided to protect us from evil and guide us in the paths of righteousness. "For if ye would hearken unto the Spirit which teacheth a man to pray," Nephi admonished his people, "ye would know that ye must pray." Likewise Satan knows the protective power of "crying unto the Lord" in prayer. As Nephi further stated, "For the evil spirit teacheth not a man to pray, but teacheth him that he must not pray" (2 Nephi 32:8).

Throughout my many years of service in the Church, I have conducted hundreds of interviews—youth interviews, temple recommend interviews, personal interviews. One of the questions I often asked was "How are your personal prayers?" From those many interviews and from my own life's experiences I have come to see the "life or death" importance of prayer. Almost always there is a striking correlation between the frequency and fervency of one's personal prayer and one's individual righteousness and faithfulness. On the other hand, almost always when I interviewed people who had been guilty of serious transgression there had been an extended period of time when either no prayers were uttered or only routine, vain-repetition-filled, quickly muttered prayers were said before drifting off to sleep. In my own life, I know that those times when I have been and am most vulnerable to the "fiery darts of the adversary" are when I am either not praying or am only hastily and casually "saying prayers."

Real communion with God through prayer is one of the most significant principles of protection found in the gospel. After teaching the Zoramites how to "experiment upon the word," Alma also taught that worship of God is not confined to a church building or a religious ritual. True worship involves communication with God through prayer. In contrast to the vain prayers they had witnessed at the Rameumptom (see Alma 31:8–24), the Zoramites were taught by Alma the true nature of prayer—real worship, pure communion with God, whenever and wherever.

> Do ye remember to have read what Zenos, the prophet of old, has said concerning prayer or worship?
>
> For he said: Thou art merciful, O God, for thou hast heard my prayer, even when I was in the wilderness; yea, thou wast merciful when I prayed concerning those who were mine enemies, and thou didst turn them to me.
>
> Yea, O God, and thou wast merciful unto me when I did cry unto thee in my field; when I did cry unto thee in my prayer, and thou didst hear me.
>
> And again, O God, when I did turn to my house thou didst hear me in my prayer.
>
> And when I did turn unto my closet, O Lord, and prayed unto thee, thou didst hear me.
>
> Yea, thou art merciful unto thy children when they cry unto thee, to be heard of thee and not of men, and thou wilt hear them.
>
> Yea, O God, thou hast been merciful unto me, and heard my cries in the midst of thy congregations.
>
> Yea, and thou hast also heard me when I have been cast out and have been despised by mine enemies; yea, thou didst hear

my cries, and wast angry with mine enemies, and thou didst visit them in thine anger with speedy destruction.

And thou didst hear me because of mine afflictions and my sincerity; and *it is because of thy Son that thou hast been thus merciful unto me*, therefore I will cry unto thee in all mine afflictions, for in thee is my joy; for thou hast turned thy judgments away from me, *because of thy Son*. (Alma 33:3–11; emphasis added.)

CONTINUAL PRAYER

It is often said that "ninety percent of success is in showing up." Something similar can be said of the efficacy of prayer. The Book of Mormon doesn't give us much of a "how to" handbook when it comes to prayer. It does, however, repeatedly teach us that we should pray often, even always, and pray fervently. "Saying your prayers" might be confined to kneeling by the bedside morning and night. Even family prayer often has a set time and location. While each of these times of prayer is important, the Book of Mormon teaches us that real communion with God can be, should be, in fact must be at all times and in all places. We can talk with our Father about all matters great and small, temporal or spiritual.

Prayer is often described as "vocalized faith." It could also be characterized as "vocalized love." There is not a day that goes by that I do not call my wife from my office or she does not call me. Often such calls might be reminders to do something or find something for me. Other times there may be requests that I pick up something at the store on my way home. Most often, however, the calls are just "check in" calls, checking on how things are going, accompanied by expressions of love and affection. We view these phone calls, however short they may be, as vital in "staying in touch"—emotionally as well as temporally—with each other and as essential nourishment to our loving relationship. Sometimes I am in meetings or in faraway places where I cannot call Wendy, but I can and do think of her always. In contrast, I am never in a place or circumstance where I cannot communicate with my Father in Heaven. He is never "out of range." I can speak with Him, express my love and gratitude, and even request a much-needed blessing, at any time, in any place, and under any circumstance. Our relationship with our Heavenly Father needs that kind of "vocalized faith" and "vocalized love"—constant "staying in touch." The prophet Amulek taught us concerning this kind of constant communication with God.

> Yea, cry unto him for mercy; for he is mighty to save.
> Yea, humble yourselves, and continue in prayer unto him.
> Cry unto him, when ye are in your fields, yea, over all your flocks.
> Cry unto him in your houses, yea, over all your household, both morning, mid-day, and evening.
> Yea, cry unto him against the power of your enemies.
> Yea, cry unto him against the devil, who is an enemy to all righteousness.
> Cry unto him over the crops of your fields, that ye may prosper in them.
> Cry over the flocks of your fields, that they may increase.
> But this is not all; ye must pour out your souls in your closets, and your secret places, and in your wilderness.
> Yea, and when you do not cry unto the Lord, let your hearts be full, drawn out in prayer unto him continually for your welfare, and also for the welfare of those who are around you. (Alma 34:18–27.)

How is it possible to "pray without ceasing"? (See 1 Thessalonians 5:17.) When the Savior admonished His disciples "always to pray, and not to faint" (see Luke 18:1), was He saying they should always be on their knees? Of course not. Continual, persistent prayer, as Amulek taught, is in the mind and the heart, not just on the knees and from the mouth. Prayer is as much an attitude as an action, if not more.

Many times when I have taught the Book of Mormon story of Enos's "wrestle" with God in "mighty prayer," my students will ask, "How can you pray all day and into the night?" To them it is a genuine question, for they can't imagine praying longer than three minutes maximum—they think they would run out of things to say. Did Enos pray vocally for a continual period of many, many hours? Perhaps. But it could also be that he "cried unto the Lord" both vocally and silently, both in formal prayer for a period of time and in deep spiritual and emotional pondering for other periods. Supplication is often more from the depths of the soul than expressed in words. I can see Enos on his knees praying, pleading with the Lord for many, many minutes. His communion continued even after getting up off his knees and sitting or walking and pondering deeply for hour upon hour. Then, perhaps, he fell on his knees again in verbal prayer. His "mighty prayer" was a process of continual communion—mouth, mind, heart, and soul.

Sometimes, as strange as it may sound, my most heartfelt and effective prayers are not offered when kneeling at the side of my bed but when I am driving to work. During the commute, I can have time alone to "talk with God." I don't close my eyes or bow my head (neither of which is highly recommended when you are driving), but I can talk aloud—talking as I would to my own earthly father. I have felt a special closeness to my Heavenly Father even in the midst of honking and heavy traffic. Even when I carpool and others in the car are talking, I can silently pray and ponder. (Sometimes those silent prayers are for safety, depending upon which of my colleagues is driving!) How thankful I am for the blessing and privilege it is to know that I can talk to and communicate with that perfectly loving and kind Father at any time and in any way I need. Whether it be on a walk observing the beauties of nature or sitting in a boring meeting staring at the walls, I can have a full heart "drawn out in prayer continually."

Many times at my office my life is chaotic—there are phone calls, visitors, tasks that need immediate attention, meetings that must be attended. I don't always have the quiet time that I need to prepare mentally and spiritually for my classes. It is a much appreciated respite when I can kneel down in my office and pray for success in my teaching or other responsibilities, but often I cannot do that. Yet I can still pray, even "cry unto the Lord." It may be while I walk across campus that I can silently "raise my voice high that it reache[s] the heavens" (see Enos 1:4). It may be that a silent yet soulful prayer is offered standing in front of my class when an important question needs an inspired answer. It may be when a teenage child is trying my patience and when I am sorely tempted to say or do something unwise that silent prayer, a cry unto the Lord, will prove most useful.

What a blessing! We can pray anytime, anywhere, even when we aren't down on our knees or opening or closing a meeting. If I will allow my heart and soul and mind to be drawn out continually in prayer I am never alone. "There is no loneliness so great, so absolute, so utterly complete," wrote Elder Richard L. Evans, "as the loneliness of a man who cannot [or who does not] call upon his God" (in *Richard Evans' Quote Book* [Salt Lake City: Publishers Press, 1971], p. 148).

PRAY FOR FORGIVENESS

"Sin keeps a man from prayer," President Brigham Young said, "and prayer keeps a man from sin." Not only is prayer essential for repentance, but repentance is essential for prayer. The blessings of heaven are obtained only "by obedience to that law upon which it is predicated" (see D&C 130:20–21). As much as our Father in Heaven may love us and as fervently as we may pray, His answers to our prayers and the blessings we desire are inextricably linked to obeying the commandments. Therefore, one of the primary purposes of prayer is to faithfully seek forgiveness of our sins and rededicate ourselves to keeping our covenants. Only in this manner can our prayers produce the desired results.

Perhaps nothing better characterizes "praying without really praying" than when the words we utter do not coincide with the life we are striving to live. "We cannot, for the purposes of real prayer," wrote Elder Neal A. Maxwell, "hurriedly dress our words and attitudes in tuxedos when our shabby life is in rags" (*All These Things Shall Give Thee Experience*, p. 96). One may "go through the motions" of prayer, yet get up off his knees knowing full well that he has no intention of keeping the commandments of God. How can such hypocrisy yield blessings? Even Huckleberry Finn recognized such incongruency. "You can't pray a lie," Mark Twain had Huck say in that classic novel.

> I about made up my mind to pray; and see if I couldn't try to quit being the kind of boy I was, and be better. So I kneeled down. But the words wouldn't come. Why wouldn't they? It warn't no use to try and hide it from [God]. Nor from *me*, neither. I knowed very well why they wouldn't come. It was because my heart warn't right; it was because I warn't square; it was because I was playing double. I was letting *on* to give up sin, but away inside of me I was holding on to the biggest one of all. I was trying to make my mouth *say* I would do the right thing and the clean thing, . . . but deep down in me I knowed it was a lie—and He knowed it. You can't pray a lie—I found that out. (*The Adventures of Huckleberry Finn* [New York: New American Library, 1959], pp. 208–9; quoted by Elder Marvin J. Ashton, "Personal Prayers," in *Prayer* [Salt Lake City: Deseret Book, 1978], p. 75.)

The Book of Mormon clearly teaches and testifies of the relationship between righteousness and answers to prayers. "When they shall cry unto me I will be slow to hear their cries," the Lord declared to the Nephites under the reign of wicked King Noah. "And except they repent in sackcloth and ashes, and cry mightily to the Lord their God, I will not hear their prayers." (Mosiah 11:24–25; see also D&C 101:6–7.)

When we understand this important relationship, we should view prayer as a continual opportunity to come before the Lord in faith and repentance in order that our petitions may be heard. For this reason, Satan would have us believe that we cannot pray when we are sinful. In contrast, our Heavenly Father beckons us to come unto Him constantly praying for forgiveness. "If the Devil says you cannot pray . . .," President Brigham Young taught, "tell him it is none of his business, and pray until that species of insanity is dispelled and serenity is restored to the mind" (*Discourses of Brigham Young*, sel. John A. Widtsoe [Salt Lake City: Deseret Book, 1977], p. 45). The command "pray always" is, in its own way, a command to "repent always," for there can be no repentance without prayer and no real prayer without repentance. What a blessing prayer provides! Not only does it give us the opportunity to petition our loving Father for much-needed blessings, but also it provides us with an opportunity for continual self-evaluation and the means whereby we can be lifted up when we have fallen down. Just as it did for Enos, "mighty prayer and supplication" for forgiveness of sins opens the door for each of us for other prayers to be heard and other blessings to be received (see Enos 1:2–18).

PRAY FOR STRENGTH TO RESIST TEMPTATION

"Yea, and I also exhort you, my brethren, that ye be watchful unto prayer continually," Amulek admonished, "that ye may not be led away by the temptations of the devil, that he may not overpower you" (Alma 34:39). There is probably no better protection against the vast array of "fiery darts" of evil we face in these last days than consistent, conscientious, and heartfelt crying unto the Lord in personal prayer. It is indeed the "armor of God" that shields us from temptation and sin.

No right-thinking law enforcement officer or soldier would enter into a skirmish with bullets flying all around without the protection of a helmet and bullet-proof vest. It is equally as foolish to think we can escape spiritual "battle wounds" if we do not avail ourselves of the very protection God has provided. The spiritual warfare we face today is of such a nature that no one can survive it by standing alone, unprotected by faith and prayer. "I will never be tempted beyond my ability to withstand," I have heard some people say. Such a view is a misinterpretation of the scripture (see 1 Corinthians 10:13). Indeed, all of us can easily be tempted beyond our mortal ability to resist if we do not avail ourselves of the means the Lord gives us for strength and protection. We can escape the tempter's grasp only if we utilize the "escape routes" the Lord provides. "Humble yourselves . . ., and call on his holy name, and watch and pray continually," Alma declared, "that ye may not be tempted above that which ye can bear, and thus be led by the Holy Spirit" (Alma 13:28).

Over the last several years I have been involved in research concerning how faith and family combine to help young people resist temptations and stand strong against negative peer pressures. While several factors were found to be significant, one in particular was most profound: Those young people who faithfully remembered to "cry unto the Lord" in daily personal prayer were better able to resist temptation. As one young woman in the study reported: "Personal prayer is one thing that cannot be done without." It is as true for adults as it is for youth and children of all ages. This kind of daily, meaningful "vocalized faith" demonstrates how temptation can be overpowered, as Alma taught his son Helaman: "Teach them to withstand every temptation of the devil, with their faith on the Lord Jesus Christ" (Alma 37:33).

Modern prophets have added their testimonies and apostolic promises to those made by the Savior and the ancient prophets of the Book of Mormon. President Heber J. Grant taught:

> I have little or no fear for the boy or the girl, the young man or the young woman, [or the older man or woman] who honestly and conscientiously supplicate God twice a day for the guidance of His Spirit. I am sure that when temptation comes they will have the strength to overcome it by the inspiration that shall be given them. Supplicating the Lord for the guidance of His Spirit places around us a safeguard, and if we earnestly and honestly seek the guidance of the Spirit of the Lord, I can assure you that we will receive it. (*Gospel Standards,* ed. G. Homer Durham [Salt Lake City: The Improvement Era, 1941], p. 26.)

President Spencer W. Kimball called prayer "an armor of protection against temptation" and promised that if we would pray "fervently and full of faith, many of your problems are solved before they begin" (*The Teachings of Spencer W. Kimball,* ed. Edward L. Kimball [Salt Lake City: Bookcraft, 1982], p.

117). Similarly, President Ezra Taft Benson promised that through faithful, fervent, personal prayer, "you will be given the strength to shun any temptation" ("A Message to the Rising Generation," *Ensign*, November 1977, p. 32). Truly, personal prayer is an enabling gift of grace from our loving Father in Heaven—a gift of guidance, a gift of strength, a gift of protection. "Behold, verily, verily, I say unto you, ye must watch and pray always lest ye enter into tempation; for Satan desireth to have you, that he may sift you as wheat. Therefore ye must always pray unto the Father in my name." (3 Nephi 18:18–19.)

PRAY FOR YOUR FAMILY

From his vision of the tree of life, Lehi perceived that because of the unspeakable joy he had experienced when he partook of the fruit of that tree, "I began to be desirous that my family should partake of it also" (1 Nephi 8:12). After he had further seen in that vision that some of his family members would not come unto the tree and partake of the fruit, he feared for them and "did exhort them then with all the feeling of a tender parent" (1 Nephi 8:37). Lehi's feelings are no different than those of almost any loving parent. We desire our own family to be blessed, guided, protected by the Lord. We desire that they come to taste of the fruits of the gospel that have been sweet to our spiritual taste and nourishing to our souls. "Pray in your families, always in my name" the resurrected Christ commanded the Nephites, "that your wives and your children may be blessed" (3 Nephi 18:21). The protective "armor of God" is forged in the home. Just as we are commanded to pray privately and personally, the Lord has commanded us to pray in our homes so that each member of the family can be spiritually shielded from the "fiery darts of the adversary" through the prayers of faith. As President Harold B. Lee taught: "Family prayer is a safeguard to the individual members of the family as they leave from the home each day and go out into the uncertainties of the world" (*The Teachings of Harold B. Lee*, ed. Clyde J. Williams [Salt Lake City: Bookcraft, 1996], p. 280).

One of the great themes of the Book of Mormon (and of all the scriptures) is that it is not enough to just pray *in* our families. We must also pray *for* our families. Even beyond kneeling together as a family each morning in a more formal family prayer, there is great power in parents—individually and together—praying for the welfare of each child and in children praying for their parents. How grateful I am for this special blessing God affords me, both as a father and as a son. Although I have had many experiences throughout my life that testify of this principle, my testimony of it was renewed and strengthened by one I had while our family lived in Israel several years ago.

Parents Praying for Children

Prior to joining us in the Holy Land for the last six months of our stay, our oldest daughter remained behind at BYU. We had occasional phone calls and letters, but it was certainly not the same as having her with us. When she encountered some serious challenges, we felt that our help was seriously limited because of the distance that separated us. I worried about her almost constantly. There were nights when I didn't get much sleep. The phone calls helped some, but mostly we felt totally helpless. How grateful I was then and am now that the Lord was mindful of her in our absence and heard our cries in her behalf, both in daily family prayer and in constant personal prayer of a parent in behalf of his child.

One can only imagine the terrible pain felt by Alma and King Mosiah and their wives over the wickedness and rebellion of their sons. Alma the Younger not only had chosen the path of personal wickedness but he also persecuted the righteous and led many Church members away from the truth. This rebellion against God came to a dramatic end and their lives were miraculously turned around with a visitation by an angel. To Alma the angel declared: "Behold, the Lord hath heard the prayers of his people, and also the prayers of his servant, Alma, who is thy father; for he has prayed with much faith concerning thee that thou mightest be brought to the knowledge of the truth; therefore, for this purpose have I come to convince thee of the power and authority of God, that the prayers of his servants might be answered according to their faith" (Mosiah 27:14).

Perhaps many parents, hurting from the wounds inflicted by a rebellious child, have read that story and wondered why the Lord has not heard their prayers and sent an angel to rescue their loved one. It may be, however, that He has sent His angels—seen and unseen, heavenly and mortal servants—in response to the pleas of faithful parents in behalf of their children. Many times there are miraculous blessings in the lives of sons and daughters that result from parental faith, fasting, and "crying unto God." Often those miracles come in a manner much different than we had expected. Sometimes we, as parents, may not even know exactly how the Lord did indeed answer our prayers, only that He did.

A dear friend of mine shared with me a personal experience that profoundly demonstrates the power of parental prayer. When he was a teenager he became involved with a group of kids who did not share the values of his family. On the weekends they would party and drink themselves into oblivion. Soon it became not just a weekend activity, but almost an everyday occurrence. Finally, the group of teens decided to see how many consecutive days they could get drunk. The days soon turned into weeks. This young man, who had been reared in a good Latter-day Saint home, had gotten drunk with his so-called friends nearly forty consecutive days.

One evening when his friends came to pick him up to go partying, he went to say good-bye to his parents (which he usually did not do). When he yelled for them and could not get an immediate response, he went up to their bedroom looking for them. He could hear his father speaking in the room, and he noticed the door was only slightly open. As he approached the room, he could hear his parents praying. Through the crack of the slightly open door he could see his father and mother kneeling at the side of their bed, with tears streaming down their faces, pleading with the Lord to bless their son, protect him, and in some way touch his heart and turn him away from evil. What he felt as he saw and heard his parents "crying unto the Lord" in his behalf miraculously turned his life around. There was no angel, no vision, no earthshaking experience. Yet his life was dramatically transformed by the simple, loving, pleading prayers of concerned parents. Such miracles—even Alma-like experiences—continue to occur today when parents pray *with* their children and *for* their children individually and continually.

Children Praying for Parents

During the time we lived in Israel I received a phone call in our Jerusalem apartment from my parents back home in America informing me that my father was to have emergency heart surgery that very day. I was stunned and afraid. I wished I could have been there with them. I wanted desperately to give my father a blessing and be there for my mother and hold them and express my love in person, but there was nothing I could do from ten thousand miles away—nothing except pray. Our Father in Heaven is as mindful of fervent "crying unto the Lord" by children on behalf of their parents as He is of parents praying for their children. When I felt most helpless I was comforted by going to the source of the greatest help possible. Just as the Lord was mindful of my prayers for my parents, He has been merciful and mindful in our behalf because of the prayers of our children. Sometimes when we feel that there is nothing more we can do than pray for them, we may in fact be doing that which is most important and effective.

Although the record does not explicitly state it, righteous sons and daughters in the Book of Mormon undoubtedly prayed for their parents. Nephi prayed for Lehi and Sariah. Moroni surely prayed for the safety of his father, Mormon, during those difficult days of Nephite history. Perhaps it was due to the faith and prayers of King Lamoni that his father responded to the preaching of Aaron. Not only do miracles occur in the lives of children, but also parents' lives can be profoundly affected by the prayers of faith on the part of caring children. It may be a simple prayer to help Mom or Dad in their Church callings or a speaking assignment, or the deep pleading of a child for the conversion or reactivation of a parent. Sometimes the simple prayer of a child for a parent can do more good than many of the combined efforts of Church programs, home teachers, or quorum leaders. Miracles, previously thought impossible, can and do occur today through the prayers of children for their parents and siblings. No matter who we are or what our circumstances, we can never outgrow family prayer. Parents and children alike need each others' prayers. Truly, "the effectual fervent prayer of a righteous man [or woman or child] availeth much" (James 5:16).

PRAY FOR YOUR ENEMIES

Just as He taught in the Old World "Sermon on the Mount," the Savior reminded the Nephite disciples to "love your enemies, bless them that curse you, do good to them that hate you, and pray for them who despitefully use you and persecute you" (3 Nephi 12:44). Book of Mormon prophets had also taught that men must also pray for their enemies (see Alma 33:4). Our prayers may not result in the dramatic change of attitude or behavior of the "enemy," but they can result in the change of our own hearts and perspective.

While attending a meeting with other bishops in my stake, I gained an insight into the Lord's command to pray for our enemies. As we were discussing some of the problems and challenges that each of us was grappling with, one of the bishops shared an experience that profoundly affected my view of that scripture. He told of a couple that was on the verge of a divorce. There had been years of contention and bitterness in the home. He had counseled with them scores of times, but all to no avail. It seemed as if nothing could save the marriage. Almost ready to give up on them, the bishop had this scripture come into his mind. This couple viewed each other as "the enemy" and perhaps it would work for them. He read the scripture to them and made them commit to daily pray for each other—not just "say prayers" but truly pray for the other's welfare and blessing, and for needed changes in their relationship. There really wasn't much more he could say, so he set a date one month later to once again meet with them. If there was no change, it seemed likely they would divorce. During the month he quietly asked them if they were keeping the commitment. They assured him they were.

By the end of the month, dramatic changes had occurred. From sincerely praying for their "enemy" this husband and wife began to view each other with new eyes and a new heart. It was hard—virtually impossible—to earnestly and consistently pray for the blessing and well-being of another yet hold on to feelings of bitterness and anger. When the heart was changed, the behavior followed. Truly, the Lord had turned these "enemies" to each other through the simple, life-changing act of prayer.

Whether it be a troubled marriage, difficult neighbors, a person at work who has offended, or other people who have used and abused us in all kinds of ways, prayer can change us even if it doesn't immediately change the "enemy." The command to pray for our enemies is not so much for *their* sake as it is for *ours*. It is evidence of our own spirituality and true communion with God. Satan stirs up hearts to contention, which leads to angry actions. God heals wounded hearts through prayer, which leads to acts of kindness, mercy, and compassion. The Prophet Joseph Smith epitomized this strength of character, this spirituality, as he would often pray for his enemies and act with kindness in their behalf. His faith and prayers often touched the hearts of even the bitterest of enemies and turned them to him. Daniel Tyler, a contemporary of the Prophet, described one such remarkable prayer.

At the time William Smith [Joseph's brother] and others rebelled against the Prophet at Kirtland, I attended a meeting "on the flats" where Joseph presided. Entering the school house a little before the meeting opened and gazing upon the man of God, I perceived sadness in his countenance and tears trickling down his cheeks. A few moments later a hymn was sung and he opened the meeting by prayer. Instead of facing the audience, however, he turned his back and bowed upon his knees, facing the wall. This, I suppose, was done to hide his sorrow and tears.

I had heard men and women pray—especially the former—from the most ignorant, both as to letters and intellect, to the most learned and eloquent. But never until then had I heard a man address his Maker as though He was present listening as a kind father would listen to the sorrows of a dutiful child. Joseph was at that time unlearned, but that prayer, which was to a considerable extent in behalf of those who accused him of having gone astray and fallen into sin, was that the Lord would forgive them and open their eyes that they might see aright. That prayer, I say, to my humble mind, partook of the learning and eloquence of heaven. . . . It appeared to me as though, in case the veil were taken away, I could see the Lord standing facing His humblest of all servants I had ever seen. It was the crowning of all the prayers I ever heard.

. . . The next Sabbath his brother William and several others made humble confessions before the public. (Quoted in *They Knew the Prophet*, comp. Hyrum L. Andrus and Helen Mae Andrus [Salt Lake City: Bookcraft, 1974], pp. 51–52.)

PRAY WITH GRATITUDE

"O how you ought to thank your heavenly king!" King Benjamin declared. "I say unto you, my brethren, . . . you should render all the thanks and praise which your whole soul has power to possess, to that God who has created you, and has kept and preserved you, and has caused that you should rejoice, and has granted that ye should live in peace one with another" (Mosiah 2:19–20). I do not believe it is coincidental or merely a matter of structural protocol that we teach that expressions of gratitude should precede requests for blessings in the pattern of prayer. There can be little real communion with the Almighty if all we do is ask for more without acknowledging what we already have received. "Gratitude is of the very essence of worship," President Gordon B. Hinckley has taught, "thanksgiving to the God of Heaven, who has given us all that we have that is good" (*Teach-*

ings of Gordon B. Hinckley [Salt Lake City: Deseret Book, 1997], p. 250).

I am reminded of a mother who not only would diligently fast and pray for needed blessings but would just as often, if not more frequently, fast and pray in thanksgiving for the blessings of God. Thinking of her example of supreme gratitude causes me to sheepishly examine my own prayers and the prayers of our family. We carefully follow the prescribed pattern of prayer, but there is an overwhelming imbalance between the "We thank thee"s and the "We ask thee"s. Yes, we have many needs, but they are still few and small in comparison to the many and mighty blessings the Lord has poured out upon us. Yet often far less time and effort is expended in expressions of gratitude than in petitioning for more.

When our prayers—both public and private, both personal and family—are more filled with profound expressions of thanksgiving we become more cognizant of how the Lord has already blessed us and answered our prayers. Gratitude opens our eyes and our hearts and leads to even more sincere "crying unto the Lord," which in turn opens the windows of heaven anew. We can never get out of debt to the Lord. We are always "unprofitable servants," but we should always be grateful ones. "Get on your knees and thank the Lord for his bounties," President Hinckley has admonished. "Cultivate a spirit of thanksgiving for the blessing of life and for the marvelous gifts and privileges you enjoy." (*Teachings of Gordon B. Hinckley,* p. 246.)

When our prayers are filled with this kind of gratitude and awe, we will recognize and receive, as Ammon did, answers to our prayers, success, and joy even beyond our expectations. "Now Ammon seeing the Spirit of the Lord poured out according to his prayers upon the Lamanites, his brethren, who had been the cause of so much mourning among the Nephites, or among all the people of God because of their iniquities and their traditions, he fell upon his knees and began to pour out his soul in prayer and thanksgiving to God for what he had done for his brethren; and he was also overpowered with joy" (Alma 19:14).

"GET UP OFF YOUR KNEES AND GO TO WORK"

"We sometimes find ourselves praying for others when we should be doing things for them," Elder Neal A. Maxwell observed. "Prayers are not to be a substitute for service, but a spur thereto." (*All These Things Shall Give Thee Experience*, p. 97.) The Book of Mormon not only teaches us the whens, whys, hows, and what fors of prayer, but also shows the relationship between faith and works, prayers and actions. After his lengthy admonition concerning the expansive scope of prayer, the prophet Amulek included this important addendum. "And now behold, my beloved brethren, I say unto you, do not suppose that this is all; for after ye have done all these things, if ye turn away the needy, and the naked, and visit not the sick and afflicted, and impart not of your substance, if ye have, to those who stand in need—I say unto you, if ye do not any of these things, behold, your prayer is vain, and availeth you nothing, and ye are as hypocrites who do deny the faith (Alma 34:28; see also James 2:14–26).

President Brigham Young often taught the practical relationship between spoken prayers and service rendered. When the beleaguered handcart pioneers who had suffered so much on the plains of Wyoming approached the Salt Lake Valley, he dismissed the afternoon session of conference and urged the Saints to be prepared to render assistance. "Go home and prepare to give those who have just arrived a mouthful of something to eat, and to wash them and nurse them up," the prophet urged those gathered in the Tabernacle.

> You know that I would give more for a dish of pudding and milk, or a baked potato and salt, were I in the situation of those persons who have just come in, than I would for all your prayers, though you were to stay here all the afternoon and pray. Prayer is good, but when baked potatoes and pudding and milk are needed, prayer will not supply their place on this occasion; give every duty its proper time and place. (As quoted in LeRoy R. Hafen and Ann W. Hafen, *Handcarts to Zion* [Glendale, Calif.: The Arthur H. Clark Co., 1960], p. 139.)

How foolish it would be to kneel in prayer and ask Heavenly Father to bless and protect the people whose car broke down in front of our house, yet be unwilling to extend help to them. I may not be able to fix the car, but giving them a ride home or letting them use my phone would be more providential than vain prayers. "I shall not ask the Lord to do what I am not willing to do," President Brigham Young taught (*Discourses of Brigham Young*, p. 43). This principle of combining our human efforts, however feeble, with our prayerful petitions, however fervent, applies as much to the acquisition of blessings for ourselves as it does for others. How can I pray for increased gospel knowledge and then be unwilling to diligently study the scriptures and the teachings of the gospel? How can I ask the Lord to help me find a good job if I am unwilling to adequately prepare myself, work hard, and diligently seek that job? How can God answer my prayers to get good grades at school if I don't study, attend class, pay attention to the teacher, and do all in my power to succeed? It may be that many times when we feel that God has not answered our prayers it is because He cannot—because we have tied His hands by our inaction and unwillingness to do our part. When prayers are offered in this way, they are nothing more than another form of "vain repetitions."

One of the guiding maxims of President Gordon B. Hinckley, not only preached but personally practiced, is: "Get on your knees and ask for help, and then get up and go to work, and you'll be able to find your way through almost any situation" (quoted in Sheri L. Dew, *Go Forward with Faith: The Biography of Gordon B. Hinckley* [Salt Lake City: Deseret Book, 1996], p. 167). In a way this reflects what Nephi taught about the grace of Christ, that is to say our prayers are answered and blessings are granted by the goodness and mercy of God, "*after all we can do*" (see 2 Nephi 25:23). My efforts are puny in comparison to the power and goodness of God, but many times I find my answers and receive the blessings I prayed for after I have gotten up from my knees and done my part.

How thankful I am for protection, guidance, comfort, joy, and peace that prayer affords. Through "crying unto the Lord" I feel the perfect love my Father has for me. Mormon taught his son, Moroni, that perfect love—that divine fruit of true communion with God—"endureth by diligence unto prayer" (Moroni 8:26). "Pray always," the Lord has admonished us. This is not merely a commandment. It is truly an invitation to come unto the Father in prayer, the language of true worship, the means of true communion with the Infinite. Prayers "said" may bounce off the ceiling, but there will always be a divine ear listening to sincere, heartfelt expressions of love and gratitude, requests for forgiveness, blessings upon ourselves and our family members, and for spiritual strength and guidance as we journey through life. We are not merely commanded to pray; we are lovingly invited. As we respond continually, even always, to the divine invitation, we will come to know in unspeakable ways how truly "prayer is the soul's sincere desire." May we always follow Alma's admonition to his son Helaman, and come to personally realize the promise to all those who faithfully "cry unto the Lord."

> Cry unto God for all thy support, yea, let all thy doings be unto the Lord, and whithersoever thou goest let it be in the Lord; yea, let . . . the affections of thy heart be placed upon the Lord forever.
>
> Counsel with the Lord in all thy doings, and he will direct thee for good; yea, when thou liest down at night lie down unto the Lord, that he may watch over you in your sleep; and when thou risest in the morning let thy heart be full of thanks unto God; and if ye do these things, ye shall be lifted up at the last day. (Alma 37:36–37.)

And thus mercy can satisfy the demands of justice, and encircles
them in the arms of safety, while he that exercises no faith unto
repentance is exposed to the whole law of the demands of justice;
therefore only unto him that has faith unto repentance is brought
about the great and eternal plan of redemption.
—ALMA 34:16

CHAPTER 4

"FAITH UNTO REPENTANCE"

While we were browsing through a bookstore several years ago, my wife grabbed me by the arm and pulled me over to a display. "You gotta see this," she said emphatically. "You aren't going to believe your eyes!" I was really excited to find out what "treasure of truth" she was leading me to. I held on to my wallet, for fear that it was going to cost me some serious money. I figured it was probably some book for husbands (like "The Key to Maintaining Strong Marriages"). It would probably say that marital Shangri-la and ultimate bliss could only be found if husbands do all the cooking, cleaning, shopping, running kids around, and, worst of all—never watch sports!

That was what I was prepared to find, but that wasn't what it was. "Check this one out!" she said as she pointed to a thin book with a simple cover but a catchy title—*Repentance Made Easy.* "What do you think about that?" Wendy asked me as she saw my "double take" and then my sly grin. "Well, I'm sure it is a best seller," was my sarcastic response.

While I haven't read the book and perhaps it is an excellent work, I must admit the title struck me as a little strange. It seemed like it was advocating some sort of "shortcut" to forgiveness. It smacked of the kind of computer books that I'm drawn to because I don't understand the software manuals—*Computers for Dummies!* Those kinds of books are very popular and serve an important purpose, but I'm not sure that spiritual things can be presented in exactly the same manner. I can't imagine a book entitled *Faith for Dummies* or *How to Repent and Still Keep Your Favorite Sins.* Yet sometimes that is how we approach some of the most important and profound teachings of the gospel. In a noble attempt to simplify complex principles or doctrines, we may end up actually oversimplifying them to the point that we fail to correctly understand and teach the doctrine in the way the scriptures intend.

This is particularly evident with the doctrine of repentance. Instead of its being recognized as a deeply spiritual process there is danger that in our attempts to simplify it and make it practical we actually mechanize the process. It becomes a "how-to" or merely a humanistic self-improvement manual. An example of this is when we codify, as it were, the "steps of repentance." The scriptures don't do that. Yet more often than not people can recite the "Rs of Repentance" even when such a step-by-step, checklist approach to this saving principle does not exist in the standard works.

The Book of Mormon, perhaps more than any other volume of scripture, teaches and exemplifies the true meaning of repentance. There we don't see an oversimplified, mechanical, humanistic approach to spiritual transformation. If we neglect the teachings of the Book of Mormon, whether through failure to seriously study it or unwillingness to believe its teachings, we are "under condemnation" and in "spiritual darkness" (see D&C 84:54–58). This is especially true with regard to the doctrine of repentance. Without an understanding of how the Book of Mormon teaches repentance, we may "look beyond the mark" and fall prey to the potential pitfalls of what I call "checklist repentance." With this unfortunate approach to repentance it is easy to see how some, through self-justification, may view repentance as easier than it really is, and others, through doctrinal distortion, make it more difficult than it needs to be.

DOCTRINAL DEFICIENCIES OF "CHECKLIST REPENTANCE"

The purpose of the Book of Mormon is to testify of Christ and to lead all to Him to partake of His goodness and mercy. This can only be done through repentance. The Book of Mormon, therefore, is a valuable tool in exposing the fallacies and deficiencies of "checklist repentance." Several deficiencies are evident, each with its own pitfalls that would prevent one from coming unto Christ.

First, without the understanding we gain from the Book of Mormon that repentance is a fruit of faith, a person may go through a repentance "checklist" and feel satisfied he has met all of the requirements of repentance but not realize that his efforts have not been adequate. "Checklist repentance" undertaken without faith in the Redeemer may produce results similar to those described by the prophet Isaiah: "It shall be be unto them, even as unto a hungry man which dreameth, and behold he eateth but he awaketh and his soul is empty; or like unto a thirsty man which dreameth, and behold he drinketh but he awaketh and behold he is faint, and his soul hath appetite" (2 Nephi 27:3).

When I served as a bishop I encountered many people, young and old, who experienced something akin to what Isaiah described. They felt they had accomplished all of the "steps" of repentance, at least according to what they thought they were, and yet they still did not feel that the burden was lifted, nor did they experience the spiritual peace and joy that follows forgiveness. Why not? In most cases it was because they had made repentance a mechanical process of their own efforts, quite devoid of a spiritual yearning that would flow from a heart filled with faith in Christ. They were trying to do it all on their own, and then they wondered why they couldn't find relief.

Second, this kind of mechanical approach to repentance may

prevent the repentant sinner from ever "catching up." Trying to apply the "steps" of some arbitrary checklist for every sin ever committed in life is like taking two steps backward for every one step forward. Because we all make mistakes and commit sins—and we will do so as long as we are mortals—it is impossible to conscientiously go through this step-by-step system for every sin. "How can I ever repent of those sins I committed shortly after I was baptized?" I have often been asked by students or ward members. "How can I do all the steps if I can't even remember those past sins?" The danger of this doctrinal deficiency of "checklist repentance" is that it often causes some to become so discouraged, thinking they can never get "caught up" and fully repent of every sin, that they may give up in despair and sink deeper into the quicksands of sin. As Elder Jeffrey R. Holland has taught:

> There are multitudes of men and women—in and out of the Church—who are struggling vainly against obstacles in their path. Many are fighting the battle of life—and losing. Indeed, there are those among us who consider themselves the vilest of sinners. . . .
>
> How many broken hearts remain broken because those people feel they are beyond the pale of God's restorative power? How many bruised and battered spirits are certain that they have sunk to a depth at which the light of redeeming hope and grace will never again shine? (*However Long and Hard the Road* [Salt Lake City: Deseret Book, 1985], p. 77.)

A third deficiency in this approach to repentance is that for some sins and situations there may not be any way to complete all of the steps on the "checklist." For example, I had a young student share with me a painful experience from her own life. She had been taught that one of the "steps" she must complete to fully repent from any sin was to confess to the person she sinned against and receive their forgiveness. In her religion class at BYU she had her conscience pricked and she desired to repent of a sin that had occurred years earlier. She had cheated on the final exam in one of her classes during her junior year in high school. She resolved that at the Christmas break she would return to her hometown, look up that teacher, confess her cheating, and ask for forgiveness. Can you imagine the emotional turmoil she must have been experiencing during the holidays?

Finally, the day before she was to return to BYU she found the address of her former teacher, mustered the courage to go and face him, and out the door she went. When she arrived at the home of the teacher she was told that he had only just recently succumbed to a year-long battle against cancer. The young woman was stunned and heartsick—not just because of the death of her former teacher, but also because she felt deep despair enveloping her. From her narrow understanding of repentance, she was overwhelmed with a feeling that she would now never be forgiven of her sins. She felt totally helpless and hopeless—all because she could not complete one of the required "steps" on the "repentance checklist."

The final and most important doctrinal fallacy in this mistaken notion of "checklist repentance" is that by concentrating on our outward actions we tend to over-emphasize our efforts and ignore the cleansing power of Christ. This approach to repentance makes it appear as though a remission of sins is something obtained primarily by our own efforts. Such a view minimizes the miraculous atonement of Jesus Christ and the grace of God that makes a remission of sins possible. If we focus all of our attention and efforts on the "steps" we must take to repent, we tend to overlook what He did to make repentance possible. A humanistic or mechanical approach to repentance promotes "pseudo self-reliance." Relying only upon our own efforts robs us of the repentance-enabling power of Christ. Thus the worst danger of this superficial view of repentance is that it causes an unwitting but crucial oversight of the most important "R of Repentance"—*Redeemer.*

FAITH IN CHRIST AS THE FOUNDATION OF ALL TRUE REPENTANCE

The Book of Mormon is replete with examples and teachings that faith in the Lord Jesus Christ is the empowering agent of repentance. In Enos's account of his "wrestle" before God, which led to a remission of his sins, we do not see him going methodically through some series of steps to repent. We see him pondering the words of eternal life, pleading with the Lord to satisfy his spiritual hunger:

> And my soul hungered; and I kneeled down before my Maker, and I cried unto him in mighty prayer and supplication for mine own soul; and all the day long did I cry unto him; yea, and when the night came I did still raise my voice high that it reached the heavens.
>
> And there came a voice unto me, saying: Enos, thy sins are forgiven thee, and thou shalt be blessed.
>
> And I, Enos, knew that God could not lie; wherefore, my guilt was swept away.
>
> And I said: Lord, how is it done?
>
> And he said unto me: Because of thy faith in Christ. . . . thy faith hath made thee whole. (Enos 1:4–8.)

Enos's question, "Lord, how is it done?" has always intrigued me. While I certainly don't know what was going on in Enos's mind, I like to superimpose the all-too-prevalent modern culture of "checklist repentance" on that situation. In that setting I can almost hear Enos adding the following to his question. "Lord, how is it done so quickly, seeing that I have NOT completed all of the steps on my checklist?" God simply stated that the most important element in any repentance is faith in the Lord Jesus Christ. It was Enos's profound faith, not his outward actions of repentance, as important as they were, that resulted in the remission of his sins.

The Book of Mormon repeatedly reminds us that forgiveness of sins as well as ultimate salvation cannot be obtained merely by righteous deeds and repentant actions but rather is attained through "unshaken faith in [Christ], relying wholly upon the merits of him who is mighty to save" (2 Nephi 31:19). "True repentance is based on and flows from faith in the Lord Jesus Christ," President Ezra Taft Benson testified. "There is no other way." (*The Teachings of Ezra Taft Benson* [Salt Lake City: Bookcraft, 1988], p. 71.)

When we rely "wholly upon the merits" of Christ, we will submit to the designated requirements of repentance as a natural consequence of faith instead of an adherence to an artificial checklist. Our actions and attitudes of penitence become evidence of our faith in the Savior and not a substitute for it.

The prophet Amulek also taught that it is the "great and last sacrifice" of Jesus Christ that gives power and efficacy to the doctrine of repentance. He emphatically declared that faith must precede repentance for the cleansing mercy of the Messiah to be enjoyed.

> And behold, this is the whole meaning of the law, every whit pointing to that great and last sacrifice; and that great and last sacrifice will be the Son of God, yea, infinite and eternal.
>
> And thus he shall bring salvation to all those who shall believe on his name; this being the intent of this last sacrifice, to bring about the bowels of mercy, which overpowereth justice, and bringeth about means unto men that they may have *faith unto repentance.*
>
> And thus mercy can satisfy the demands of justice, and encircles them in the arms of safety, while he that exercises no *faith unto repentance* is exposed to the whole law of the demands of justice; therefore only unto him that has *faith unto repentance* is brought about the great and eternal plan of redemption.
>
> Therefore may God grant unto you, my brethren, that ye may begin to exercise your *faith unto repentance*, that ye begin to call upon his holy name, that he would have mercy upon you;
>
> Yea, cry unto him for mercy; for he is mighty to save. (Alma 34:14–18; emphasis added.)

Perhaps no scriptural example better illustrates Amulek's teaching of "faith unto repentance" than the Book of Mormon account of Alma the Younger's dramatic conversion. Alma was a sinner who was "racked with torment" and "harrowed up by the memory of [his] sins," who pleaded with the Lord to do something for him that he could not do for himself. Again, we do not see Alma mechanically going through a series of steps to repentance. In fact, there is no scriptural evidence that he had previously performed any of the actions traditionally taught as sequential steps to forgiveness. There was no "Repentance Made Easy" program of self-improvement for him—no 13-step recovery program, nor even the "5 Rs of Repentance." The Book of Mormon reveals, however, that Alma's miraculous change from a life of sin to a life of service and spirituality resulted from his "faith unto repentance."

> And it came to pass that as I was thus racked with torment, while I was harrowed up by the memory of my many sins, behold, I remembered also to have heard my father prophesy unto the people concerning the coming of one Jesus Christ, a Son of God, to atone for the sins of the world.
>
> Now, as my mind caught hold upon this thought, I cried within my heart: O Jesus, thou Son of God, have mercy on me, who am in the gall of bitterness, and am encircled about by the everlasting chains of death.
>
> And now, behold, when I thought this, I could remember my pains no more; yea, I was harrowed up by the memory of my sins no more.
>
> And oh, what joy, and what marvelous light I did behold; yea, my soul was filled with joy as exceeding as was my pain! (Alma 36:17–20.)

Merciful relief was extended to Alma because of his newly exercised faith in the atonement of Jesus Christ. Alma's subsequent abandonment of sinful practices, his restitution for past mistakes, and his life of continued commitment to the kingdom of God grew out of his faith in the cleansing power of Christ's atonement. Other scriptural examples in the Book of Mormon also affirm this principle. Nephi saw in vision the Savior's twelve Apostles who "because of their faith in the Lamb of God their garments are made white in his blood. . . . These are made white in the blood of the Lamb, because of their faith in him." (1 Nephi 12:8–11.) Our lives are cleansed of sin in the same manner as Enos, Alma, and the ancient Apostles. This cleansing and sanctifying comes to us not because of our own righteous acts but, as Lehi declared, "because of the righteousness of thy Redeemer" (2 Nephi 2:3)—because of His infinite atonement.

Indeed, faith in the Lord Jesus Christ as the first principle of the gospel and repentance as the second, along with all other principles and ordinances of the gospel, have their foundation in the Savior's atoning sacrifice. Truly, then, repentance stems only from faith in the redemptive and cleansing power of Christ. Elder Orson Pratt taught: "The first effect of true faith is a sincere, true, and thorough repentance of all sins. . . . Faith is the starting point—the foundation and cause of our repentance." ("The True Faith," *A Series of Pamphlets by Orson Pratt* [Liverpool: Franklin D. Richards, 1852], pp. 5, 6; republished in *Orson Pratt: Writings of an Apostle* [Salt Lake City: Mormon Heritage Publishers, 1976].)

Without the merciful atonement there could be no forgiveness of our sins. And without unwavering faith in that atonement there can be neither repentance nor saving works of righteousness. Thus, paraphrasing Nephi's familiar teaching, it is by God's grace that we receive a remission of sins, "after all we can do" (see 2 Nephi 25:23).

While there really is no set recipe or checklist of steps for repentance that must be taken in every case, we must still do all we can do. The Lord has specified that "all we can do" begins with unshaken faith in Christ. Other than this, the Book of Mormon (and the other standard works) gives no list of "Rs of Repentance." It does, however, provide doctrinal teachings and examples of how "faith unto repentance" leads us, both by inward attitudes and outward actions, to fulfill the Lord's stated requirements of repentance revealed in our day. "By this ye may know if a man repenteth of his sins—behold, he will confess them and forsake them" (D&C 58:43).

CONFESSION OF SINS: INWARD ATTITUDES AND OUTWARD ACTIONS

Speaking of the Nephite Church, Moroni wrote that "they were strict to observe that there should be no iniquity among them; . . . and if they repented not, and confessed not, their names were blotted out, and they were not numbered among the people of Christ" (Moroni 6:7). The Book of Mormon confirms the concept taught in both the Old and New Testaments, as well as in modern revelation, that confession is an integral part of true repentance. The act of verbal confession serves as an outward reminder of what should be happening inside the soul. Confession is like a mirror in which a person can examine himself spiritually and recognize his need for the cleansing power of Christ. The Apostle Paul spoke of confession that involves both the heart and the mouth (see Romans 10:10). Similarly, the Book of Mormon teaches that true repentance, born of faith in Christ, yields an *action* of confession coming from the mouth that mirrors an *attitude* of confession born in the heart.

"A Broken Heart and a Contrite Spirit"

As a bishop, I heard many confessions of sins from people—each different and unique in its own right. Some approached confession with deep humility and sorrow, having shed many tears, and others approached it rather matter-of-factly. One such was a young woman who had committed many grievous transgressions. She knew that she must confess to the bishop—she had been taught all of her life that confession was one of the "steps" of repentance. She was very open in her discussion of the sins and did not leave out any necessary detail. I was deeply troubled as I listened to her—troubled not so much because of what she was telling me, but rather what was missing. It was readily apparent that she was "going through the motions"— confessing with her *mouth*, but her *heart* wasn't in it. There was no "godly sorrow," as Paul describes it, that would reflect "faith unto repentance" (see 2 Corinthians 7:9–10). The Book of Mormon describes the attitude of "godly sorrow" as "a broken heart and a contrite spirit" (see 2 Nephi 2:7; 3 Nephi 9:19–20; 12:19; Ether 4:15; Moroni 6:2). This concept of "godly sorrow"—feeling the sorrow for our sins that God would have us feel—is the true indicator of faith in Christ and the only genuine motivation for bringing forth "fruit meet for repentance" (see Alma 12:15).

Godly sorrow—the broken heart and contrite spirit—is much more than remorse or regret over having sinned. Mormon observed anguish in his own people and described it as "the sorrowing of the damned" (see Mormon 2:12–14). It was sorrow born of sins and circumstances but which did not produce "faith unto repentance." Many may be remorseful for past actions and regret the consequences that have befallen them, but do nothing to change, to come unto Christ and partake of His mercy and to comply with the requirements of the gospel.

A "broken heart and contrite spirit" is an attitude that always leads to a commitment to change. Alma spoke of this kind of motivational sorrow for sin when he declared to Corianton, "Let your sins trouble you, with that trouble which shall bring you down unto repentance" (Alma 42:29). Elder Orson Pratt wrote:

> The sorrow that is acceptable in the sight of God, is that which leads to true Repentance, or reformation of conduct. . . . This kind of sorrow will lead us to obey every commandment of God; it will make us humble and childlike in our dispositions; it will impart unto us meekness and lowliness of mind; it will cause our hearts to be broken and our spirits to be contrite; it will cause us to watch, with great carefulness, every word, thought, and deed; it will call up our past dealings with mankind, and we feel most anxious to make restitution to all whom we may have, in any way, injured. . . . These, and many other good things, are the results of a Godly sorrow for sin. This is Repentance not in word but in deed: this is the sorrow with which the heavens are well pleased. ("True Repentance," *A Series of Pamphlets by Orson Pratt*, p. 31.)

When the Book of Mormon uses the term "broken heart and

contrite spirit" it implies considerably more than just a repentant attitude. We gain a better understanding of it by examining what the Book of Mormon teaches about two important elements of godly sorrow—an "awful awareness" of our sinful state and a willing submission to the will of God in our lives.

An "Awful Awareness" of Our Unworthiness Before God.

Before we can exercise "faith unto repentance" and obtain a remission of sins, we must experience something akin to what King Benjamin described as "an awful view of their own guilt and abominations, which doth cause them to shrink from the presence of the Lord" (Mosiah 3:25). That stark realization of guilt, King Benjamin declared, awakens "you to a sense of your nothingness, and your worthless and fallen state" (Mosiah 4:5). It thus produces a total dependence upon the Lord and a humility of soul that permits the seeds of repentance to take root. This "awful awareness" must include a self-inflicted stripping away of all rationalization and self-justification. There is no room in a broken heart for feeble excuses. There is no room in a contrite spirit for blaming others for our sins. Accompanying this "awful awareness" of our unworthiness before the Lord and our total dependence upon His mercy is a spiritual yearning to be clean again and to stand approved with God. It is much more than mere recognition of wrongdoing. It is a sackcloth-and-ashes humility that promotes spiritual growth and leads one to a condition described as a "change of nature befitting heaven" (statement quoted by David O. McKay, *Gospel Ideals* [Salt Lake City: Improvement Era, 1953], p. 13).

Willing Submission and Surrender to God's Will.

The Book of Mormon also teaches that one of the most important indicators of "godly sorrow" is a willingness to submit to whatever the Lord requires of us in order to obtain a remission of sins. Not only did King Benjamin teach his people about the necessity of an "awful awareness" of their sinful state, but he also taught them that their faith in Christ would lead them to voluntarily surrender to the Lord. A person who has "faith unto repentance" and desires to be forgiven of sins is willing to do whatever is necessary to have those burdens lifted. He yields his own will "to the enticings of the Holy Spirit, and putteth off the natural man and becometh a saint through the atonement of Christ the Lord, and becometh as a child, submissive, meek, humble, patient, full of love, willing to submit to all things which the Lord seeth fit to inflict upon him" (Mosiah 3:19). Helaman, speaking of Church members in his day, described how such submission, born of faith, leads to "the purifying and the sanctification of their hearts, which sanctification cometh because of their yielding their hearts unto God" (Helaman 3:35).

In contrast to the people of King Benjamin and Helaman, some today desire repentance whose hearts are not yet broken and whose spirits are less than contrite. Some become selectively submissive—desiring to repent on their own terms rather than on the Lord's. They desire to make repentance easy, pain-free, and convenient. In reality the process is difficult and demanding and sometimes may require humiliation, public embarrassment, restrictions, and inconvenience. Lehi warned such people that Christ offered "himself a sacrifice for sin, to answer the ends of the law, unto all those who have a broken heart and a contrite spirit; and unto none else can the ends of the law be answered" (2 Nephi 2:7). "There can be no conditions attached to unconditional surrender to God," wrote Elder Neal A. Maxwell. "Unconditional surrender means we cannot keep our obsessions, possessions, or cheering constituencies. . . . Every obsession or preoccupation must give way in total submission." (*"Not My Will, But Thine"* [Salt Lake City: Bookcraft, 1988], pp. 92–93.)

If we truly possess the proper attitude of confession, as taught in the Book of Mormon, our hearts will be broken with a piercing sorrow for sin and an "awful awareness" of our unworthiness and total dependence upon the mercy of the Savior. Our spirits will be contrite—filled with a desire to submit to God's will and to learn from Him what we must do to obtain a remission of our sins.

"If He Confess His Sins Before Thee and Me . . . I Will Forgive Him"

To confess without a proper repentant attitude is merely to take another ineffectual step in the "repentance checklist." Confession should be a natural response to faith and godly sorrow. When our hearts are broken and our spirits contrite, the desire to set things right will lead us to follow the Spirit and away from groping for the letter of the law.

The most frequently asked questions about repentance that my students have posed through the many years I have been a religious educator seem to always revolve around the issue of confession. "Why is confession even necessary?" "Why do I have to talk to my bishop? Can't I talk to someone else?" "What sins must be confessed?" "How much do I have to tell?" "What will happen to me after I confess? Will I be excommunicated?" These represent the many questions I have heard—all concerning the specific action of confession. One Book of Mormon contribution to an understanding of the doctrine of repentance is its confirmation of the role of confession to the Lord and to proper priesthood leaders. The Lord instructed Alma that "whosoever transgresseth against me, him shall ye judge according to the sins which he has committed; and if he confess his sins before thee and me, and repenteth in the sincerity of his heart, him shall ye forgive, and I will forgive him also" (Mosiah 26:29). From Alma's account we learn that there are two types of confession and two types of forgiveness. Elder Bruce R. McConkie explained the significance of these two types of confession:

> There are thus two confessions and two sources of forgiveness. A sinner must always confess all sins, great and small, to the Lord; in addition, any sins involving moral turpitude and any serious sins for which a person might be disfellowshipped or excommunicated must also be confessed to the Lord's agent, who in most instances is the bishop. The bishop is empowered to forgive sins as far as the church is concerned, meaning that he can choose to retain the repentant person in full fellowship and not impose [disciplinary council] penalties upon him. Ultimate

forgiveness in all instances and for all sins comes from the Lord and from the Lord only. (*A New Witness for the Articles of Faith* [Salt Lake City: Deseret Book, 1985], p. 236.)

The Lord does not require confession in order to humiliate, embarrass, or cause one to feel punished by a vindictive God. Neither is confession a mere disclosure of deeds. It is, rather, an opportunity to covenant with the Lord that we are turning away from sin and will make the necessary adjustments in our lives. Confession without a solemn commitment to change does not guarantee any enduring effects. When we understand how "faith unto repentance" and confession are related, we recognize that confession is provided by a merciful and loving Savior to impart the inspired counsel, comfort, and direction that is only available from the Lord and His authorized servants. When we "cast our burdens upon the Lord" through complete confession and commitment to forsake sin, we are in a position to be taught by the Master. His guidance far surpasses any emotional lift or well-meant advice from mere mortals. The spiritual motivation to confess, characterized in the Book of Mormon as "willful submission to the Lord," will prompt us to approach the Lord and the proper priesthood leader, as necessary, in humble confession to receive his counsel and support. Under such conditions, the necessary *action* of confession as taught by Alma, as a fruit of the *attitude* of confession, as taught by King Benjamin, becomes a blessing rather than a burden.

FORSAKING SIN: THE "MIGHTY CHANGE"

When I ask my students what "forsaking" means, I usually get the answer, "Stop doing it!" They mean by that, cease and desist committing that particular sin. While that is certainly important, it isn't all that repentance requires. As spiritually dangerous as "checklist repentance" is, another common misconception about repentance can derail a person's spiritual progress—"fragmentary forsaking." A person who confesses a major moral transgression and promises to forsake *that* sin but continues to blatantly disregard the Word of Wisdom by drinking and indulging in illicit drug use is guilty of "fragmentary forsaking." The Book of Mormon teaches that forsaking requires the abandonment of sinfulness, not of just a particular sin. One cannot merely forsake one specific sin or sinful situation and yet cling tenaciously to other sins. It is not just the stopping of a sinful practice that is required, but rather a complete change in one's disposition and desire for sin.

There are several examples in the Book of Mormon of how forsaking sin, in the truest sense, brings about a total transformation of one's life. King Lamoni's father understood forsaking sin to be an element of genuine repentance when he declared: "I will give away all my sins to know thee . . . and be saved at the last day" (Alma 22:18). His forsaking of sin was not fragmented or selective but rather was a total surrender. "True repentance is not only sorrow for sins, and humble penitence and contrition before God," President Joseph F. Smith taught, "but it involves the necessity of turning away from them, a discontinuance of all evil practices and deeds, a thorough reformation of life, a vital change from evil to good, from vice to virtue, from darkness to light" (*Gospel Doctrine* [Salt Lake City: Deseret Book, 1939], p. 100).

Forsaking sin, like confession, requires a change in both inward attitudes and outward behaviors. It is not just the abandonment of an action. It is the changing of one's entire being. Alma described this mortal metamorphosis as a "mighty change in your hearts" which causes one to "sing the song of redeeming love" (see Alma 5:14, 26). Such forsaking, as an indicator of true repentance, involves a mighty change of one's heart—one's desires and deeds—and a mighty change of direction and devotion.

A "Mighty Change" of Heart

The Lord has promised that if we will indeed abandon our wicked deeds and desires, he will perform a great miracle in our behalf that will bring about a newness of attitude, character, and being. He has promised to create in us "a new heart and a new spirit" (Ezekiel 18:31). The Lamanite prophet Samuel held up the works of the repentant and faithful Lamanites as an example to the wicked Nephites of the miracle of a new heart that occurs through "faith unto repentance." He explained that his Lamanite brethren had been "led to believe the holy scriptures, yea, the prophecies of the holy prophets, which are written, which leadeth them to faith on the Lord, and unto repentance, which faith and repentance bringeth a change of heart unto them" (Helaman 15:7). This mighty change of behavior, thoughts, attitudes, and desires comes as a merciful gift of grace—"after all we can do." When we have demonstrated our faith, repentant determination, and renewed devotion, the indispensable gift of God is what brings about a remission of sins.

True repentance, as taught in the Book of Mormon, is a demanding process. No "Repentance Made Easy" is found within its pages. Once we commit to the process there can be no hesitation or holding back—we cannot straddle the line of demarcation between good and evil. We cannot, figuratively speaking, have one hand reaching for the fruit of the tree of life while continuing to dance and dine in the "great and spacious building," for it requires both hands and our whole heart and soul to cling to the iron rod (see 1 Nephi 11:8–36). The examples of individuals in the Book of Mormon who were transformed through their "faith unto repentance" make it clear that we must do all that we can as mortals so that God, through His grace and mercy, can make us "new creatures."

A "Mighty Change" of Direction and Devotion

Forsaking sin involves not only turning *from* evil practices but also turning *to* God in greater righteousness and service. Just as Paul taught King Agrippa that repentance means to "turn to God, and do works meet for repentance" (Acts 26:20), so does the Book of Mormon teach that repentance requires actions that demonstrate renewed love for God and increased commitment to a life of righteousness. The resulting "works meet for repentance" are naturally two-directional—we cannot demonstrate greater love and worship of God without also gaining an intensified desire to serve and bless the lives of others. Alma taught that the covenants associated with baptism and a remission of sins require an increased devotion on our part to both God and our fellowmen (see Mosiah 18:8–10).

Increased Devotion to God.

Alma taught his people at the waters of Mormon that the covenant of baptism for the remission of sins involves a commitment, or solemn promise, to God "that ye will serve him and keep his commandments" (Mosiah 18:10). Writing to his son Moroni, Mormon taught that "fulfilling the commandments [of God] bringeth remission of sins" (Moroni 8:25). King Benjamin taught his people that in order to obtain and retain a remission of sin, they must continue "calling on the name of the Lord daily, and standing steadfastly in the faith," and continue to "grow in the knowledge of the glory of him that created [them]" (Mosiah 4:11–12). This renewed and intensified devotion to God, King Benjamin further taught, will also affect our relationships with others. "And ye will not have a mind to injure one another, but to live peaceably, and to render to every man according to that which is his due" (Mosiah 4:13). Just as Alma and the sons of Mosiah demonstrated their true repentance by their desire to serve God, so too must we if we are truly repentant. A person cannot really repent and then be inactive in the Church or indifferent to the expectations and responsibilities that accompany gospel living. "Though one may have abandoned a particular sin and even confessed it to his bishop, yet he is not repentant if he has not developed a life of action and service and righteousness," explained President Spencer W. Kimball ("What is True Repentance?" *New Era,* May 1974, p. 7).

Increased Love and Service to our Fellowmen.

In all of the standard works there is perhaps no more profound example of how service and love for others flow naturally out of "faith unto repentance" than the Book of Mormon story of the sons of Mosiah. Before their remarkable conversion, these young men were, according to the scriptural record, "the very vilest of sinners" (Mosiah 28:4). Because of the sincerity of their repentance and the intensity of their faith in and gratitude for the atonement of Christ, they were later "zealously striving to repair all the injuries which they had done to the church, confessing all their sins, and publishing all the things which they had seen, and explaining the prophecies and the scriptures to all who desired to hear them. And thus they were instruments in the hands of God in bringing many to the knowledge of the truth. . . . Now they were desirous that salvation should be declared to every creature." (Mosiah 27:35–36; 28:3; see also Helaman 5:17.)

The subsequent lives of righteousness and service of the sons of Mosiah are evidence that it was indeed true repentance that prompted them to make spiritual restitution for their sins. While it is true that we can in no way, of ourselves, repay the Savior, make full restitution for our sins, or overcome our sinfulness by our efforts alone, we can show our appreciation for His sacrifice through lifelong devotion to God and our fellowmen. Although we will always be "unprofitable servants" (Mosiah 2:21), if we truly have "faith unto repentance" we will strive to follow the example of the sons of Mosiah, who spent their lives serving God and loving their fellowmen, teaching the gospel to others, and living lives of personal righteousness.

There is no "short-cut" to repentance. No man-made "checklist" can yield a remission of sins. There is no surefire do-it-yourself program, no "Repentance Made Easy" quick fix. Yet even with all the self-discipline, pure willpower, or inner strength that mortal man can muster, he can only change his attitude and his behavior. Christ, on the other hand, can change his very being. It is only by coming unto Him—the Physician of men's souls—with "faith unto repentance" that lives stained as scarlet can become white as wool. Alma, who spoke not only as a prophet but also as one who had experienced the "mighty change" that comes through the atonement of Jesus Christ, reiterated the Lord's injunction to repent and partake of the blessings of forgiveness. This is one of the most timeless themes of the Book of Mormon and one of our greatest needs today.

> There can no man be saved except his garments are washed white; yea, his garments must be purified until they are cleansed from all stain, through the blood of him of whom it has been spoken by our fathers, who should come to redeem his people from their sins. . . .
>
> Behold, he sendeth an invitation unto all men, for the arms of mercy are extended towards them, and he saith: Repent, and I will receive you.
>
> Yea, he saith: Come unto me and ye shall partake of the fruit of the tree of life; yea, ye shall eat and drink of the bread and waters of life freely;
>
> Yea, come unto me and bring forth works of righteousness. (Alma 5:21, 33–35.)

Marvel not that all mankind, yea, men and women, all nations,
kindreds, tongues and people, must be born again; yea, born of God,
changed from their carnal and fallen state, to a state of righteousness,
being redeemed of God, becoming his sons and daughters.
—MOSIAH 27:25

CHAPTER 5

HAVE YOU BEEN BORN AGAIN?

At a large gathering of Latter-day Saints several years ago, something was said to me by one of the guests that both surprised and troubled me. The speaker was addressing the important doctrinal topic of salvation by grace and spiritual rebirth—being "born again." After the talk was completed, one of the people in attendance approached me with this question, "We don't believe that stuff, do we?"

The "we" in his question meant Latter-day Saints, and the "that stuff" obviously referred to the doctrine of spiritual rebirth that we had just heard addressed. "Of course we do," I responded. "Why would you even ask?" His response was, "Because that is what the 'born-agains' believe."

I was surprised that he had never heard that Latter-day Saints believe in being "born again." And I was even more troubled by the fact that he seemed to dismiss the doctrine just because other devout Christians professed something similar. His attitude seemed to be, "Well, if *they* believe it, then *we* must surely not believe it."

"Haven't you read in the New Testament where Jesus said

that a person must be 'born of the water and of the Spirit' in order to enter into the kingdom of heaven?" I asked. "What do you think that means?"

"That just means being baptized and confirmed a member of the Church," he answered.

"Do you believe that a remission of sins is necessary to gain exaltation?" I asked.

"Of course," he said, a little frustrated with the question, thinking I was changing the subject.

"Then you believe in being 'born again,'" I concluded. "Receiving forgiveness from our sins is part and parcel with spiritual rebirth. You can't have one without the other."

I was troubled by this man's misunderstanding of one of the most important and profound doctrines of the Restoration—spiritual regeneration that results through the atonement of Christ. We often hear the phrase "born-again Christians." Unfortunately, more often than not that term is used in a negative sense, both by the secular world in general and by some uninformed Latter-day Saints. In the truest sense of the phrase, however, being "born again" not only is a positive Christian characteristic but is also an imperative for salvation. As Latter-day Saints we not only believe in spiritual rebirth but we also realize that we must become "born-again" Christians ourselves.

When our family lived in Virginia many years ago, we had several friends that would be characterized as "born-again Christians." They were evangelicals from various denominations. We had many cordial discussions with them about religion in general and "Mormonism" in particular. I was always fascinated that these friends spoke often of the day they were "saved" or "born again." They knew the exact date—sometimes the precise moment. Many celebrated the anniversary of that event in much the same way we would celebrate a birthday. To them, however, they were celebrating a "re-birthday." When they would ask me, "Have you been 'born again'?" I would readily admit that I had.

The confusion came, however, when they asked me for the date of my "rebirth." At first, I didn't know what to say. And then, being the smart alec that I am, I decided that I could just as easily give any date—better yet, give several dates in several different years. I was just trying to be funny, but in reality I was also teaching them that while Latter-day Saints do, indeed, believe in being born again, they are not content to be reborn only once. They were as incredulous to that idea as was the Latter-day Saint who had approached me with the question, "Do we really believe all that stuff?" Both were guilty of a misunderstanding of the true doctrine of spiritual rebirth.

While my Latter-day Saint friend may have misunderstood the doctrine because of his aversion to the evangelical use of the term "born again," my evangelical friends were suspicious of our view of being born again repeatedly—thinking that somehow diminished or demeaned the significance of spiritual rebirth. Whatever the cause, both were deficient in their doctrinal understanding. Both were Bible believing and were familiar with New Testament passages on the subject, yet despite the teachings of the Bible there was still misunderstanding and many differing views. Perhaps the differences of opinions on the subject and the misunderstandings of the doctrine are as much a result of a different doctrinal vocabulary as almost anything else. Being "born again" may mean different things to different people. Thus they may use a different terminology, but often are describing the same things.

A national study was brought to my attention recently that illustrates this problem. When asked on a survey, "Have you been spiritually born again?" there was great diversity in the responses of Christians from many different denominations and religious traditions. Some churches showed very high percentages of respondents who said they had, indeed, been "born again." Others had very low percentages. Of significant interest to me was the results for Latter-day Saints. Over twenty-five percent of the LDS respondents reported having been "born again." That statistic could be read as both positive and negative. My immediate reaction was, "What about the other seventy-five percent?" The more I thought about this study, the more I was convinced that the diversity of the results was due more to differences in definition than to doctrine or experience.

For example, for some Christians "born again" would be the same as commitment to Christ. For others it may mean when they experienced a spiritual change in their life's direction. I am convinced that had the question been posed to Latter-day Saints, "Have you been converted?" or "Have you ever felt a remission of sins in your life?" or "Have you received the Holy Ghost?" the results would have been drastically different. The difference would be because of our use of different terms to describe what appears to be the same phenomenon—spiritual rebirth. This confusion of terms and misunderstanding of doctrine could be part of the spiritual darkness spoken of in Doctrine and Covenants 84:54–58 that is lifted through greater study of the Book of Mormon and its teachings on this important subject. The Bible may teach the need for spiritual rebirth and give some guidance and explanation of the doctrine, but in the Book of Mormon we really begin to see what is meant by the phrase "born again." Through studying and applying the Book of Mormon teachings on this subject, not only would understanding dramatically increase but so too would the percentage of Latter-day Saints who could affirmatively respond to the question, "Have you been born again?"

There are brief glimpses in the New Testament of what is meant by the injunction, "Ye must be born again." They are like small pieces of a giant jigsaw puzzle. John the Baptist taught his disciples that he baptized with "water unto repentance; but he that cometh after me is mightier than I, whose shoes I am not worthy to bear; he shall baptize you with the Holy Ghost, and with fire" (Matthew 3:11). At the Last Supper Jesus promised the Apostles that He would pray to the Father asking Him to bestow upon them "another Comforter, that he may abide with you forever" (John 14:16). The Apostle Paul also taught of a "spiritual birth" (see Galatians 4:29) whereby a person becomes a "new creature" in Christ (see 2 Corinthians 5:17) and walks thereafter in a "newness of life" (see Romans 6:2–6; Ephesians 4:24). All these passages are important pieces of the puzzle and indirectly refer to the spiritual rebirth of which Jesus spoke as He commanded Nicodemus, "Ye must be born again," yet they do not fully explain *what* the "baptism of fire" really is and *how* it is obtained. It is only through the doctrines of the Restoration in general and the Book of Mormon specifically that more and more pieces of the puzzle are revealed and fitted together. Only then can we see the true "picture" of the doctrine of spiritual rebirth. Through a careful examination of the doctrinal teachings of Book of Mormon prophets we can more fully understand what it means to be born again, how one comes to experience spiritual rebirth, and what are the "fruits" or indicators of that transformation, and how one retains a remission of sins.

WHAT IT MEANS TO BE BORN AGAIN

Spiritual rebirth—also described in the scriptures by such terms as "born again," "baptism of fire," or "a mighty change"—is the spiritual transformation that results when one has actually received the Holy Ghost and experienced the remission of sins that accompanies it. Nephi explained that *after* one has followed the Savior "with full purpose of heart, acting no hypocrisy and no deception before God, but with real intent, repenting of your sins, witnessing unto the Father that ye are willing to take upon you the name of Christ, by baptism," *only then* will that person "receive the Holy Ghost; yea, then cometh the baptism of fire and of the Holy Ghost; and then can ye speak with the tongue of angels, and shout praises unto the Holy One of Israel" (2 Nephi 31:13). Two of the most illustrative examples in the Book of Mormon of how the process described by Nephi actually works are the accounts of the conversion of King Benjamin's people and the dramatic transformation of Alma the Younger.

King Benjamin taught his people that there was "no other name given nor any other way nor means whereby salvation can come unto the children of men" except through the atonement of Jesus Christ (see Mosiah 3:17; also 4:8). He further explained that the natural man, which is "an enemy to God," could only be overcome through submitting to Christ's redemptive power (Mosiah 3:19) and by continually repenting of and forsaking

their sins, calling on the Lord daily, and through continual obedience (Mosiah 3:10–12). Benjamin's people were already members of the Church. They had already received the ordinance of
baptism and perhaps had previously received the "baptism of
fire," but now as Benjamin taught them anew concerning the
principles of the gospel and how to "retain a remission of [their]
sins" (Mosiah 3:12), a remarkable thing occurred.

> And now, it came to pass that when king Benjamin had thus
> spoken to his people, he sent among them, desiring to know of
> his people if they believed the words which he had spoken unto
> them.
> And they all cried with one voice, saying: Yea, we believe all
> the words which thou has spoken unto us; and also, we know of
> their surety and truth, because of the Spirit of the Lord
> Omnipotent, which has wrought a mighty change in us, or in
> our hearts, that we have no more disposition to do evil, but to
> do good continually. (Mosiah 5:1–2.)

King Benjamin's doctrinal explanation to his people regarding what had indeed occurred within the hearts of his people
also serves as one of the best definitions of the phrase "born
again."

> And now, these are the words which king Benjamin desired
> of them; and therefore he said unto them: Ye have spoken the
> words that I desired; and the covenant which ye have made is a
> righteous covenant.
> And now, because of the covenant which ye have made ye
> shall be called the children of Christ, his sons and his daughters;
> for behold this day he hath spiritually begotten you; for ye say
> that *your hearts are changed* through faith on his name; there-
> fore, ye are *born of him* and have become *his sons and his daugh-
> ters.* (Mosiah 5:6–7; emphasis added.)

Experiencing a similar yet even more dramatic conversion,
Alma the Younger described his spiritual tranformation—being
changed by the power of the Holy Ghost from an enemy of God

to a "new creature," one who is converted and committed to the cause of righteousness.

> For, said he, I have repented of my sins, and have been redeemed of the Lord; behold I am born of the Spirit.
>
> And the Lord said unto me: Marvel not that all mankind, yea, men and women, all nations, kindreds, tongues and people, must be born again; yea, born of God, changed from their carnal and fallen state, to a state of righteousness, being redeemed of God, becoming his sons and daughters;
>
> And thus they become new creatures; and unless they do this, they can in nowise inherit the kingdom of God. (Mosiah 27:24–26.)

The Book of Mormon clearly teaches that while the ordinance of baptism allows one to enter in at the gate ("For the gate by which ye should enter is repentance and baptism by water"), salvation cannot be obtained without also experiencing the spiritual rebirth—"then cometh a remission of your sins by fire and by the Holy Ghost" (2 Nephi 31:17). "Water baptism is only a preparatory cleansing of the believing penitent . . . ," explained Elder Orson Pratt; "whereas, the Baptism of fire and the Holy Ghost cleanses more thoroughly, by renewing the inner man, and by purifying the affections, desires, and thoughts which have long been habituated in the impure ways of sin" ("The Holy Spirit," *A Series of Pamphlets by Orson Pratt* [Liverpool: Franklin D. Richards, 1852], p. 57; republished in *Orson Pratt: Writings of an Apostle* [Salt Lake City: Mormon Heritage Publishers, 1976]). Several Book of Mormon passages illustrate, as well as define, this spiritual rebirth (see Enos 1:1–6; Alma 13:1–12; 18:41–43; 19:6, 33; Helaman 5:41–49; 3 Nephi 9:20–22). The spiritual rebirth that Jesus told Nicodemus was required "to see the kingdom of heaven" is the same baptism of fire that we experience when we fulfill the commandment given at confirmation, "Receive the Holy Ghost." Being born again is the actual *reception* of the Holy Ghost, which brings a remission of our sins and a "newness of life"—our being raised from a lower or carnal state to a state of righteousness and increased spiritual enlightenment. "The baptism of the Holy Ghost is the baptism of fire," Elder Bruce R. McConkie wrote. "Sins are remitted not in the waters of baptism, as we say in speaking figuratively, but when we receive the Holy Ghost. It is the Holy Spirit of God that erases carnality and brings us into a state of righteousness. We become clean when we actually receive the fellowship and companionship of the Holy Ghost. It is then that sin and dross and evil are burned out of our souls as though by fire." (*A New Witness for the Articles of Faith* [Salt Lake City: Deseret Book, 1985], p. 290.)

HOW ONE COMES TO EXPERIENCE SPIRITUAL REBIRTH

Most of the scriptural accounts of men and women whose lives were transformed by the "baptism of fire" and whose sins were remitted involve dramatic or almost sensational events. Alma (see Mosiah 27; Alma 36), Paul (see Acts 9), King Benjamin's people (see Mosiah 5), King Lamoni and his wife (see Alma 18–19), and the general gathering of Saints on the day of Pentecost (see Acts 2) are among the many who were "born again" in a most remarkable manner, in a singular and overwhelming event. These miraculous conversion stories often leave the reader wondering if he/she must be "born again" in the same manner. The Book of Mormon also provides us with less obvious accounts that describe this same spiritual transformation as a less visible, gradual process rather than a single event. The resurrected Christ declared: "And whoso cometh unto me with a broken heart and a contrite spirit, him will I baptize with fire and with the Holy Ghost, even as the Lamanites, because of their faith in me at the time of their conversion, were baptized with fire and with the Holy Ghost, and *they knew it not*" (3 Nephi 9:20; emphasis added). Even in our day there are those who receive the Holy Ghost and become "new creatures" in Christ through sudden, miraculous conversions, and yet others likewise are baptized by fire and become "quickened in the inner man" (see Moses 6:65–66) and still, like the Lamanites of old, may not even recognize it. "A person may get converted in a moment, miraculously," Elder Bruce R. McConkie taught. "But that is not the way it happens with most people."

With most people conversion [spiritual rebirth and the accompanying remission of sins] is a process; and it goes step by step, degree by degree, level by level, from a lower state to a higher, from grace to grace, until the time that individual is wholly turned to the cause of righteousness. Now this means that an individual overcomes one sin today and another sin tomorrow. He perfects his life in one field now, and in another field later on. And the process goes on until it is complete, until we become, literally, as the Book of Mormon says, saints of God instead of natural men. (Address delivered at Brigham Young University First Stake conference, 11 February 1968.)

We say that a man has to be born again, meaning that he has to die as pertaining to the unrighteous things in the world. Paul said, "Crucify the old man of sin and come forth in a newness of life" (see Romans 6:6). We are born again when we die as pertaining to unrighteousness and when we live as pertaining to the things of the Spirit. But that doesn't happen in an instant, suddenly. That also is a process. Being born again is a gradual thing, except in a few isolated instances that are so miraculous they get written up in the scriptures. As far as the generality of the members of the Church are concerned, we are born again by degrees, and we are born again to added light and added knowledge and added desires for righteousness as we keep the commandments. ("Jesus Christ and Him Crucified," in *1976 Devotional Speeches of the Year* [Provo, Utah: Brigham Young University Press, 1977], p. 399.)

Thus there is no real difference in the quality of the conversion or spiritual rebirth, whether it comes gradually over time or suddenly in a singular event. The *process* may differ but the *results* are the same. It could perhaps be compared to "the difference between suddenly emerging from a dark room into bright sunlight as opposed to experiencing the dawning of the day. The dawning is more gradual, but results in just as much light." (Larry E. Dahl, "The Doctrine of Christ," in *The Book of Mormon: Second Nephi, the Doctrinal Structure*, ed. Monte S. Nyman and Charles D. Tate, Jr. [Provo, Utah: Religious Studies Center, Brigham Young University, 1989], p. 366.)

SOME SPIRITUAL "FRUITS" OR INDICATORS OF THE "BAPTISM OF FIRE"

Whether it be a sudden and singular transformation or a slow process of growth with almost imperceptible changes, becoming "born again," becoming Christ's sons and daughters with a "baptism of fire," brings with it "fruits" that can be felt and discerned within the heart and life of one who has overcome the natural man through the atonement of Christ. Just as spiritual rebirth can be a process as well as an event, so can this spiritual transformation occur on various levels and at different times in one's life. The Book of Mormon, perhaps better than any other volume of scripture, teaches and illustrates not only how one can tell if he/she has been "born of God," but also to what extent. The following "fruits" or indicators of spiritual rebirth, taught in the Book of Mormon, are not given to be an exhaustive, all-inclusive inventory checklist of experiences one must have in order to be considered "born again," but rather may serve as inspiring examples and illustrative guides. The Book of Mormon can bring us comfort in helping us to recognize how the Atonement has indeed transformed us, and also inspire us to continue to "press forward with steadfastness in Christ" that we may be "born again" and again—from one level to a higher until finally we hear the blessed pronouncement, "Behold, thus saith the Father: Ye shall have eternal life" (2 Nephi 31:20).

Peace of Conscience

One of the most significant indicators or by-products of spiritual rebirth is found in Enos's declaration, "My guilt was swept away" (Enos 1:6). Approximately four centuries after Enos's "wrestle" with God that resulted in a "baptism of fire," King Benjamin's people experienced similar feelings after their prayer of faith and penitence: "O have mercy, and apply the atoning blood of Christ that we may receive forgiveness of our sins, and our hearts may be purified" (Mosiah 4:2). The Book of Mormon records their miraculous spiritual rebirth, which effected a remission of their sins and was accompanied by a "peace of conscience, because of the exceeding faith which they had in Jesus Christ" (Mosiah 4:3). Like Enos, King Benjamin's people experienced a sweet spiritual "fruit" of conversion that "swept away" feelings of guilt and pain and replaced them with a peace of conscience that permeated their very souls. Spiritual rebirth does not eliminate our memory of our sins but instead affects us in much the same manner as Alma, who explained to his son, "I could remember my pains no more; yea, I was harrowed up by the memory of my sins no more" (Alma 36:19). Although he continued to remember his sins and even the pain he suffered as a result, after his spiritual rebirth he was no longer tortured by guilt. Each of us, like Alma, may continue to remember our sins, and to a degree the feelings of remorse and pain associated with them, even after we have been "born of God," but through faith and repentance the "harrowing" or debilitating effects of a guilty conscience are removed, and with that "baptism of fire" will come a peace of conscience that will cause us to feel as Alma testified, "My soul was racked with eternal torment; but I am snatched, and my soul is pained no more" (Mosiah 27:29).

A Feeling of Joy and Divine Love

Another indicator of the "mighty change of heart" often cited in the Book of Mormon conversion accounts is that of an overwhelming feeling of joy and being enveloped in the divine love of God. Alma contrasted this divine feeling with the pains of his wickedness when he declared: "And oh, what joy, and what marvelous light I did behold; yea, my soul was filled with joy as exceeding as was my pain! Yea, I say unto you, my son, that there could be nothing so exquisite and so bitter as were my pains. Yea, and again I say unto you, my son, that on the other hand, there can be nothing so exquisite and sweet as was my joy." (Alma 36:20–21.)

Another example of this kind of joy that accompanies spiritual rebirth is found in the scriptural account of the conversion of King Lamoni and his wife. After being taught the gospel by Ammon they were "overpowered by the Spirit" and they all fell to the ground "as though they were dead" (see Alma 19:13, 18). Witnessing this remarkable scene, Abish, the converted Lamanite woman, took the queen by the hand, who arose and testified of her remarkable spiritual transformation. "O blessed Jesus, who has saved me from an awful hell" (Alma 19:29). The record continues: "And when she had said this, she clasped her hands, being filled with joy" (Alma 19:30). King Benjamin's people experienced something akin to this. "Behold they had fallen to the earth, for fear of the Lord had come upon them," the scriptural account records. After they petitioned the Lord for forgiveness of their sins "the Spirit of the Lord came upon them, and they were filled with joy." (Mosiah 4:1, 3.)

Although we may not become so overwhelmed by the "baptism of the Holy Ghost" that we fall to the earth in a spiritual trance, we can nonetheless feel the "exquisite joy" that comes with conversion and a remission of sins. Associated with this increased sense of joy is also an intensified awareness of divine love. Alma characterized this "fruit" of being "born again" as a joyful desire to "sing the song of redeeming love" (Alma 5:26). This in turn heightens our love, appreciation, respect, reverence, and awe for God. This intense love for God and from God causes those who have experienced the "mighty change" to echo Nephi's declaration: "He hath filled me with his love, even unto the consuming of my flesh" (2 Nephi 4:21).

Moroni taught that "despair cometh because of iniquity" (Moroni 10:22). Darkness, despondency, and discouragement are destroyed by the joy that blesses those who are "born of God." Hearts heavy with hopelessness are lifted and illuminated by a hope instilled by the companionship of the Comforter. "The remission of sins bringeth meekness, and lowliness of heart," declared Mormon, "and because of meekness and lowliness of heart cometh the visitation of the Holy Ghost, which Comforter filleth with hope and perfect love" (Moroni 8:26).

No Desire to Do Evil, but to Do Good Continually

Another testament of the spiritual transformation is a "mighty change" in dispositions and desires. King Benjamin's people experienced this "fruit" and joyfully declared: "The Spirit of the Lord Omnipotent . . . has wrought a mighty change in us, or in our hearts, that we have no more disposition to do evil, but to do good continually" (Mosiah 5:2). King Lamoni, his wife, and all those who on that occasion had been converted following Ammon's ministrations likewise testified of the "mighty change" that took place in their lives when they were spiritually reborn and forgiven of their sins. "They did all declare unto the people the self-same thing—that their hearts had been changed; that they had no more desire to do evil" (Alma 19:33). Similarly, Alma spoke of the high priests whose "garments were washed white through the blood of the Lamb" and whose hearts and lives were changed by the sanctifying power of the Holy Ghost so that they "could not look upon sin save it were with abhorrence" (Alma 13:11–12).

Thus we can determine the degree to which we have been "born again" by examining our disposition toward evil and our desires to "do good continually." This condition does not mean that we will never again succumb to any of the temptations surrounding us, but it does mean that sinfulness becomes repugnant to us and the desires of our hearts are turned to righteousness, to doing good. This "fruit" of spiritual rebirth is reflected in the following experience of President Joseph F. Smith.

The feeling that came upon me was that of pure peace, of love and of light. I felt in my soul that if I had sinned—and surely I was not without sin—that it had been forgiven me; that I was indeed cleansed from sin; my heart was touched, and I felt that I would not injure the smallest insect beneath my feet. I felt as if I wanted to do good everywhere to everybody and to everything. I felt a newness of life, a newness of desire to that which was right. There was not one particle of desire for evil left in my soul. . . .

Oh! that I could have kept that same spirit and that same earnest desire in my heart every moment of my life from that day to this. Yet many of us who have received that witness, that new birth, that change of heart, while we may have erred in judgment or have made many mistakes, and often perhaps come short of the true standard in our lives, we have repented of the evil, and we have sought from time to time forgiveness at the hand of the Lord; so that until this day the same desire and purpose which pervaded our souls when we . . . received a remission of our sins, still holds possession of our hearts, and is still the ruling sentiment and passion of our souls. (*Gospel Doctrine* [Salt Lake City: Deseret Book, 1939], p. 96.)

Increased Love for Our Fellowman

The spiritual transformation that comes with the reception of the Holy Ghost also creates a "new heart" and a "new spirit" (see Ezekiel 36:25–27), a heart softened by the mercy of Christ and that is filled with greater love and compassion toward others. Enos exemplified this when, after the Lord assured him that his sins were forgiven, his compassion and concern extended beyond self to his brethren, the Nephites, and even to his enemies, the Lamanites (see Enos 1:9–13). After the remarkable conversion of the sons of Mosiah "they were desirous that salvation should be declared to every creature, for they could not bear that any human soul should perish; yea, even the very thoughts that any soul should endure endless torment did cause them to quake and tremble" (Mosiah 28:3). The love of God and the joy of the Lord that fills our hearts when we are "born again" naturally becomes reflected in our desire to "bring [others] to taste of the exceeding joy of which [we] did taste; that they might also be born of God, and be filled with the Holy Ghost" (Alma 36:24).

King Benjamin perhaps explained it best as he counseled his people regarding the "mighty change" they had experienced: "If ye have known of [God's] goodness and have tasted of his love, and have received a remission of your sins, which causeth such exceedingly great joy in your souls. . . . ye will not have a mind to injure one another, but to live peaceably, and to render to every man according to that which is his due. . . . And also ye yourselves will succor those that stand in need of your succor; ye will administer of your substance unto him that standeth in need." (Mosiah 4:11, 13, 16.)

Increased Spiritual Understanding

Several of the Book of Mormon accounts of the remarkable spiritual metamorphosis experienced by those who were "baptized by fire" speak of souls being filled with *light.* A natural or sinful man is spiritually darkened, whereas one who has overcome the natural man and has become a "new creature" in Christ is enlightened by the Holy Ghost. Such spiritual enlightenment is evident in the conversion of King Lamoni—"the dark veil of unbelief was being cast away from his mind, and the light which did light up his mind, which was the light of the glory of God, which was a marvelous light of his goodness—yea, this light had infused such joy into his soul, the cloud of darkness having been dispelled, and that the light of everlasting life was lit up in his soul" (Alma 19:6).

This increased guidance of the Holy Spirit not only brings comfort, peace, and joy, but also an increased spiritual perspective on life. Elder Wilford Woodruff testified of the increased spiritual discernment that comes with the reception and companionship of the Holy Ghost. "The veil of darkness, of doubt, and fear is taken from our minds," he explained, "and we can see clearly where to go and what to do; and we feel that our spirit is right—that we are acceptable before the Lord our God, and are the subjects of his blessings." (In *Journal of Discourses* 8:268.)

King Benjamin's people witnessed that accompanying their "baptism of fire" were "the manifestations of his Spirit" and "great views of that which is to come" (see Mosiah 5:3). These "great views of that which is to come" not only instruct the spiritually reborn concerning the doctrines of the kingdom and the "mysteries of God" (see Alma 26:19–22), but also give them strength in times of uncertainty and troubles and provide practical insight into the daily challenges of life. Those "quickened" by this spiritual outpouring are drawn to spiritual things more than the "natural man." This baptism of the Spirit has "enlightened our minds, enlarged our understandings, extended our feelings, informed our judgment," Elder John Taylor taught. "[It] has warmed up our affections to God and holiness, has nourished and cherished us, and put us in possession of principles that we know will abide for ever and for ever." (In *Journal of Discourses* 7:318.) Men and women who are "born of the Spirit"—who are changed and renewed through the atonement of Christ—"come to see and feel and understand things that the spiritually inert can never know. They become participants in the realm of divine experience." (Robert L. Millet, *The Power of the Word* [Salt Lake City: Deseret Book, 1994], p. 112.)

Having the Image of God Engraven upon Our Countenances

Speaking to the Church in Zarahemla, Alma asked a simple yet significant question of the Saints regarding their level of spiritual rebirth and conversion. "Have ye received [God's] image in your countenances?" (Alma 5:14.) Perhaps Alma was referring to a literal and discernible change that comes upon a person who is spiritually reborn and whose life is redirected to righteousness—a real spiritual appearance that bespeaks a new life of goodness and purity. However, rather than referring to an outward, visible aura, Alma may have been speaking more of an inward spiritual transformation that manifests itself in the actions of the recipient of that "mighty change." As Andrew Skinner, an LDS scholar on the scriptures, explained:

An "image" is not just an outward visual impression but

also a vivid representation, a graphic display, or a total likeness of something. It is a person or thing very much like another, a copy or counterpart. Likewise, *countenance* does not simply mean a facial expression or visual appearance. The word comes from an Old French term originally denoting "behavior," "demeanor," or "conduct." In earlier times the word *countenance* was used with these meanings in mind.

Therefore, to receive Christ's image in one's countenance means to acquire the Savior's likeness in behavior, to be a copy or reflection of the Master's life. This is not possible without a mighty change in one's pattern of living. It requires, too, a change in feelings, attitudes, desires, and spiritual commitment. ("Alma's Pure Testimony," in *Studies in Scripture, vol. 7, 1 Nephi to Alma 29*, ed. Kent P. Jackson [Salt Lake City: Deseret Book, 1987], p. 301.)

Determining whether we have been "born again" and to what extent we have experienced this "mighty change" requires a self-examination of our countenances. This examination is not conducted in front of any mortal mirror, but rather through sincere soul-searching and by listening to the still, small voice of the Spirit. The Holy Ghost will help us to answer the question: Is our renewed commitment to follow the Savior discernible in our countenance, both in our appearance and, more important, in our actions? Sometimes we may recognize the level of spiritual regeneration we have experienced as much by what we do as by what we feel. "If a man bringeth forth good works," declared Alma, "he hearkeneth unto the voice of the good shepherd" (Alma 5:41). Our countenance becomes engraven with the image of God as we continue to exercise faith in the Redeemer, repent of our sins, and strive to keep the commandments of God. As we are "spiritually reborn" again and again and again—each time being elevated to a higher level of righteousness—our countenance, or more precisely, our behavior, becomes more like Him whom we seek to emulate (see 3 Nephi 27:21, 27). C. S. Lewis offers the following insightful word-picture that Latter-day Saints may find helpful as regards Alma's question, "Have ye received his image in your countenances?"

Christ, here and now, in that very room where you are saying your prayers, is doing things to you. It is not a question of a good man who died two thousand years ago. It is a living Man, still as much a man as you, and still as much God as He was when He created the world, really coming and interfering with your very self; killing the old natural self in you and replacing it with the kind of self He has. At first, only for moments. Then for longer periods. Finally, if all goes well, turning you permanently into a different sort of thing; into . . . a being which, in its own small way, has the same kind of life as God; which shares His power, joy, knowledge and eternity. (*Mere Christianity* [New York: Macmillan, 1952], p. 164.)

RETAINING A REMISSION OF ONE'S SINS

Being "born again" and forgiven of our sins does not mean that we have "arrived" at spiritual maturity or that we are guaranteed of eternal life, nor does it mean that we can never lose the "fruits" of that spiritual rebirth. "It is a possibility that one may be born of the Spirit and then, because of his sinfulness or slothfulness, he may lose the Spirit and fall from grace," President Harold B. Lee stated. "The Spirit will not dwell in unholy tabernacles." (Address to seminary and institute personnel, Brigham Young University, 26 June 1962.) This important realization is reflected in the searching question posed by Alma as he taught the Saints in Zarahemla concerning the spiritual rebirth he called the "mighty change." It is a question that we today must continually ask of ourselves: "If ye have experienced a change of heart, and if ye have felt to sing the song of redeeming love, I would ask, can ye feel so now?" (Alma 5:26.) Implicit in Alma's question is the reality that once a person has received the "baptism of fire" and has known and experienced the "fruits" of spiritual rebirth, if he becomes slothful or sinful he may lose the desire "to sing the song of redeeming love." What then can be done to recapture that spiritual regeneration?

"I would that ye should remember to retain the name written always in your hearts," King Benjamin admonished his people after their hearts had been changed, "that ye are not found on the left hand of God, but that ye hear and know the voice by which ye shall be called, and also, the name by which he shall call you" (Mosiah 5:12; see also verses 7–10). King Benjamin counseled his people that in order for them to retain or regain their spiritual rebirth in Christ, they must exercise faith in Christ and repent of their sins, and strive to keep the commandments all the days of their lives. Those attitudes and actions that initially led them to be "born of God" would also result in a retention or reclamation of that "newness of life."

> And again, believe that ye must repent of your sins and forsake them, and humble yourselves before God; and ask in sincerity of heart that he would forgive you; and now, if you believe all these things see that ye do them.
> And again I say unto you as I have said before, that as ye have come to the knowledge of the glory of God, or if ye have known of his goodness and have tasted of his love, and have received a remission of your sins, which causeth such exceedingly great joy in your souls, even so I would that ye should remember, and always retain in remembrance, the greatness of God, and your own nothingness, and his goodness and long-suffering towards you, unworthy creatures, and humble yourselves even in the depths of humility, calling on the name of the Lord daily, and standing steadfastly in the faith. . . .
> And behold, I say unto you that if ye do this ye shall always rejoice, and be filled with the love of God, and always retain a remission of your sins; and ye shall grow in the knowledge of the glory of him that created you, or in the knowledge of that which is just and true. (Mosiah 4:10–12.)

King Benjamin's exhortations are as relevant to us today as they were when given to his own people. If we are to retain the Savior's image in our countenances and His divine love in our hearts we will, as Nephi declared, "press forward with steadfastness in Christ, having a perfect brightness of hope, and a love of God and of all men. Wherefore, if ye shall press forward, feasting upon the word of Christ, and endure to the end, behold, thus saith the Father: Ye shall have eternal life." (2 Nephi 31:20.)

Through the teachings and examples given in the Book of Mormon we learn what being "born again" really entails, how it is to be achieved, and what it does for and to us. This is truly one of the timeless themes of that sacred book. But perhaps even more important than just doctrinal clarification, we learn from the Book of Mormon that becoming a "new creature" in Christ is a lifetime endeavor. Birth, even spiritual rebirth, is just a beginning. Just because we may have once had our "hearts changed through faith on [Christ's] name" and our sins burned from our souls through the "baptism of fire," we cannot let go of the iron rod. "Pressing forward," holding on to the iron rod unceasingly, will inevitably lead us to the tree of life. For this reason King Benjamin's final exhortation to his people—a people who had been "born of God" and had commenced a "new life"—is our charge today as well.

Therefore, I would that ye should be *steadfast and immovable, always abounding in good works,* that Christ, the Lord God Omnipotent, may seal you his, that you may be brought to heaven, that ye may have everlasting salvation and eternal life, through the wisdom, and power, and justice, and mercy of him who created all things, in heaven and in earth, who is God above all. Amen. (Mosiah 5:15; emphasis added.)

*Wherefore, men are free according to the flesh. . . . And
they are free to choose liberty and eternal life, through the great
Mediator of all men, or to choose captivity and death, according
to the captivity and power of the devil; for he seeketh that all men
might be miserable like unto himself.*
—2 NEPHI 2:27

CHAPTER 6

OBEDIENCE: THE DOORWAY TO FREEDOM

As a parent, I think I have heard just about everything from my children—feeble excuses for disobedience, lame explanations for missing curfew, impassioned pleas for permission to do something, direct criticism of my parenting skills, begging for money, mumblings and murmurings of all kinds, and sometimes, however rarely, even expressions of love. I've gotten so that a lot of what they say, especially when it is intended to provoke me, does not immediately cause my blood pressure to elevate to dangerous levels. As I get older I have noticed that I am slower to become agitated with some of the irritating things they say and do. There is one thing, however, that my kids say, and though I have heard it a zillion times it still "pushes my buttons." It is the rhetorical question, "Don't you trust me?"

Usually that question is raised when we have denied them permission to do something, go somewhere, or be with someone. It is a rhetorical question, because as I have learned many times they really don't want an answer; they just want permission to do what they want to do, right now! I find it interesting that most of the time my children ask that notorious question "Don't you trust me?" they have done things that would cause us as parents concern about granting them permission. If I totally trusted them I would have given permission in the first place and then they wouldn't have had to ask that aggravating, argumentative, rhetorical question that they know drives me up the wall!

What disturbs me most when my children ask, "Don't you trust me?" is the implication that trust is something that just automatically happens, like one of those "unalienable rights" mentioned in the Declaration of Independence. Trust, like freedom, doesn't just exist in a vacuum, as it were. It must be earned. There is a price that must be paid for trust and the freedom that it affords. My children sometimes can't see the relationship between the two. Mom and Dad don't just arbitrarily decide if and when they trust their children. They don't grant or deny permission and freedom merely on a whim. Trust and freedom are directly linked to other factors.

"If you feel pressed in and pressured and not free," Elder Boyd K. Packer observed, "it may be for one of two reasons. One, if you have lost freedom, possibly it has been through some irresponsible act of your own. Now you must regain it. You may be indentured—indentured to some habits of laziness or indolence; some even become slaves to addiction. The other reason is that maybe if you are not free you have not earned it. Freedom is not a self-preserving gift. It has to be earned, and it has to be protected." (*"That All May Be Edified"* [Salt Lake City: Bookcraft, 1982], p. 254.)

In high school I came to understand in an interesting and personal way how trust and freedom are directly linked to behavior. During my senior year, my friends and I decided that we were going to take a "college day" absence to go visit a college campus to determine if we wanted to attend that university. Our high school allowed graduating seniors a few school-excused "college days" absences for this purpose. In reality, we had no intention of attending that school, but we wanted a school-

authorized and approved absence that was really a "vacation"—
kind of like the movie *Ferris Bueller's Day Off.* We selected a
weekend for our trip that not-so-accidentally coincided with a
girls' drill team competition for the state. Our girlfriends were in
the drill team and would be conveniently in that city the same
weekend. The plans were made, but an obstacle or two remained
in the way—permission to go and then being able to take the
family car. Our biggest concern was the car—it's far easier to get
permission to go somewhere than to get permission to take the
car.

"Top, you ask your parents for permission to take your car,"
my buddies requested. "Your parents trust you, and if they let
you take the car then our parents will surely let us go along."
What my friends said was true. My parents did seem to trust me
a great deal and I seemed to have more freedom and privileges
than most. I assumed that it was just because I was the "baby" of
the family and "spoiled rotten"—deservedly so I might add! It
was, however, on this trip that I began to put two and two
together regarding my parents' trust. What I learned was
enlightening and has stayed with me all the years since. I have
tried to teach the same principle to my own children.

When the long-awaited and planned-for weekend arrived, we
excitedly drove across the state—not with an intention of visiting
the college, but rather playing and partying with friends. There
we were—boyfriends and girlfriends alone and without parental
supervision. There were many opportunities to fall prey to temptations and the foolish activities of youth. But when I came face
to face with some of the temptations we had actually planned for
and "courted," one thought repeatedly and powerfully pierced
my mind and heart. "Your parents trust you." I could hear over
and over again my friends stating that to me. It was almost like
an epiphany to me—a revelation as to why I was where I was,
doing what I wanted to be doing. It dawned on me like a thun-
derbolt that I was able to take the car and go away with friends
for a weekend—even in the presence of sin and temptation—
because my parents trusted me. They trusted me because I had
not been rebellious, fighting them for my independence and

resisting their supervision and expectations. They trusted me because I had been obedient.

Now, don't get me wrong—I wasn't a perfect little angel, but neither was I a perfect little devil. I *generally* tried to live the standards of the gospel, obey family rules, and respect the wishes of my parents. As the temptations to "sow wild oats" or "go off the deep end" presented themselves to me I was reminded that if I did those things I would lose my parents' trust (and certainly break their hearts) and as a result I would lose the freedom I so much enjoyed. My much-treasured independence was inextricably linked to their trust of me and their trust was linked to my obedience. You can't have one without the other. I am grateful for the lesson learned that weekend in Boise so many years ago. I wish I had understood it sooner. It could have averted many arguments and allowed me to enjoy even greater freedom.

One of the most important messages of the Book of Mormon for our day—for young and old alike—is how agency really operates and the relationship of freedom to choose to the consequences resulting from those choices. Through the doctrinal teachings and examples of the lives of men and women we read about in the Book of Mormon, we see how some, through obedience, obtained "perfect liberty"—what President Marion G. Romney defined as "freedom of the soul"—while others became enslaved, physically and spiritually, through their sinful choices.

Agency is a great blessing. "Next to the bestowal of life itself, the right to direct our lives is God's greatest gift to man," President David O. McKay declared. "Freedom of choice is more to be treasured than any possession earth can give. . . . It is the impelling source of the soul's progress." ("Man's Free Agency— an Eternal Principle of Progress," *Improvement Era*, December 1965, p. 1073.) Although agency is a divine gift and a monumental blessing to mankind, it also has its serious side effects. Not only can free exercise of agency yield great spiritual growth, bounteous blessings, and personal progress, but it can also end in bondage, misery, and spiritual death. Every choice we make leads us in one direction or the other. As Lehi explained to his own family, specifically his son Jacob: "Wherefore, men are free according to the flesh; and all things are given them which are expedient unto man. And they are free to choose liberty and eternal life, through the great Mediator of all men, or to choose captivity and death, according to the captivity and power of the devil; for he seeketh that all men might be miserable like unto himself." (2 Nephi 2:27; see also 2 Nephi 10:23.)

When we speak of *agency* there is another word that must also be used and understood in conjunction with it—*accountability*. It is the companion of agency and cannot be separated from it. Similarly, the word *choice* also has an inseparable companion—*consequence*. There are no real choices without accompanying consequences. If accountability is eliminated, so also is agency. There is a law of physics that I may not fully understand in its scientific context, yet I see a spiritual corollary—"For every action there is an equal and opposite reaction." Every choice we make—leading either to action or inaction—has a reaction, a consequence. While I am free to make my choices, I am not always free to choose the consequences—it is a package deal! When my children disobey resulting in a loss of privileges or some other form of punishment, they sometimes say, "You're taking away my free agency!" In reality, it is not we who have restricted them, but they themselves. Their choices yielded certain consequences—consequences they did not want but which cannot be separated from the choices. Many years ago there was a popular LDS musical entitled *My Turn On Earth*. In that musical play was a cute song with a profound and powerful message that illustrated the relationship between choice and consequence—agency and accountability. "When you choose the very first step on the road, you also choose the last. So if you don't like the end of the road, you'd better back up fast."

When I served as a bishop several years ago I had many experiences with disciplinary councils that also testified of this principle. When one man was disfellowshipped for serious moral transgressions, he accused me of wrongfully taking away blessings that he felt were rightfully his as a member of the Church, such as attending the temple, holding a calling, and participating in Church meetings. In his case, the Church discipline also adversely affected his vocational pursuits. "You're taking away my freedom!" he stated repeatedly. "No," I responded, "*you* took away your own freedom! You gave it away for sin." That is the essence of agency and accountability, choice and consequence. They always go hand in hand. As Elder Neal A. Maxwell succinctly stated, "We'd better want the consequences of what we want!" (" 'Swallowed Up in the Will of the Father,' " *Ensign*, November 1995, p. 23.) Samuel the Lamanite prophet, in calling the wicked Nephites to repentance, further taught this principle.

> And now remember, remember, my brethren, that whosoever perisheth, perisheth unto himself; and whosoever doeth iniquity, doeth it unto himself; for behold, ye are free; ye are permitted to act for yourselves; for behold, God hath given unto you a knowledge and he hath made you free.
>
> He hath given unto you that ye might know good from evil, and he hath given unto you that ye might choose life or death; and ye can do good and be restored unto that which is good or have that which is good restored unto you; or ye can do evil, and have that which is evil restored unto you. (Helaman 14:30–31.)

As Lehi taught, there are two ends of the continuum of agency—"liberty and eternal life" or "captivity and death." The Book of Mormon gives us graphic illustrations of each. Individuals as well as entire nations are seen in the scriptures as obtaining through their own choices either freedom, both political and spiritual, or captivity—enslavement by their enemies and spiritual bondage to sin. One of my favorite illustrations in the Book of Mormon of how "perfect liberty" is obtained through righteousness is the example of Nephi, son of Helaman. Weighed down by the wickedness of the Nephites—their secret combinations, murders, immorality, dishonesty, and "all manner of iniquities," Nephi poured out his soul to the Lord. "And it came to pass as he was thus pondering in his heart," the scriptures record, "behold, a voice came unto him saying:"

Blessed art thou, Nephi, for those things which thou hast done; for I have beheld how thou hast with unwearyingness declared the word, which I have given unto thee, unto this people. And thou hast not feared them, and hast not sought thine own life, but hast sought my will, and to keep my commandments.

And now because thou hast done this with such unwearyingness, behold, I will bless thee forever; and I will make thee mighty in word and in deed, in faith and in works; yea, even that all things shall be done unto thee according to thy word, for thou shalt not ask that which is contrary to my will. (Helaman 10:3–5; see also verses 6–11.)

Nephi was given all power because of his righteousness. He could seal the heavens and cause a famine if he wanted to. He could destroy the wicked Nephites if he desired. He could move mountains or perform any other remarkable miracle. God gave him that power—that freedom to do anything he wanted—because God trusted him totally. That kind of trust came because of continual, "unwearying" obedience. The Lord knew that Nephi would not "ask that which is contrary to my will" because Nephi had already demonstrated that his choices and will were in harmony with the mind of God. That is freedom!

At the other end of the continuum I see Korihor as one whose choices led to terrible consequences. He certainly would not have desired those outcomes at the outset, yet they came as the natural by-product of his evil desires and deeds. Undoubtedly he was a man of great talent and ability, blessed with the gifts of a keen intellect and the powers of persuasion. He had just as much freedom to choose as anyone else. Instead of choices that would lead to the kind of "perfect liberty" that Nephi would enjoy, he exercised his will to choose the path that led to complete captivity, both physical and spiritual. Korihor's own words describe the consequences that followed his choices.

I always knew that there was a God.

But behold, the devil hath deceived me; for he appeared

unto me in the form of an angel, and said unto me: Go and reclaim this people, for they have all gone astray after an unknown God. And he said unto me: There is no God; yea, and he taught me that which I should say. And I have taught his words; and I taught them because they were pleasing unto the carnal mind; and I taught them, even until I had much success, insomuch that I verily believed that they were true; and for this cause I withstood the truth, even until I have brought this curse upon me. (Alma 30:52–53.)

The scriptural account shows Korihor at the end of his life being rejected and derided by the very people who once supported him and made him popular. In the end, he was left to the humiliation of going from "house to house begging for his food" (Alma 30:56). While in this pitiful bondage he was "run upon and trodden down, even until he was dead" (Alma 30:59). What a contrast to righteous Nephi who had total freedom and ultimate power! God grants the obedient perfect liberty, whereas Satan only offers the wicked complete captivity. The "moral of the story" surely is as the prophet Mormon states it: "And thus we see the end of him who perverteth the ways of the Lord; and thus we see that the devil will not support his children at the last day, but doth speedily drag them down to hell" (Alma 30:60).

It was the sum of the choices made by the "more righteous part" of the Nephites that allowed them the freedom to behold the resurrected Lord and to one by one feel the prints in His hands and His feet (see 3 Nephi 11). It was the sum of their choices that led to freedom from contention and crime, prejudice and persecution (see 4 Nephi 1). The resulting blessings of their righteous choices included hearts filled with love of God, and spiritual and economic prosperity. "Surely there could not be a happier people among all the people who had been created by the hand of God" (4 Nephi 1:16). There are many similar accounts in the Book of Mormon of individuals and entire peoples who, through the righteous exercise of their agency, experienced "perfect liberty"—both temporal freedom and progression and spiritual "freedom of the soul."

In contrast, it was the sum of the choices made by Laman and Lemuel that left them in ultimate spiritual bondage—"past feeling" (see 1 Nephi 17:45). It was the sum of the wicked choices made by the Nephites that led to their bondage to Gadianton robbers, to rampant corruption and crime at all levels, which in turn led to the ultimate undermining of their very government (see Helaman 6). Because of their unrighteous exercise of their divine gift of agency, they "did trample under their feet the commandments of God, and did turn unto their own ways" (Helaman 6:31), which resulted in the Spirit of the Lord withdrawing from them. The consequences of their choices led to ultimate bondage—"the sorrowing of the damned" (see Mormon 2). Mormon stated that because of their wickedness "they did curse God, and wish to die" and "that the day of grace was passed with them, both temporally and spiritually" (Mormon 2:14–15).

Each group, both ends of the continuum, started out with the same divine gift of agency. Each was blessed with the Light of Christ which "inviteth and enticeth to do good continually" (Moroni 7:13) and helps all "know good from evil" (Moroni 7:15–16). Yet the "end of the road" for each was poles apart—all because of the sum of choices, both small and large. There is probably no greater illustration of the reality that men are "free to act for [themselves]—to choose the way of everlasting death or the way of eternal life" (2 Nephi 10:23) than the Book of Mormon. And as the familiar saying states, "Those who fail to learn from the past are doomed to repeat it." Truly, the Book of Mormon was written for our day.

There is a diagram that I use with my classes at Brigham Young University when I talk about agency and accountability that visually reflects the Book of Mormon teaching on the subject. I think it is helpful to take a complex spiritual concept and make it simple to understand. For me, this visual diagram helps me to see how choice is directly linked to consequences. It shows how the consequences of wrong choices can restrict freedom and how obedience is truly, as Elder Boyd K. Packer called it, "the doorway to freedom."

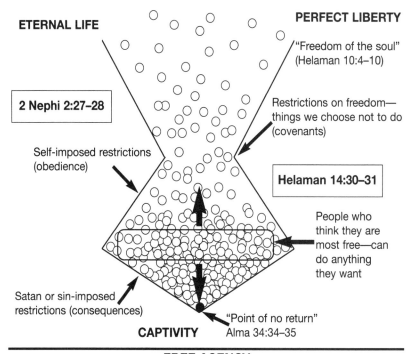

ETERNAL LIFE

PERFECT LIBERTY

"Freedom of the soul"
(Helaman 10:4–10)

2 Nephi 2:27–28

Restrictions on freedom—
things we choose not to do
(covenants)

Self-imposed restrictions
(obedience)

Helaman 14:30–31

People who
think they are
most free—can
do anything
they want

Satan or sin-imposed
restrictions (consequences)

"Point of no return"
Alma 34:34–35

CAPTIVITY

FREE AGENCY
A Summary

1. Agency does not mean we can do anything we want and have the results we want. There is a "given" consequence to every choice. Agency, therefore, is not "free"—it is bounded by irrevocable laws.

2. Correct choices preserve agency and expand the parameters within which it can be exercised. Incorrect choices limit these parameters.

3. Although forgiveness is always available, we can get to a point where that availability will be of no value to us—we can move so deeply and so long into sin that we can lose the *desire* and eventually the *power* to choose right (see Spencer W. Kimball, *The Miracle of Forgiveness* [Salt Lake City: Bookcraft, 1969], p. 117; Alma 34:35).

4. When we *exercise* our agency, entering into agreements (BYU standards, for example) or covenants (baptismal, priesthood, temple, marriage), we cannot then claim our agency as being violated when we are expected to honor these agreements or covenants, or when we suffer the consequences of not honoring them.

5. From an eternal perspective, those who bind (govern, discipline) themselves most closely to the gospel standards are the most "free," or have the most agency, while those who insist on being "free" from gospel standards are ultimately the most restricted.

(Diagram and summary developed by Larry E. Dahl, Professor of Church History and Doctrine, Brigham Young University)

All of us are familiar with people who *feel* they are free to do anything they want. Sometimes these people even mock and persecute those of us who do not feel the same freedom and who do not engage in the activities they advocate. "You Mormons can't do anything," they sometimes mockingly declare. "You are not free. You can't smoke, drink, or do any of the 'fun things' we can do." In reality we all begin with the same divine gift of agency, but every choice we make either adds to our freedom or restricts it. As Lehi anciently taught, every significant choice we make is either leading us to liberty and eternal life or captivity and spiritual death. So those people who think they are most free will soon come to realize that their wicked choices have left them far less free than they had intended. Even when they felt most free there were limitations on and parameters surrounding their freedom. They may have used their agency to choose evil, but they usually forget that "every action has an equal and opposite reaction"—every choice has an accompanying consequence. "With respect to the loss of personal liberty through the misuse of agency," President Marion G. Romney explained, "our lives are filled with tragic evidence."

> We see the alcoholic with his craving for drink, the dope fiend in his frenzy, and worse, the pervert with his irretrievable loss of manhood. Who will say that such persons enjoy liberty?
>
> Notwithstanding the fact that through its misuse, political, economic, and personal liberty are lost, free agency will always endure because it is an eternal principle. However, the free agency possessed by any one person is increased or diminished by the use to which he puts it. Every wrong decision one makes restricts the area in which he can thereafter exercise his agency. The further one goes in the making of wrong decisions in the exercise of free agency, the more difficult it is for him to recover the lost ground. One can, by persisting long enough, reach the point of no return. He then becomes an abject slave. By the exercising of his free agency, he has decreased the area in which he can act, almost to the vanishing point. ("The Perfect Law of Liberty," *Ensign*, November 1981, p. 45.)

President Romney uses two interesting phrases in his description of the end result of making wrong choices and choosing evil rather than righteousness: "the point of no return" and "the vanishing point." Sin is extremely addicting. Without repentance, it is possible to become a "spiritual junkie"—addicted to all manner of evil—just as powerfully as drug "junkies" or alcoholics are addicted to their substances of choice. "From an initial experiment thought to be trivial," Elder Russell M. Nelson observed: "A vicious cycle may follow. From trial comes a habit. From habit comes dependence. From dependence comes addiction. Its grasp is so gradual. Enslaving shackles of habit are too small to be sensed until they are too strong to be broken. . . . Addiction surrenders later freedom to choose." ("Addiction or Freedom," *Ensign*, November 1988, pp. 6–7.)

The Book of Mormon warns of the binding power of sin by using such terms as "awful chains" (2 Nephi 1:13), "chains of hell" (Alma 13:30), "bands of iniquity" (Mosiah 23:12), "bands of death" (Alma 5:7), and other images of spiritual bondage. The prophet Amulek warned of the binding powers of sin when he urged his people to not procrastinate their repentance. "For behold, if ye have procrastinated the day of your repentance . . . ," he warned, "ye have become subjected to the spirit of the devil, and he doth seal you his; therefore, the Spirit of the Lord hath withdrawn from you, and hath no place in you, and the devil hath all power over you" (Alma 34:35). In the full context of his sermon, Amulek was speaking of the final state of the wicked "in that eternal world," but the "night of darkness" when Satan "doth seal you his" can also occur in this life. Through continually choosing evil and suffering the freedom-restricting consequences of those choices it is possible to reach that terrible "point of no return"—"the vanishing point" of personal liberty. Elder Spencer W. Kimball testified:

> It is true that the great principle of repentance is always available, but for the wicked and rebellious there are serious reservations to this statement. For instance, sin is intensely habit-forming and sometimes moves men to the tragic point of

no return. Without repentance there can be no forgiveness, and without forgiveness all the blessings of eternity hang in jeopardy. As the transgressor moves deeper and deeper in his sin, and the error is entrenched more deeply and the will to change is weakened, it becomes increasingly nearer hopeless and he skids down and down until either he does not want to climb back up or he has lost the power to do so. (*The Miracle of Forgiveness* [Salt Lake City: Bookcraft, 1969], p. 117.)

When I discuss the lower half of this diagram with my students and show how the sin-caused and Satan-imposed consequences of bad choices continually constrict freedom, I ask them to think of specific "friends" in high school who mocked them for not being "free" to do the things these so-called friends were doing. "Where are they now?" I ask. "What has happened to their so-called freedom? And where are you in comparison?" It is interesting to discuss how so often many of those who thought they were most free become slaves to all manner of sins. Doors of opportunity are slammed in their faces by their own choices. In contrast, those who were persecuted as being "not free to do whatever you want" now have greater freedom to feel, to do, to be—because righteous use of agency always opens "the doorway to freedom."

It is readily apparent by examining the diagram that there are constrictions and restrictions in both the upper and the lower portions. There is, however, a big difference between the two, and that difference makes all the difference. When a person once chooses to sin, he may not choose the consequences that restrict his freedom, yet they occur as the natural side effects of sin—Satan-imposed and sin-induced. On the other hand, there are indeed restrictions of a positive nature, self-imposed restrictions of freedom in order to preserve freedom and expand the parameters of choice. These self-imposed restraints constitute self-control—the "best control,"—the most important "freedom of choice" (see Boyd K. Packer, "Agency and Control," chapter 16 in *The Shield of Faith* [Salt Lake City: Bookcraft, 1998], pp.128–29). Choosing to obey a divine commandment or exercise self-discipline in some manner may temporarily restrict what we can or cannot do in some areas, but it always leads to greater freedom in those areas we desire most.

For example, I am always amazed by gifted musicians who can perform some of the most difficult, complex, yet remarkably beautiful compositions. It is like a miracle to me. It brings great joy to them as well as the audience. Sometimes I am inspired as much by the joy they exude in their performing as in the music itself. The most gifted musicians perform with such passion and poise that they make what they are doing almost look easy. But easy it's not, and usually the audience has no idea of the "price" that has been paid for such musical freedom.

I have a small inkling and large regrets. As a boy I took piano lessons for a few years. My teacher even told me I had talent, but I didn't have self-discipline—I hated to practice. It took time, concentration, and energy that I wanted to spend on baseball instead. Because I was unwilling to "restrict" my freedom at that time, I have neither piano playing talent nor am I a major-league baseball player. Mom and Dad exerted all kinds of external pressure on me to practice and to develop that talent. Nothing worked. Not even gentle proddings, financial incentives, loss of privileges, and angry confrontations caused me to practice—at least for very long. In the end, however, only internal pressure, self-imposed discipline, will yield the desired results. When I do things only because of external pressures I am not really free. I only become free when I choose to do those things all by myself. This is as true with spiritual matters as it is with the temporal.

My children have often said, usually after they have been told they can't do something inappropriate, "I can't wait to grow up, because then I can do whatever I want!" As parents we often worry about what they are *doing*, but should also be attentive to what they are *wanting*. Our desires are closely linked to our freedom to choose. We are not totally free just because we may, because of any number of external factors, choose to *do* right. We become truly free, however, when choosing to do right is also what we, from within ourselves, want. President Boyd K. Packer has taught:

I am free, and I am very jealous of my independence. I am quick to declare my independence and my freedom. Choice among my freedoms is my freedom to be obedient. I obey because I want to: I choose to.

Some people are always suspicious that one is only obedient because he is compelled to be. They indict themselves with the very thought that one is only obedient because he is compelled to be. They feel that one would obey only through compulsion. They speak for themselves. I am free to be obedient, and I decided that—all by myself. I pondered on it; I reasoned it; I even experimented a little. I learned some sad lessons from disobedience. Then I tested it in the great laboratory of spiritual inquiry—the most sophisticated, accurate, and refined test that we can make of any principle. So I am not hesitant to say that I want to be obedient to the principles of the gospel. *I want to.* I have decided that. My volition, my agency, has been turned in that direction. The Lord knows that. (*"That All May Be Edified,"* p. 255.)

When our desires for righteousness coincide with our choice to obey we feel a liberty—a "freedom of the soul"—that the world cannot offer in any form. In my own life I have felt this freedom even in the face of worldly ridicule for my "blind obedience" and "lack of freedom." I feel no restriction to my freedom because of the law of chastity. I don't look at beautiful women and disgustedly think to myself: "Top, you poor soul. You are not free to commit adultery. The Church is taking away not only your free agency but also all the fun out of life." What a ridiculous thought! There is not one nanosecond when I entertain such a thought, because I live the law of chastity because I chose, even covenanted, to do so, not out of external Church pressure or because my job depends on temple worthiness, but because *I desire* to do so. By doing so I have greater freedoms, joys, and blessings than a worldly person can imagine. And so it is, not only with chastity but with every principle of the gospel—obeying because we really want to opens the door of freedom. "Subjection to God," Elder Neal A. Maxwell stated, "is really emancipation" (" 'Willing to Submit,' " *Ensign,* May 1985, p. 71).

With each righteous choice, coupled with righteous desires, come greater blessings and opportunities, ever expanding until there remain no parameters, no limitations to the freedom that one can enjoy. "Just as following wrong alternatives restricts free agency and leads to slavery," President Romney explained, "so pursuing correct alternatives widens the scope of one's agency and leads to perfect liberty."

> Freedom thus obtained—that is, by obedience to the law of Christ—is freedom of the soul, the highest form of liberty. And the most glorious thing about it is that it is within the reach of every one of us, regardless of what people about us, or even nations, do. All we have to do is learn the law of Christ and obey it. To learn it and obey it is the primary purpose of every soul's mortal life. ("The Perfect Law of Liberty," p. 45.)

The Book of Mormon teaches and illustrates this timeless theme best of all. Not only was Nephi, son of Helaman, granted all power and perfect liberty because of his obedience and righteousness, but others too experienced the expansive nature of freedom of the soul. The people of Nephi who repented of their sins and exercised their agency in righteousness were blessed with economic prosperity, political liberty, and more. Mormon tells us that they experienced an unsurpassed spiritual freedom because "they did fast and pray oft, and did wax stronger and stronger in their humility, and firmer and firmer in the faith of Christ, unto the filling their souls with joy and consolation, yea, even to the purifying and the sanctification of their hearts, which sanctification cometh because of their yielding their hearts unto God" (Helaman 3:35; see also Mosiah 3:19).

They, like Nephi, learned that freedom isn't really free. It has its "price"—submission of one's desires and deeds to the will of God. In reality, that "cost" is not exorbitant—it returns to us our initial investment and much, much more in dividends. "When you and I finally submit ourselves," Elder Neal A. Maxwell stated, "by letting our individual wills be swallowed up in God's will, then we are really giving something to Him! It is the only possession which is truly ours to give!" (" 'Swallowed Up in the Will of the Father,' " p. 24.) This kind of obedience—"the only unconditional surrender which is also a total victory"—is the key that turns the lock and opens up to us the freedom of heaven. As Elder Boyd K. Packer taught:

> Obedience—that which God will never take by force—He will accept when freely given. And He will then return to you freedom that you can hardly dream of—the freedom to feel and to know, the freedom to do, and the freedom to *be*, at least a thousandfold more than we offer Him. Strangely enough, the key to freedom is obedience.
>
> . . . Perhaps the greatest discovery of my life, without question the greatest commitment, came when I finally had the confidence in God that I would loan or yield my agency to Him—without compulsion or pressure, without any duress, as a single individual alone, by myself, no counterfeiting, nothing expected other than the privilege. In a sense, speaking figuratively, to take one's agency, that precious gift which the scriptures make plain is essential to life itself, and say, "I will do as thou directs," is afterward to learn that in so doing you possess it all the more. (*"That All May Be Edified,"* pp. 256–57.)

In the many years since that weekend trip to Boise, I have repeatedly gained a witness of the truthfulness of the lesson I learned then—that freedom is dependent upon trust, and trust comes with obedience. My children have heard this story many times and have heard me say, "If you want to have total freedom, then earn my total trust by desiring and doing only that which is right." But this lesson, as taught in the Book of Mormon, is far bigger than just adolescents gaining independence from parental supervision. It is about achieving perfect liberty—that freedom of the soul—that is promised to those who exercise their God-given agency in faithful obedience—in yielding their will and wishes to the will of the Father. We all have agency; that is not the issue. The burning issue of the day, the relevant question that faces all of us today is, what will we choose? In this age of personal independence—"doing your own thing"—Lehi's message is perhaps needed now more than ever. To what and to whom will we look for freedom? The Book of Mormon provides us the only answer that will ultimately lead to the personal freedom mankind desperately seeks.

> I would that ye should look to the great Mediator, and hearken unto his great commandments; and be faithful unto his words, and choose eternal life, according to the will of his Holy Spirit;
>
> And not choose eternal death, according to the will of the flesh and the evil which is therein, which giveth the spirit of the devil power to captivate, to bring you down to hell, that he may reign over you in his own kingdom (2 Nephi 2:28–29).

And now, as the preaching of the word had a great
tendency to lead the people to do that which was just—
yea, it had had more powerful effect upon the minds of the
people than the sword, or anything else, which had happened
unto them—therefore Alma thought it was expedient
that they should try the virtue of the word of God.
—ALMA 31:5

CHAPTER 7

THE POWER
OF THE WORD

My children have taught me a great deal about effective discipline.
The lessons have come from observing how they respond to my
efforts to discipline them. Sometimes the things that I think are
most effective in punishing them when they have done wrong
and in altering inappropriate behaviors have little or no effect—
much to my chagrin. I have learned that often the most simple
things are actually the most powerful in changing attitudes and
actions.

For example, on more than one occasion after a child had
broken family rules and gotten into some kind of trouble, he or
she would say to me something like: "Ground me, lecture me,
spank me, yell at me, even take away the car keys, but don't let
Mom loose on me!" Of course, I am exaggerating a tad, but
nonetheless I was taken aback by their extreme aversion to how
Mom dealt with their misbehavior. My wife is far more gentle
and kind in teaching and training the children than I, yet they
seemed to be more afraid of the discipline she dispensed than

what I might do. She was never harsh, abusive, or overly punitive in her dealings with the children. She is the "softy" and I am the "hard guy"—I am the "iron fist" and she is the "velvet glove." Then why would they express those kinds of feelings? What made her discipline so potent that it was dreaded?

One of the children once made a statement that perhaps explains their feelings about Mom's discipline: "Oh, you know how Mom is. She has a scripture for everything!" So that was it! The dreaded discipline—that which my children feared more than grounding, yelling, going to bed without supper, even spanking—was to have Mom quote a relevant scripture.

There was something they felt when Mom would recite or read a scripture that cut to the very core—that pierced their very souls. This could not be rationalized away or escaped. While my children might think that their mother's disciplinary scriptural sermons were "cheesy" (that's the word they used to describe anything too "churchy" or "goody-goody"), they readily admitted that it affected them in ways that they did not always like. They usually didn't like it, because it often made them feel guilty for wrongdoing and always reminded them of what the Lord has taught. For them that was the problem—you can argue with Dad and fight against his discipline, but how do you argue with the Lord? How can you tell God that His words found in the scriptures are wrong? It is easier to resent and rebel against the authority and discipline of men than God's. That is one of the values of the scriptures and the doctrines revealed from heaven. To his young friend Timothy, the Apostle Paul taught the value of the scriptures that can be applied in all aspects of life. "And that from a child thou hast known the holy scriptures, which are able to make thee wise unto salvation through faith which is in Christ Jesus. And all scripture given by inspiration of God, is profitable for doctrine, for reproof, for correction, for instruction in righteousness: that the man of God may be perfect, thoroughly furnished unto all good works." (JST 2 Timothy 3:15–17.)

In modern revelation the Lord Himself speaks not only of the value of the scriptures but also of their power to cut to the very core of the heart, mind, and soul. "Behold, I am God; give heed unto my word, which is quick and powerful, sharper than a two-edged sword, to the dividing asunder of both joints and marrow; therefore give heed unto my words" (D&C 6:2; see also D&C 15:2; 33:1). The scriptures have not only instructional value, but also a power to touch hearts and transform lives.

The Book of Mormon testifies of this inherent power of the scriptures, both by its doctrine and by the numerous examples it cites of lives lifted and souls saved by the "power of the word." One of my favorite examples is of the prophet Alma. Having served in a variety of priesthood leadership callings in the Church—high councils, bishoprics, bishop, and stake presidency—I can relate in some small measure to the feelings of Alma as he encountered apostasy, iniquity, and spiritual slackness among his people. The Book of Mormon records that Alma's "heart again began to sicken because of the iniquity of the people" (Alma 31:1).

> For it was the cause of great sorrow to Alma to know of iniquity among his people; therefore his heart was exceedingly sorrowful because of the separation of the Zoramites from the Nephites. . . .
>
> Now the Zoramites were dissenters from the Nephites; therefore they had had the word of God preached unto them.
>
> But they had fallen into great errors, for they would not observe to keep the commandments of God, and his statutes, according to the law of Moses.
>
> Neither would they observe the performances of the church, to continue in prayer and supplication to God daily, that they might not enter into temptation.
>
> Yea, in fine, they did pervert the ways of the Lord in very many instances; therefore, for this cause, Alma and his brethren went into the land to preach the word unto them. (Alma 31:2, 8–11.)

What a monumental reactivation task faced Alma! He could have easily felt that it was hopeless. How could those who had sunk so deep be pulled out of their spiritual hole and turned around? What could he do? Where would he start?

How he went about that mission of reformation and redemption is both enlightening and applicable to us and our own challenges today. He did not create any new programs. He did not organize a ward social, establish an intramural basketball league, or plan some super-duper water-skiing excursion. Now, don't get me wrong—I am not making fun of these kinds of activities. They have their place and purpose, but Alma seems to be telling us—showing us the way—that there are more powerful reactivation and spiritual reformation tools at our disposal than mere activities. Alma wasn't desirous of reclaiming the Zoramites only as "cultural converts" or "social Saints." He wanted them truly converted and committed to Christ—heart, might, mind, and soul turned to righteousness.

> And now, as the preaching of the word had a great tendency to lead the people to do that which was just—yea, it had had more powerful effect upon the minds of the people than the sword, or anything else, which had happened unto them— therefore Alma thought it was expedient that they should try the virtue of the word of God (Alma 31:5).

President Gordon B. Hinckley has taught that three things are required to retain converts—a friend, a responsibility, and "nurturing with the good word of God" (see "Some Thoughts on Temples, Retention of Converts, and Missionary Service," *Ensign*, November 1997, p. 51). These three things are vital not only to retention of converts and reactivation of those members who have drifted from full activity in the Church, but are also vital for each of us in order to keep the fires of testimony and conversion blazing in our own souls. Without the spiritual nourishment that comes from "the good word of God" the other two—friends and responsibilities—will not have the power to permanently transform lives. The Book of Mormon illustrates this "power of the word" over and over again.

Recently a colleague shared with me an insightful observation of how we obtain the profound doctrinal teachings of the Book of Mormon. I was able to see something in the scriptures that had previously escaped my notice. I was familiar with all of the doctrines taught in the scriptures, but my friend pointed out to me something a little different that gave even greater meaning to those teachings. "You know *what* is taught in those chapters," he explained, "but look carefully at *to whom* those doctrines are addressed and *why*."

As I took this challenge and read carefully the context of those many important passages, something jumped off the pages at me. Interestingly, many, if not most, of the doctrinal discourses and foundational gospel teachings in the Book of Mormon were addressed to dissidents, apostates, "inactives," or blatant sinners in need of repentance. Why? Because, as Alma knew and testified of, the "preaching of the word had a great tendency to lead the people to do that which was just—yea, it had a more powerful effect upon the minds of the people than the sword, or anything else" (Alma 31:5). The scriptures and the doctrines of the kingdom of God, accompanied by the witness of the Holy Spirit, will affect a profound and permanent change in hearts and souls and behavior of men and women. In fact, it appears that many of the problems we read about in the Book of Mormon came as result of the people failing to study, comprehend, and apply the scriptures. Take a look at just a few of the examples:

We learn the "doctrine of Christ" and gain much understanding regarding the scattering and gathering of Israel and the latter-day restoration from Nephi, who was trying to break down the skepticism and hard-heartedness of his brothers.

From Abinadi's encounter with King Noah and his wicked priests we gain a greater understanding of the purposes of the ancient law of Moses and its relationship to the Atonement. We gain great insights into the plan of redemption and the resurrection that the Messiah will bring (see Mosiah chapters 11–16).

We learn more about the Atonement, the doctrine of restoration and resurrection, as well as how to obtain spiritual knowledge and to become sanctified through the power of the Holy

Ghost, from Alma's mission of reactivation throughout the land and his subsequent encounter with Zeezrom (see Alma chapters 5–16).

Perhaps there are no greater discourses on faith, true worship, the power of prayer and the "infinite and eternal sacrifice" of the Son of God than what we find in the words of Alma and Amulek as they taught the humble Zoramites, in an effort to reclaim them for the true Church (see Alma chapters 31–35).

From the top of the city walls, Samuel the Lamanite prophet called the wicked Nephites to repentance and declared doctrine to them. From his prophecies regarding the coming Christ we also learn how the atoning sacrifice of the Great Redeemer unconditionally redeems all mankind from the Fall and how redemption from our own personal sins is achieved through faith, repentance, and the ordinances of the gospel. Perhaps the most profound discussion of the indispensable role of agency in the plan of salvation is given in this context (see Helaman chapters 13–15).

There are many, many more examples. But there is one that is my personal favorite—Alma's correction of his wayward son, Corianton. Most of us are quite familiar with the setting for this story. Corianton had been called as one of many missionaries that accompanied Alma on his mission of reform among the Zoramites. While on that mission, Corianton did "forsake the ministry" and became involved with a harlot (see Alma 39:3–4). It is a tragic story, and one can only imagine Alma's heartbreak. What is most enlightening to me, however, is that despite the terrible nature of Corianton's immorality and the negative impact it had on missionary work, that is not the major thrust of Alma's reproof. He could have easily given a long and impassioned lecture about chastity. Or perhaps he could have played upon the "guilt complex" of Corianton—"grounding" him forever and continually reminding him of the damage that was done to the family, the Church, and the Zoramites because of his sins. There are many other things that any other parent might have naturally done or said, but Alma chose a different approach—different from the "natural man," he chose the "power of the word."

It is interesting to me that the context of this story is immorality, yet there is very little on chastity—only a verse or two in the entire discourse. Why? It appears to me that Alma knew that there was something else that would affect the heart of Corianton, lead him to repentance, and turn him from immorality to virtue, from abandonment of responsibilities to a life of service. That which would be of spiritual significance and would produce an enduring transformation was not merely a lesson on chastity but rather an expounding of the doctrine of the Atonement, explaining the justice and mercy of God, and testifying of the "great plan of happiness" (see Alma chapters 39–42).

So what does all this mean? What application is there for us today? How can we "liken" these scriptures to our own unique challenges and circumstances? Each of these examples illustrates the power of pure doctrine—the inherent power of the holy scriptures—taught, understood, and lived. "True doctrine, understood, changes attitudes and behavior," Elder Boyd K. Packer declared. "The study of the doctrines of the gospel will improve behavior quicker than a study of behavior will improve behavior. Preoccupation with unworthy behavior can lead to unworthy behavior. That is why we stress so forcefully the study of the doctrines of the gospel." (In Conference Report, October 1986, p. 20.)

One of the timeless themes of the Book of Mormon is that the "power of the word"—the studying, pondering, preaching and teaching from, and applying the scriptures—can powerfully affect our personal lives and our service to Heavenly Father's children in whatever circumstances in life we may encounter. Nephi invited his brethren anciently and us today to "feast upon the words of Christ" (see 2 Nephi 31:20). There is no feast anything like it. It is delicious to the soul and life-sustaining for the spirit. "Feasting upon the word of Christ. What a banquet of choice food is laid before us in holy writ!" declared Elder Bruce R. McConkie. "Feasting upon the word of Christ. How we ought to partake of the good word of God, and feast upon the bread from heaven which if men eat they shall never hunger more (John 6:35, 51)!" (*Doctrines of the Restoration: Sermons*

and Writings of Bruce R. McConkie, ed. Mark L. McConkie [Salt
Lake City: Bookcraft, 1989], p. 240.)

WHAT THE SCRIPTURES CAN DO FOR US

Not only does the Apostle Paul enumerate the purposes and
value of the scriptures. So too does the Book of Mormon repeatedly testify and illustrate the "power of the word" and what
"feasting upon the words of Christ" can do *for* us and *to* us personally. The power of the scriptures in general, and the Book of
Mormon in particular, includes intellectual benefits as well as
spiritual blessings and protections. We are taught truth, our
questions can be answered, and other principles are clarified. But
more than mere intellectual stretching comes with a serious
study of scripture. The spiritual benefits far exceed earthly comprehension.

Answers to Gospel Questions

Each of us has questions—things in the gospel we may not
fully understand; things in life that seem inexplicable or unfair. It
was no different for the peoples of the Book of Mormon. I find
it useful to read how Nephi expounded the scriptures to his
questioning and criticizing brothers. When anti-Christs like
Sherem, Nehor, and Korihor sought to lead people astray, the
Book of Mormon prophets used the scriptures to put down false
doctrines, expose evil philosophies and designs, and lead people
again to the strait and narrow path. The sons of Mosiah were
powerful instruments in the hand of God, as missionaries,
because they knew the answers to the difficult questions. They
knew how to teach the gospel to others, because "they had
waxed strong in the knowledge of the truth; for they were men
of a sound understanding and they had searched the scriptures
diligently, that they might know the word of God" (Alma 17:2).
It is no different in our day. Answers to the most difficult questions and disturbing dilemmas are to be found in the scriptures.
That is one of the most significant "powers" of the word for us

today—the power of instruction, the power of finding answers, the power of putting down false notions. It should say something to us that when angels visited the Prophet Joseph Smith much of the content of their messages were the words of scripture. Similarly, it is no accident or coincidence that many of the great revelations of the Restoration came as a direct result of studying, pondering, or translating the scriptures. So it is with us. Personal revelation and spiritual guidance will come to us in direct proportion to our study of the scriptures.

When I was called as a missionary many years ago there was no Missionary Training Center. We first went to the old "Mission Home" in Salt Lake City for a few days in preparation for language training, and then left for our assigned fields of labor. One of the highlights of that experience was being able to attend endowment sessions in the Salt Lake Temple and a special meeting in the Solemn Assembly room with a member of the First Presidency. It was our privilege to have President Harold B. Lee address us and answer questions from the missionaries in attendance. While I cannot remember everything that transpired in that meeting, I can remember one thing as vividly as if it were yesterday. I remember that in the question-answer session President Lee answered so profoundly and so completely a wide array of questions—but most impressive to me was that he answered every question from the scriptures. He would make a comment on and counsel concerning the issue at hand, but if there wasn't something in the scriptures addressing it, neither did he. In the years since that experience I have become even more impressed and inspired by his example of finding answers in the scriptures—especially as I read President Lee's own words concerning this responsibility.

> One of the anxieties I have about our people today arises out of an experience I have had with every company of missionaries. Before they leave for their missions I am assigned to go over to the temple, and in the upper room of the temple . . . they are permitted for an hour or so to ask questions about the temple ordinances and matters they might not have understood. . . . We always say to them repeatedly as we have finished, "I

want you to notice that all the answers I have given have been given from out of the scriptures. I wouldn't dare attempt to make an answer to your questions anywhere else but from the scriptures or from the statements of a President of the Church, which, to us as they give inspired utterances, are scripture." (*The Teachings of Harold B. Lee*, ed. Clyde J. Williams [Salt Lake City: Bookcraft, 1996], pp.153–54.)

If only each of us would be wise enough to say that we aren't able to answer any question unless we can find a doctrinal answer in the scriptures! And if we hear someone teaching something that is contrary to what is in the scriptures, each of us may know whether the things spoken are false—it is as simple as that. But the unfortunate thing is that so many of us are not reading the scriptures. We do not know what is in them, and therefore we speculate about the things that we ought to have found in the scriptures themselves. I think that therein is one of our biggest dangers of today. (*The Teachings of Harold B. Lee*, p. 153.)

We don't find just answers to gospel questions from a serious study of scriptures. Answers to almost all of life's problems and challenges can be addressed by the scriptures, the doctrines of the gospel, and through the guidance of the Spirit that accompanies such purposeful and diligent gospel study. I remember hearing Elder Boyd K. Packer, in speaking to religious educators, testify of how the scriptures can provide answers to life's most difficult questions. "If [you] are acquainted with the scriptures, there is no question—personal or social or political or occupational—that need go unanswered," he declared. "In the scriptures we find the principles of truth that will resolve every confusion and every problem and every dilemma that will face the human family or any individual of it." (*Teach the Scriptures* [address to religious educators, 14 October 1977], p. 5.)

Conversion and Testimony

In our dispensation the Lord has declared that the scriptures and the Holy Spirit possess "the power of God unto the convincing of men" (see D&C 11:21). The Book of Mormon is one of the most important tools in this convincing and converting process. One might become *convinced* of the truth by intellectual means alone, but it takes the "power of the word" to not only convince the mind but also *convert* the heart and soul and turn one totally to God. This is as true for Latter-day Saints as it is for those not of our faith who are investigating our message. Moroni gave us a promise that we can know for a surety of the truthfulness of that book (see Moroni 10:3–5). The promise applies to all—member and nonmember, male and female, black and white, young and old.

The Prophet Joseph Smith declared that the Book of Mormon is the "keystone of our religion" (see Introduction to the Book of Mormon). In our day President Ezra Taft Benson explained that one of the ways that it is the "keystone of our religion" is that it is the "keystone of testimony." "Just as the arch crumbles if the keystone is removed," he taught, "so does all the Church stand or fall with the truthfulness of the Book of Mormon. The enemies of the Church understand this clearly. This is why they go to such great lengths to try to disprove the Book of Mormon, for if it can be discredited, the Prophet Joseph Smith goes with it. So does our claim to priesthood keys, and revelation, and the restored Church. But in like manner, if the Book of Mormon be true—and millions have now testified that they have the witness of the Spirit that it is indeed true—then one must accept the claims of the Restoration and all that accompanies it." (*A Witness and a Warning* [Salt Lake City: Deseret Book, 1988], p. 19.)

The Book of Mormon stands not only as the "keystone of testimony" *institutionally*, but also it is the very keystone of *individual* testimony. Just as we urge friends and neighbors, relatives and acquaintances to come to know the truthfulness of the gospel and the reality of the Restoration by putting Moroni's promise to the test, so too must we. There can be no real conversion, no constant commitment to the kingdom of God, no determined discipleship, no enduring in faith to the end, without a personal testimony of the Book of Mormon. President Joseph Fielding Smith testified:

> It seems to me that any member of this Church would never be satisfied until he or she had read the Book of Mormon time and time again, and thoroughly considered it so that he or she could bear witness that it is in very deed a record with the inspiration of the Almighty upon it, and that its history is true. . . .
>
> No member of this Church can stand approved in the presence of God who has not seriously and carefully read the Book of Mormon. (In Conference Report, October 1961, p. 18.)

The more I study the scriptures, "feasting upon the words of Christ," the more I realize that none of us ever outgrow them, particularly the Book of Mormon. The more I search that book of books, the more there is to yet discover and the more I realize that my understanding and witness of it is linked to all of my other beliefs. In fact, I have come to realize that virtually every aspect of my testimony, the personal witness of specific doctrines and principles, comes to me because I have a testimony of the truthfulness of the Book of Mormon.

Just as it is impossible to physically survive on a meal long since eaten, so too is it impossible to spiritually survive in this day and age on a testimony—a personal witness of the truth of the Book of Mormon—that was obtained years or even decades ago. Spiritual nourishment of a testimony requires daily feeding upon the food that is delicious and life-sustaining to the soul and that is found in the words of holy writ. Perhaps we should periodically ask ourselves questions like: "Have you really studied the Book of Mormon or just superficially skimmed through it?" "Have you ever put Moroni's promise to the test and received your own personal witness of the truthfulness of the Book of Mormon?" And perhaps the most important question of all— "When was the last time you searched the scriptures, prayed for a stronger testimony, and received a witness by the power of the Holy Ghost?" As we seriously consider these questions we may sadly discover that perhaps it's been too long.

"Are you continually increasing your testimony by diligent study of the scriptures? Do you have a daily habit of reading the scriptures?" asked President Harold B. Lee. "If we are not reading the scriptures daily, our testimonies are growing thinner, our spirituality isn't increasing in depth." (Address delivered at regional representatives' seminar, 12 December 1970, p. 10.) The "power of the word," when forged by study, pondering, and prayer, brings with it a "keystone" testimony that can strengthen us and empower us in other important ways.

Strength to Resist Temptation

The scriptures give us not only doctrinal insights, answers to gospel questions, and strengthened testimonies, but also an inherent "power of the word" in the strength it affords us against the temptations and evils of the day, both philosophical and behavioral. Shortly before His death, the Savior foretold of the conditions and calamities that would precede His second coming. Especially relevant among those signs was His statement regarding false Messiahs and false prophets who would work mighty miracles and perform wondrous deeds, so much so that "if possible, they shall deceive the very elect according to the covenant" (see JST Matthew 24:23). What protection does God extend to His Saints from such deception and the "cunning snares of the devil"? The answer is found in the same prophecy. Jesus declared: "And whoso treasureth up my word, shall not be deceived" (see JST Matthew 24:39).

I often hear people (even my own family) complain about studying the scriptures. "I don't get anything out of it," they protest. "I don't always understand what I read." The Book of Mormon reminds us that it is through the "power of the word"—the scriptures and the companionship of the Holy Ghost—that we are not blinded by the adversary (see 1 Nephi 15:24) and have the means of "divid[ing] asunder the cunning snares of the devil" (see Helaman 3:29–30). Whether we are two or a hundred, whether we have to have someone read to us because we are too young to read or too old to see the words, or

whether we are a "gospel scholar" or a "scripture novice," studying the scriptures, particularly the Book of Mormon, blesses our
lives. Even if I can't understand everything I read, I am still
being infused with spiritual strength and a protective power that
can, often even unbeknown to me, cause the power of darkness
to be dispersed before me (see D&C 21:6). There is truly power
that comes from serious, consistent study of the word of God.
President Benson explained and prophetically promised:

> It is not just that the Book of Mormon teaches us truth,
> though it indeed does that. It is not just that the Book of Mor-
> mon bears testimony of Christ, though it indeed does that, too.
> But there is something more. There is a power in the book
> which will begin to flow into your lives the moment you begin
> a serious study of the book. You will find greater power to resist
> temptation. You will find the power to avoid deception. You
> will find the power to stay on the strait and narrow path. The
> scriptures are called "the words of life" (see D&C 84:85), and
> nowhere is that more true than it is of the Book of Mormon.
> When you begin to hunger and thirst after those words, you will
> find life in greater and greater abundance. (*A Witness and a
> Warning*, pp. 21–22.)

Personal Spirituality

We all need greater spirituality in our lives. As "iniquity
abounds" and "love waxeth cold" in our modern world, there is
and will be a greater need for us to draw closer to our Heavenly
Father. Spirituality is an oasis, rich with the "living waters" and
the soul-sustaining "bread of life." Surrounding that fertile oasis
is the barren wilderness of the world and the worldly, devoid of
that which brings lasting joy and "the peace which passeth all
understanding." Each day, in our responsibilities of mortality, we
have to journey into that wilderness, but we can take the spiritual
nourishment of the oasis with us—when we are daily being fed
by "the good word of God." Without that daily feeding of the
soul, the sands of sin and the wasteland of the world encroach

further and further into our oasis. We cannot survive long in that wasteland without the refreshment of "feasting upon the words of Christ"—we will quickly become spiritually dehydrated. "I find that when I get casual in my relationships with divinity and when it seems that no divine ear is listening and no divine voice is speaking, that I am far, far away," President Spencer W. Kimball observed. "If I immerse myself in the scriptures the distance narrows and the spirituality returns." (*The Teachings of Spencer W. Kimball*, ed. Edward L. Kimball [Salt Lake City: Bookcraft, 1982], p. 135.)

"Faith cometh by hearing, and hearing by the word of God," the Apostle Paul declared (Romans 10:17). Perhaps we could paraphrase Paul's words and capture the same essence: Spirituality comes by hearing the voice of God, and hearing His voice comes by studying the scriptures (see D&C 18:33–36). The personal spiritual growth and development that comes from reading and studying scriptures, even "feasting" upon them as a starving man would approach a banquet table, not only enlightens the mind and strengthens the spirit but also leads to gospel living and Christlike behaviors. Samuel the Lamanite prophet described the spiritual transformation that came upon the Lamanites as they were brought to a knowledge of the truth (see Helaman chapter 15). They sought to keep the commandments, to serve God and their fellowmen with diligence and honor. These converted Lamanites did "walk circumspectly before God" because they had been "led to believe the holy scriptures, yea, the prophecies of the holy prophets, which are written, which leadeth them to faith on the Lord, and unto repentance, which faith and repentance bringeth a change of heart unto them" (Helaman 15:7).

That kind of faith, that kind of true spirituality that leads to a change of heart comes as we conscientiously and regularly partake of the "power of the word" through scripture study. Elder Bruce R. McConkie, a spiritual giant and a consummate student of the scriptures, stated:

> I think that people who study the scriptures get a dimension

to their life that nobody else gets and that can't be gained in any way except by studying the scriptures. There's an increase in faith and desire to do what's right and a feeling of inspiration and understanding that comes to people who study the gospel—meaning particularly the standard works—and who ponder the principles, that can't come in any other way. (*Church News*, 24 January 1976, p. 4.)

STRENGTHENING OUR FAMILIES THROUGH THE POWER OF THE SCRIPTURES

In the account of Lehi's dream of the tree of life, we see a touching image of a loving father concerned for the welfare of his family. "And as I partook of the fruit thereof it filled my soul with exceedingly great joy," Lehi stated, "wherefore I began to be desirous that my family should partake of it also; for I knew that it was desirable above all other fruit" (1 Nephi 8:12). When Lehi saw later in his vision that some of his family would not come unto him and partake of the fruit, he was heartsick. Afterwards, as he gathered his children about him to describe what he had seen in his dream, he expressed his desires that they all partake of the fruit of God's love and his concerns over those who did not possess those same desires. "And he did exhort them then with all the feeling of a tender parent, that they would hearken to his words" (1 Nephi 8:37).

Each of us, as parents, can relate to Lehi's feelings. When our lives have been so richly blessed by the goodness and mercy of God, we too desire that our families should partake. Each of the blessings and benefits of scripture study that flow into our own individual lives can likewise bless our children and grandchildren. They can experience the "power of the word" in their own lives through personal scripture study, but we can provide them with an extra spiritual coating of the "armor of God" by studying and teaching from the scriptures more in our homes and with our families. Unfortunately some of us have scriptures in our houses, but not in our hearts or heads. They even may be prominently displayed and ornately embossed, yet the pages are still crisp from never having been turned. There is a humorous poem that perhaps illustrates this all-too-common condition. That is, I guess it would be funny if it wasn't so true.

> Old Brother Higgins built a shelf,
>   For the family Bible to rest itself,
> Lest a sticky finger or a grimy thumb,
>   Injure the delicate pages some.
> He cautioned his children to touch it not,
>   And it rested there with never a blot,
> Though the Higgins tribe are a troublesome lot.
>
> His neighbor Miggins built a shelf.
>   "Come children," he said, "and help yourself."
> Now his book is old and ragged and worn,
>   With some of the delicate pages torn,
> Where children had fingered and thumbed and read,
>   But of the Miggins children I've heard it said,
> That each carries a Bible in his head.

The leaders of the Church have long admonished us to study the scriptures as families. "Scripture study as individuals and as a family is most fundamental to learning the gospel," President Spencer W. Kimball declared. "Daily reading of the scriptures and discussing them together has long been suggested as a powerful tool against ignorance and the temptations of Satan. This practice will produce great happiness and will help family members love the Lord and his goodness. . . . Home is where we become experts and scholars in gospel righteousness." (*The Teachings of Spencer W. Kimball,* p. 129.)

Even when our children were very young we tried to follow this counsel and study the scriptures each morning as a family. I must admit, however, that I probably had the *practice* down better than the *principle* attending it. I think we were guilty of viewing family scripture study as some kind of a race or something we just had to "get through." We wanted to hurry up and get through the volume of scripture we were reading at the time. I would get frustrated if we were slowed down in our progress by such things as questions from the kids. I really had things backwards, thinking there was more value in merely reading *through* the scriptures rapidly than in teaching and answering questions *from* the scriptures. Don't get me wrong. There is indeed value in regular scripture reading as a family. But there are even greater blessings when together we search, study, and discuss the scriptures and thus come to understand them, not just wade through them. So what if it takes two years or ten to make it all the way through the Bible or the Book of Mormon if we are gaining increased understanding of the gospel and learning what the scriptures *mean*, not just what they *say*?

In our home, morning family scripture study time was often stressful, chaotic, and sometimes even contentious. "Hurry up! I've got to catch the school bus," one child might say. "We don't have time for questions," I might say. "We've got to get through this chapter before we can quit!" It didn't seem much like a time of contemplation and study, a time when the Spirit of the Lord could teach us anything significant, as we hurried and scurried about or grumbled about having to read at such an early hour. But in the years since, I have come to realize that even when it seemed that nothing significant spiritually was taking place the "power of the word" was strengthening, enlightening, and building faith, little by little, day by day—compounded with interest over time.

In a similar way I came to realize that lessons taught from the scriptures in family home evening—as crazy and stressful as many Monday nights were in our house—also added to the "power of the word" drop by drop, here a little and there a little, until there were stored up "reservoirs of righteousness" in the lives of our family. I have experienced over and over again that there is a power in teaching our families from the standard works that far surpasses sweet stories or animated videos or any other lesson manual or teaching methodology. Each of these is important in its own right and can serve an important function, but they must only be "side dishes" and never the "main course." As parents we wouldn't allow our children to only eat chocolate cake and drink sodas for every meal. We wouldn't even allow it if they agreed to eat a carrot stick. We know that too little of the most nourishing things and too much of those things that may taste good but lack vital nutrients will leave them malnourished, sick, and out of shape.

The same is true in homes when it comes to teaching the gospel to our children. The "main course"—that which contains the spiritual nourishment needed to build faith and protect from evil—must be the scriptures. These are the words of Christ we are commanded to "feast" upon. Just as Alma discovered on his mission to reclaim those who had spiritually lost their way that the "power of the word" was greater than anything else in turning people's hearts to God and leading them to do right, so is it within the walls of our own homes. President Marion G. Romney promised parents in Zion:

> I feel certain that if, in our homes, parents will read from the Book of Mormon [and all the Standard Works] prayerfully and regularly, both by themselves and with their children, the spirit of that great book will come to permeate our homes and all who dwell therein. The spirit of reverence will increase; mutual respect and consideration for each other will grow. The spirit of contention will depart. Parents will counsel their children in greater love and wisdom. Children will be more responsive and submissive to the counsel of their parents. Righteousness will increase. Faith, hope, and charity—the pure love of Christ—will abound in our homes and lives, bringing in their wake peace, joy, and happiness. (In Conference Report, April 1980, p. 90.)

SUCCESS IN OUR CHURCH CALLINGS BY "TRYING THE VIRTUE OF THE WORD OF GOD"

When my son was in Primary he was enthused about taking his own set of scriptures to church each Sunday. His teacher had promised a "treat" each time the class members remembered to bring their own copy of the standard works to class. The teacher would distribute a piece of candy to each child who had his scriptures in class. I thought it sounded like a really good idea. (In fact I often wished that my Gospel Doctrine teacher or high priests group instructor would have done the same thing.) But this tasty inducement soon lost its power. "Why aren't you taking your scriptures?" I asked my son one Sabbath when he left for Church without them. "It's not worth it," he quickly responded. "I'm tired of lugging them around. It's only a piece of candy, and besides, we never open our scriptures anyway." ("Out of the mouth of babes!")

His words hit me like a brick. At first, I was irritated with the teacher. "Why would he encourage the children to bring their scriptures and then not use them?" I murmured. It wasn't long, however, until I could see that I had been guilty of much the same thing in my own service in the kingdom. As a bishop I often counseled couples who had marriage problems, people with serious transgressions, or others with feelings of discouragement, or depression, or other struggles with feelings of self-worth. Yet when I think back now I see how guilty I was of spouting off counsel from my own head—even though it may have been good or based on common sense and experience— rather than turning to the scriptures. On my desk sat the standard works, yet often I didn't even turn to them. My counsel and words of advice pale in comparison to the "power of the word." I could have done so much more good if I had used the scriptures more and relied less on myself and man-made solutions. Similarly, as a teacher in the many quorums and classes of the Church I was guilty at times of worrying more about maintaining a high interest level or having a stimulating discussion than in reading and teaching from the scriptures themselves. How many times did I answer questions "off the top of my head" rather than letting the Lord answer the questions in His own words. These were painful memories. I was left sheepish and humbled and I resolved that I must do better in using the scriptures in my callings and service in the Church.

President Ezra Taft Benson urged all leaders and teachers in the priesthood quorums and organizations of the Church to use the scriptures, particularly the Book of Mormon, more in our leading, counseling, and teaching. "I have a vision of homes alerted, of classes alive, and of pulpits aflame with the spirit of Book of Mormon messages," he declared. "I have a vision of home teachers and visiting teachers, ward and branch officers, and stake and mission leaders counseling our people out of the most correct of any book on earth—the Book of Mormon." (In Conference Report, October 1988, pp. 4–5.) Are we doing our part to make that vision a reality?

Just as Alma, Ammon, Aaron, and numerous others found success in their ministry by using "the virtue of the word of God," so too will we in the modern Church find greater success if our labors—whatever and wherever they are—are firmly founded on the scriptures. "One of the most important things you can do as priesthood leaders [and auxiliary leaders and teachers] is to immerse yourselves in the scriptures," President Benson admonished. "Search them diligently. Feast upon the words of Christ. Learn the doctrine. Master the principles that are found therein. There are few other efforts that will bring greater dividends to your calling. There are few other ways to gain greater inspiration as you serve." ("The Power of the Word," *Ensign*, May 1986, p. 81.)

Not only must we immerse ourselves in them to be filled with the Spirit to guide us in our callings, but we must also use them in everything we do in the Church—teaching, administering, fellow-shipping, leading. "Buildings and budgets, and reports and programs and procedures are very important," Elder Boyd K. Packer counseled priesthood leaders. "But, by themselves, they do not carry that essential spiritual nourishment and will not accomplish what the Lord has given us to do. . . . The right things, those with true spiritual nourishment, are centered in the scriptures." (Quoted in Ezra Taft Benson, "The Power of the Word," p. 81.)

Serving in a stake presidency has afforded me many opportunities to teach and train, counsel and instruct, and give more talks than I enjoy doing. Each time I am asked to do such things, the stake president reminds me, "Teach them from the scriptures!" Even when I am called up to conduct more technical and procedural training with bishops and high councilors, he will say: "Be sure to use the scriptures!" This is wise counsel for all of us. Handbooks may contain polices and procedures, lesson manuals may give helpful teaching tips, ideas, and methodologies, but the scriptures provide us with the principles—the "doctrine of Christ." How arrogant or ignorant it is to think that anything we might say, any story we might tell, or any handout we might distribute, could have any greater influence than the "power of the word." The influence of the Spirit coupled with the gospel insights and answers to difficult questions that are gained through a serious study of the scriptures can teach lessons or solve problems in ways we might not imagine.

I have heard mission presidents talk about the problems they often have with their missionaries—companion problems, discouragement, homesickness, and many other kinds of challenges. One mission president shared an experience that illustrates the "power of the word" in our callings. He reported that the mission was at an all-time low in morale as well as in baptisms. He could hardly focus his attention on missionary efforts because all of his efforts went to meeting with missionaries, seeking to help solve their problems, and encouraging some to stay in the mission field. The thought entered his mind that he should have the entire mission rededicate themselves to a serious, intense study of the Book of Mormon for a perod of one month. A miracle occurred! At the end of the month, the numbers of baptisms had dramatically increased, enthusiasm for the work was rekindled, companion problems virtually disappeared, and the Spirit of the Lord was once again evident in the work. When this president visited with the missionaries he had scheduled interviews with the previous month, he would ask, "Well, what problem is troubling you?" Most of the missionaries who before had been weighed down with worries and problems now said, "It's okay now, President. I found my answers in the scriptures."

Similarly, a bishop reported that when he met with young people bogged down by the weight of serious transgressions, he would have them commit themselves to prayerfully study the scriptures—even read the Book of Mormon through, cover-to-cover, in a very short period of time. The results were that hearts were softened, "godly sorrow [that] worketh repentance" was obtained (see 2 Corinthians 7:10), discipline was humbly received, and subsequent falling prey to the same old temptations ceased. It wasn't what the bishop said or did that brought about these mighty transformations. The word of God—contained in the scriptures—"which is quick and powerful, sharper than a two-edged sword" was the catalyst for change, a change of behavior and a change of heart. Likewise, this good bishop had ward members who could not forgive themselves of past mistakes do the same thing, with a special focus on the scriptural teachings regarding the Atonement. Others who harbored heartaches of many kinds were also directed to the scriptures. They discovered the literal power of the "pleasing word of God" in very personal and poignant ways, just as the prophet Jacob declared—"the word which healeth the wounded soul" (Jacob 2:8).

I am inspired by the example of Nephi, Jacob, Abinadi, Alma, and others in the Book of Mormon who filled their minds and hearts with the scriptures and the words of eternal life. Anti-Christs were exposed and their evil efforts thwarted by the "power of the word." Apostates were reformed and reclaimed into the kingdom of God. Entire nations were converted to Christ and turned to righteousness. The Church was fortified spiritually and prospered exceedingly. Individual testimonies were strengthened—hearts changed, repentance realized, protection from temptations acquired. All of this because of the "power of the word." This certainly stands out to me as one of the most important, most timely, and relevant of Book of Mormon themes.

Today we too can realize these same kinds of blessings and experience similar miracles if in our own lives, in our homes with our children, and in our callings in the Church, we follow Alma's example and "try the virtue of the word of God" (Alma 31:5). These blessings will come to us in proportion to our love for, our understanding, and our use of the scriptures. As Elder Neal A. Maxwell insightfully reminds us, it is not enough to possess the scriptures—"Now they must come to possess us!" (In Conference Report, April 1986, p. 45.) When we become thus possessed we will understand better than ever what Nephi really meant when he declared:

> My soul delighteth in the scriptures, and my heart pondereth them, and writeth them for the learning and the profit of my children.
>
> Behold, my soul delighteth in the things of the Lord; and my heart pondereth continually upon the things which I have seen and heard. (2 Nephi 4:15–16.)

Yea, come unto Christ, and be perfected in him, and
deny yourselves of all ungodliness; and if ye shall deny
yourselves of all ungodliness, and love God with all your
might, mind and strength, then is his grace sufficient
for you, that by his grace ye may be perfect in Christ.
—MORONI 10:32

CHAPTER 8

PERFECT IN CHRIST

When I was a young boy the most popular movies and television programs included westerns and pirate adventures. Like most normal children, I enjoyed going to these kinds of movies on Saturday mornings or watching television episodes of some of my favorite programs—"Roy Rogers," "Gunsmoke," "Bonanza," "Rawhide," "Wild Wild West."

Those adventure programs of yesteryear pale in comparison to today's action movies. Instead of all the explosions that characterize modern adventure films, the dangers portrayed in cowboy shows were less sensational, but hazardous nonetheless.

One of those hazards that I always found intriguing was quicksand. Usually one of the heroes of the story would somehow get trapped in this strange mixture of sand and water. What was so interesting about quicksand (at least as it was portrayed on television and in the movies) was that it could not support heavy weight, but a person would not immediately sink in it either. Since it is not completely liquid, swimming in it is impossible; and it is not completely solid, so one cannot stand on it or walk out of it. One of the characteristics of these quicksands that make them so hazardous is that a person who is trapped in it actually sinks faster and deeper the more he tries to extricate himself from the sandy bog. The only hope for escape is to be rescued from outside the quicksand by someone who has sure footing and is anchored on a firm foundation.

Almost as if in quicksand, sometimes we can become bogged down with discouragement and frustration in our attempts to live up to the spiritual expectations of the gospel. "When comparing one's personal performance with the supreme standard of the Lord's expectation," Elder Russell M. Nelson observed, "the reality of imperfection can at times be depressing" ("Perfection Pending," *Ensign*, November 1995, p. 86). The Savior's command "Be ye therefore perfect" is as soul-stretching as it is mind-boggling. We want to be able to keep all of the commandments, even this one, but sometimes we compound the daunting task of becoming more Christlike in our lives by adding other expectations for ourselves, expectations that are often unrealistic and usually impossible to achieve. There is a difference between a person who is striving for the perfection the Savior commands and a "perfectionist" who thinks he or she must be perfect in every expectation and every aspect of our mortal existence.

Jesus commanded us to become perfect, not to be perfectionists. The one leads to perfect liberty and the other leads to bondage—a bondage of emotions and "spiritual burnout" that we often bring upon ourselves. When we fall short, not only of the Savior's charge to be perfect but also of our own self-appointed expectations, we often feel an overwhelming sense of guilt, inadequacy, frustration, and even hopelessness. These counterproductive feelings of discouragement and helplessness can have a detrimental effect on every aspect of our lives and our relationships with others. It may not be visible like quicksand, but it is nonetheless a spiritual trap that can destroy us if we are left alone to flail helplessly in these "quicksands of perfectionism." Elder Dean L. Larsen identified emotional and spiritual "burnout" as one of the destructive side effects of having unrealistic and unhealthy expectations regarding the process of perfection.

Some of us create such a complexity of expectations for ourselves that it is difficult to cope with the magnitude of them. Sometimes we establish so many particulars by which to evaluate and rate ourselves that it becomes difficult to feel successful and worthy to any degree at any time. We can drive ourselves unmercifully toward perfection on such a broad plane. When this compulsion is intensified by sources outside ourselves, the problem is compounded. Confronting these demands can bring mental and emotional despair.

Everyone needs to feel successful and worthy in some ways at least part of the time. The recognition of our frailties need not propel us to try to achieve perfection in one dramatic commitment of effort. The best progress sometimes comes when we are not under intense duress. Overzealousness is at least as much to be feared as apathy. Trying to measure up to too many particular expectations without some sense of self-tolerance can cause spiritual and emotional "burn-out." ("The Peaceable Things of the Kingdom," in *Brigham Young University 1984–85 Devotional and Fireside Speeches* [Provo, Utah: University Publications, 1985], p. 72.)

In our family we have had to struggle with these kinds of challenges—discerning between the real expectations of the gospel and false expectations, whether they be from ourselves or from some other external source. It is a daily struggle. One of the dangers of unhealthy perfectionism is the unrealistic expectations that we place not only upon ourselves but also upon others. Failing to adequately measure up to those expectations, we then feel even more guilt, frustration, and failure. As with the quicksand, we keep sinking deeper and deeper. My wife and I had an interesting experience that taught us a valuable lesson about this principle.

Several years ago when we lived in Arizona and our children were quite young, Wendy and I met with our bishop for a temple recommend renewal interview. It was common for our bishop, after the official questions were all asked, to ask us some general questions about how we were doing in our family duties, such as: "Do you have regular family prayer and family home evening?

Are you offering your personal prayers? Do you pray together as companions?"

I had my interview first, and everything went well. I answered the questions as honestly as I could. The bishop signed my recommend and I waited in the foyer for Wendy to have her interview. Several minutes later, she emerged from the bishop's office with recommend in hand. "Brother Top, I need to visit with you again," the bishop said to me, motioning me back to his office. "We need to get the stories straight." What in the world could he mean by that last statement? I wondered.

The bishop had heard a discrepancy between something I reported and what Wendy had told him, and he wanted now to find out the "straight scoop." When he had asked me, "Do you have regular family prayer?" I answered yes—and that was the honest-to-goodness truth. When he asked the same question to Wendy, she answered no—and that was the truth, as she perceived it. Well, how can both be true? To me, regular meant just that—regular, but sometimes we might miss because of extenuating circumstances. Wendy, however, interpreted "regular" to mean "never missing." To her, regular meant perfect. To me, regular meant almost always—"pretty good," but not perfect. We were both truthful, but both wrong in some way. Wendy may have had an unrealistic expectation, and I may have had too liberal an interpretation. While this may seem like a very small and simple misunderstanding, we have since come to realize that we are not the only ones who have had disparate expectations and misunderstandings of what the Lord really requires of us with regard to perfection.

Both Wendy and I have encountered hundreds of people who feel frustrated with their feeble attempts to emulate the Savior. Many feel like giving up in despair and giving in to the adversary because they fall far short of their preconceived notions of the standard of perfection. "My heart goes out to conscientious Saints, who, because of their shortcomings, allow feelings of depression to rob them of happiness in life," Elder Russell M. Nelson stated. "We all need to remember: men are that they might have joy—not guilt trips! We also need to remember that the Lord gives no commandments that are impossible to obey. But sometimes we fail to comprehend them fully." ("Perfection Pending," p. 86.)

As Elder Nelson pointed out, much of the frustration and discouragement that perfectionists in particular and all of us in general experience in our quest for Christlike perfection comes out of a misunderstanding of the doctrine of perfection and/or from a lack of faith in the grace and love of the Savior. Too often when we read, "Be ye therefore perfect, even as your Father which is in heaven is perfect" (Matthew 5:48) we think this means we should be perfect in every aspect of our lives—right now. Such a narrow, literalistic view of this scripture can create a spiritual form of quicksand. When we misunderstand the doctrine of becoming perfect and assume that we ought to be perfect now—without sin, never making mistakes, and always doing the ideal in every situation, or in every calling—we are like one in quicksand who, the more he attempts to extricate himself by his sole efforts, the more he is actually sinking dangerously deeper.

To escape the quicksands of perfectionism and to save our spiritual lives we must correctly understand what the Lord expects of us and how we can actually become perfect. The Book of Mormon coupled with the teachings of modern prophets can dispel the doctrinal darkness regarding perfection that has clouded some people's view to the point that gospel living becomes a burden rather than a blessing. This, I believe, is one of the most important ways in which a serious study of the Book of Mormon can lift the spiritual condemnation that, as President Benson taught, has adversely affected the Church and individual members in the past.

The word *perfect* has different meanings in the scriptures and is used in several different contexts. For example, there are two different Hebrew words used in the Old Testament for the one word that is translated as *perfect* in the King James version of the Bible. Having a "perfect heart" is spoken of (see 1 Kings 8:61; 15:14; 2 Kings 20:3). The Hebrew word in this context is *shalem*, which means "finished" or "whole." (It is interesting to note that *shalem* shares the same root as *shalom*, which means "peace." This seems to indicate that one with a "perfect heart" would be one with an inner peace and spiritual wholeness that comes from a relationship with God.) The other word used in the Old Testament for perfect is *tammim*. The Lord commanded Abraham, "Walk before me, and be thou perfect" (Genesis 17:1). In this context *perfect*, or *tammim*, means "complete," "upright," "undefiled," or "complete, whole, fully initiated, mature." (See *Encyclopedia of Mormonism* [New York: Macmillan, 1992], 3:1074; see also 2 Timothy 3:17; Ephesians 4:13; James 3:2.)

Even outside the scriptures the word *perfect* can mean different things to different people. For example, perfection in the eternal sense means something dramatically different than an earthly action that may be characterized as perfect. As Elder Russell M. Nelson explained:

> In this life, certain actions can be perfected. A baseball pitcher can throw a no-hit, no-run ball game. A surgeon can perform an operation without an error. A musician can render a selection without a mistake. One can likewise achieve perfection in being punctual, paying tithing, keeping the Word of Wisdom, and so on. . . .
>
> Scriptures have described Noah, Seth, and Job as *perfect* men. No doubt the same term might apply to a large number of faithful disciples in various dispensations. Alma said that "there were many, exceedingly great many," who were pure before the Lord.
>
> This does not mean that these people never made mistakes or never had need of correction. ("Perfection Pending," p. 86.)

It is clear from the above words and phrases, as well as the definition and examples of "mortal perfection" given by Elder Nelson, that the term *perfect*, as used in the scriptures, means something different than we usually think. It does not exclusively mean "without sin," or "making no mistakes," or "never falling short." Most often the scriptural emphasis is on the completion

of man. We understand what is meant by perfection being the
end product of man by examining how the Savior's commandment to be perfect is different in the Book of Mormon than
what is recorded in the New Testament.

In the Sermon on the Mount, Jesus declared to His disciples,
"Be ye therefore perfect, even as your Father which is in heaven
is perfect" (Matthew 5:48). But to the Nephites, at the temple in
Bountiful, the now-resurrected Christ gave the same command,
but with an important and interesting addition. "I would that ye
should be perfect *even as I*, or your Father who is in heaven is
perfect" (3 Nephi 12:48; emphasis added). In the one account
the model of perfection is Heavenly Father, and in the other it is
both—the exalted Father and the resurrected Lord. Why is there
a difference? Does that distinction have a doctrinal significance?
Wasn't Jesus sinless when He gave that command in the Sermon
on the Mount? Of course He was! Then why doesn't He include
Himself with the Father as the embodiment of perfection? Elder
Russell M. Nelson authoritatively addressed these questions in
general conference. His answers help us to better understand
why the Book of Mormon makes the distinction. His in-depth
discussion helps us to better distinguish between the *process* of
perfection and the ultimate *state* of perfection.

Recently, I studied the English and Greek editions of the
New Testament, concentrating on each use of the term *perfect*
and its derivatives. Studying both languages together provided
some interesting insights, since Greek was the original language
of the New Testament.

In Matthew 5:48, the term *perfect* was translated from the
Greek *teleios*, which means "complete." *Teleios* is an adjective
derived from the noun *telos*, which means "end." The infinitive
form of the verb is *teleiono*, which means "to reach a distant
end, to be fully developed, to consummate, or to finish." Please
note that the word does not imply "freedom from error"; it
implies "achieving a distant objective." In fact, when writers of
the Greek New Testament wished to describe perfection of
behavior—precision or excellence of human effort—they did

not employ a form of *teleios*; instead, they chose different words. . . .

With that background in mind, let us consider another highly significant statement made by the Lord. Just prior to his crucifixion, he said that on "the third day I *shall be perfected*." Think of that! The sinless, errorless Lord—already perfect by mortal standards—proclaimed his own state of perfection yet to be in the future. His *eternal* perfection would follow his resurrection and receipt of "all power . . . in heaven and in earth."

The perfection that the Savior envisions for us is much more than errorless performance. It is the eternal expectation as expressed by the Lord in his great intercessory prayer to his Father—that we might be made perfect and be able to dwell with them in the eternities ahead. . . .

That Jesus attained eternal perfection *following* his resurrection is confirmed in the Book of Mormon. It records the visit of the resurrected Lord to the people of ancient America. There he repeated the important injunction previously cited, but with one very significant addition. He said, "I would that ye should be perfect *even as I*, or your Father who is in heaven is perfect." This time he listed himself along with his Father as a perfected personage. Previously, he had not.

Resurrection is requisite for eternal perfection. . . .

Eternal perfection is reserved for those who overcome all things and inherit the fulness of the Father in his heavenly mansions. Perfection consists in gaining eternal life—the kind of life that God lives. ("Perfection Pending," pp. 86, 87.)

Thus the Savior is not demanding perfect lives—no sin, no mistakes, no weaknesses or inadequacies. What He is admonishing us is to *become* perfect or exalted by partaking of His atonement and the rest of the plan of salvation through faith, repentance, obedience, and faithful endurance. It is the Book of Mormon, specifically Nephi, that reminds us that drawing upon our own spiritual resources we are to make every effort to overcome our sins and weaknesses in this life as we steadily extend our reach toward perfection. That is, as Nephi said, "all we can do" (see 2 Nephi 25:23). In the end, however, we only become *perfect*—"complete," "finished," "whole"—as we are resurrected and exalted through the tender mercies of Christ.

"I believe the Lord meant just what he said: that we should be perfect, as our Father in heaven is perfect," President Joseph Fielding Smith declared, and then he added an important clarification. "That will not come at once, but line upon line, and precept upon precept, example upon example, and even then not as long as we live in this mortal life, for we will have to go even beyond the grave before we reach that perfection and shall be like God." (*Doctrines of Salvation,* comp. Bruce R. McConkie, 3 vols. [Salt Lake City: Bookcraft, 1954–56], 2:18–19.)

The great, encouraging message of the gospel is that God does not often require sensational or extraordinary deeds in our quest toward perfection, but merely that we continually try to do a little better each day than we did yesterday. In contrast to that message of hope, an unrealistic expectation that we must be perfect in all we do in this life becomes an overwhelming burden. That false notion actually retards our progress, stifles our spiritual development, and interferes with real gospel living. When we fall short of our preconceived notions of perfection (as we always will in mortality), we tend to browbeat ourselves with undeserved self-criticism and guilt, or we exhaust ourselves with unrealistic efforts to "perfect ourselves." I loathe that phrase! I know what we usually mean by it and that how it is often interpreted is not the way it is intended. However, to me, the phrase "perfect ourselves" leaves the impression that perfection is something I can—I ought, or worse yet, that I must—do all on my own.

In fact, the more we stubbornly seek to "perfect ourselves" in this manner, solely by our own efforts and self-discipline, and knowingly and subconsciously refuse the grace and mercy of Christ, we sink deeper into the quicksands of that devilish, dangerous, and destructive trait—perfectionism. Just as the cowboy heroes of those movies and television programs of my youth could only be rescued from quicksand through the assistance of another, we too can only be saved by someone else whose strength alone can save us—Jesus Christ, our "sure foundation."

That is the great message, the timeless theme, of the Book of Mormon. Nephi taught that the only way we can become perfect is by "unshaken faith in [Christ], relying wholly upon the merits of him who is mighty to save," at the same time "[pressing] forward with a steadfastness in Christ" (see 2 Nephi 31:19–20). When we use and/or hear the phrase "perfect ourselves" we must never construe it to mean that we must do it all on our own, but rather that we do our part, by doing the best we can, and the Savior will do the rest.

The Book of Mormon reminds us that although we can never "perfect ourselves" we can *become* "perfect in Christ." Moroni declared:

> Yea, come unto Christ, and be perfected in him, and deny yourselves of all ungodliness; and if ye shall deny yourselves of all ungodliness, and love God with all your might, mind and strength, then is his grace sufficient for you, that by his grace ye may be perfect in Christ; and if by the grace of God ye are perfect in Christ, ye can in nowise deny the power of God.
>
> And again, if ye by the grace of God are perfect in Christ, and deny not his power, then are ye sanctified in Christ by the grace of God, through the shedding of the blood of Christ, which is in the covenant of the Father unto the remission of your sins, that ye become holy, without spot. (Moroni 10:32–33.)

Through the many years I have conducted temple recommend interviews I have encountered hundreds of people who, when asked "Do you keep the covenants you made in the temple?" or "Do you consider yourself worthy to enter the temple and participate in temple ordinances?" will answer with something like, "Well, I'm not perfect." They are overly apologetic that they are not perfect in their lives. But that was not the question. Worthiness is not the same as perfection. Yet right here and now most of us demand perfection of ourselves when, in reality, the Lord may only require worthiness now. If we do all we can, He'll take care of the perfection later on. "Worthiness is a process, and perfection is an eternal trek," declared Elder Marvin J. Ashton. "I am also convinced of the fact that the speed with which we head along the straight and narrow path isn't as important as the direction in which we are travelling. That direction, if it is leading toward eternal goals, is the all-important factor." ("On Being Worthy," *Ensign*, May 1989, pp. 20–21.)

Understanding the doctrine of perfection, as taught in the scriptures and the Book of Mormon specifically, can liberate us from self-defeating behaviors and destructive attitudes that destroy that trust in the Master that is necessary to allow Him to make us perfect. When we come to know in our minds and accept in our hearts that it is only through Christ that we *become* perfect—that He is the means whereby we can be rescued from the quicksands of perfectionism—then our quest for perfection can become a joyful journey. "God's demand for perfection need not discourage you in the least in your present attempts to be good, or even in your present failures," wrote the noted Christian author C. S. Lewis.

Each time you fall He will pick you up again. And He knows perfectly well that your own efforts are never going to bring you anywhere near perfection. On the other hand, you must realise from the outset that the goal toward which He is beginning to guide you is absolute perfection; and no power in the whole universe, except you yourself, can prevent Him from taking you to that goal. . . .

. . . The command *Be ye perfect* is not idealistic gas. Nor is it a command to do the impossible. He is going to make us into creatures that can obey that command. He said (in the Bible) that we were "gods" and He is going to make good His words. If we let Him—for we can prevent Him, if we choose—He will make the feeblest and filthiest of us into a god or goddess, dazzling, radiant, immortal creature, pulsating all through with such energy and joy and wisdom and love as we cannot now imagine, a bright stainless mirror which reflects back to God perfectly. . . His own boundless power and delight and goodness. The process will be long and in parts very painful; but that is what we are in for. Nothing less. He meant what He said. (*Mere Christianity* [New York: Macmillan, 1952], pp. 172, 174–75.)

Some people may fully understand the doctrinal relationship between the grace of Christ and our own quest for perfection. They may likewise acknowledge that we cannot be perfect, in the truest sense of the word, while yet in mortality. They may even acknowledge our total dependence upon the Lord, yet fall prey to another aspect of perfectionism that can also adversely affect their own spirituality. This dangerous attitude manifests itself not just in matters of sin and righteousness but also in our efforts to be the "perfect mother" or "perfect father" *and* the "perfect spouse" *and* the "perfect neighbor" *and* the "perfect church worker." The list could go on and on. So many of us have guilt feelings that we are not all we should be because we cannot be all things to all people and perfect in all of those expectations.

It is not uncommon for some to exhaust themselves physically and become drained emotionally in their attempts to be perfect in all things and at all times. (My wife is kind of like this. Not only does she often feel frustration in her attempts to be "Patty Perfect" in her own life, but she is even more frustrated that I am not perfect—not a perfect husband, not a perfect father, not perfect at cleaning up after myself, not perfect at remembering what I was supposed to get at the grocery store on my way home, and so forth. Much to my wife's frustration, not only am I not perfect, but in her estimation I am not trying very hard to be perfect in some of those areas.) We sometimes find ourselves fretting over little things—like saying just the perfect thing at the perfect time, reacting in the perfect way to a difficult situation, or giving the perfect lesson, or doing the perfect job at whatever we undertake. This attitude of perfectionism is also like quicksand, because the harder we try to be as perfect as we think we should, and to do the perfect job at everything others expect of us, the more distraught we can become because we never quite "measure up." That's the problem with perfectionism— nothing is ever good enough! Elder M. Russell Ballard, in speaking to the women of the Church, described this common dilemma that afflicts not only many women but also many men.

> Some of you very likely are striving to be "super-moms." You feel a need to spend time with your husband and children. You want to be sure to have family prayer, read the scriptures, and have family home evening. You also feel the need to help children with homework and music lessons; keep your home presentable; prepare nutritious meals; keep clothes clean and mended; chauffeur children and possibly their friends to school and to a variety of lessons, practices, and games; and keep everyone in the family on schedule, making sure they are where they should be when they should be there. And that is all within your family and home. It makes me weary just reviewing all of this! It doesn't include PTA, volunteer service, or caring for family members who are ill or aged. You feel the need to protect your family from the many evil influences in the world such as suggestive television, films, and videos; alcohol; drugs; and pornography. You are committed to and faithfully fulfill your Church callings. In addition, many of you must earn a living because financial pressures are real and cannot be ignored. If anything is left or neglected, you may feel that you have failed.
>
> . . . I saw a bumper sticker the other day . . . that may say it all:
>
> "God put me on earth to accomplish a certain number of things. Right now I am so far behind, I will never die!" ("Be an Example of the Believers," *Ensign*, November 1991, p. 95.)

How can we manage these vexing feelings of inadequacy? How can we overcome the unhealthy "guilt trips" we often encounter on our quest toward perfection? How can we escape emotional and spiritual "burnout" and the quicksand of overexpectation before we, figuratively speaking, drown in our own perfectionism?

The Book of Mormon provides us with important counsel, as well as pure doctrine, that can liberate us from undeserved guilt and unneccessary discouragement. Both Nephi and King Benjamin taught valuable lessons that may, in fact, be more needed by us today in our frenetic world than the people of their day. Nephi reminds us that eternal life—ultimate perfection—will be ours if we but "press forward with a steadfastness in Christ," loving God and our fellowmen, "feasting upon the word of Christ, and endure to the end" (2 Nephi 31:20). King Benjamin reminds us that "all . . . things [are to be] done in . . . order" and that "it is not requisite that a man should run faster than he has strength." All that God requires of us, as King Benjamin declared, is to "be diligent" and "keep his commandments" (see Mosiah 4:27; 2:22). This counsel to "not run faster than [we have] strength" is significant to us both spiritually and emotionally. The key phrases that should guide us in our quest for perfection and in our approach to the "spiritual demands" placed upon us would be "press forward" and "be diligent." When we plug along the best we can, "pressing forward" with faith and hope in Christ, staying diligent—not necessarily perfect—in our obedience and service, we will find abundance rather than anguish, delight rather than discouragement, and fulfillment rather than frustration.

We must remember that much spiritual progress occurs not suddenly but usually through time and experience. The encouraging message of the gospel, as we find particularly in the Book of Mormon, is that God does not often require sensational or extraordinary deeds of us but merely requires that we keep "pressing forward"—trying to do a little better today that we did yesterday. He desires that we do things, as King Benjamin taught, "in wisdom and order"—steady progress, not spurts of spirituality; firmness of resolve, not flashy but fleeting results. The Lord neither expects nor desires us to do more than we can, or more than that which is wise, but He desires that we diligently and steadily keep moving in the right direction. Elder B. H. Roberts explained that the "little things" we do each day are often those things that matter most in our ongoing quest for perfection. The cumulative effect of the small and simple things will be ultimate salvation.

> There is no one great thing that man can do and then do no more and obtain salvation. After entering into the kingdom of

God, . . . it is by learning "precept upon precept; line upon line; here a little and there a little," that salvation will be made secure. It is by resisting temptation today, overcoming a weakness tomorrow, forsaking evil associations the next day, and thus day by day, month after month, year after year, pruning, restraining and weeding out that which is evil in the disposition, that the character is purged of its imperfections. Salvation is a matter of character-building under the Gospel laws and ordinances, and more especially with the direct aid of the Holy Spirit. (*The Gospel and Man's Relationship to Deity* [Salt Lake City: Deseret Book, 1965], p. 197.)

The author John Steinbeck wrote of one of his characters in the novel *East of Eden*, "Now that she knew that she didn't have to be perfect, she could be good." That is one of the great messages of the gospel and the scriptures. We cannot "perfect ourselves," but we can be good and do good. Being good and doing the best we can, whatever that may be, is doing the "all we can do" (2 Nephi 25:23) that will lead to our ultimate perfection. It is truly by the grace and love of Jesus Christ that we are made "perfect in Christ" while yet in mortality. That does not mean that we do everything right or that we will never sin. It does mean, however, that through our faith in the atoning sacrifice of the Savior and through our continual "pressing forward with steadfastness" in Him, we can become pure—justified, sanctified, "whole," "at peace with God"—perfect. President Brigham Young declared:

Those who do right, and seek the glory of the Father in heaven, . . . whether they can do little or much, if they do the very best they know how, they are perfect. . . . To be as perfect as we possibly can according to our knowledge, is to be just as perfect as our Father in Heaven is. . . . When we are doing as well as we know how in the sphere, and station which we occupy here, we are justified. . . . We are as justified as the angels who are before the throne of God. (In *Deseret News Weekly*, 31 August 1854, p. 1; see also *Journal of Discourses* 2:129–30.)

What a blessing it is to know, by virtue of the Book of Mormon, that God realizes that I cannot be totally error-free in this life—always saying, doing, and thinking the perfect things. What comfort it is to me to know that "perfect in Christ" means just that—*in Christ*. For I could never do it on my own—no, not even get close. How grateful I am that what I am able to do in mortality, through His grace coupled with my faith, I can do. He makes that possible. "When our imperfections appear, we can keep trying to correct them," Elder Russell M. Nelson encouraged. "We can be more forgiving of flaws in ourselves and among those we love."

> We can be comforted and forbearing. The Lord taught, "Ye are not able to abide the presence of God now. . . ; wherefore continue in patience until ye are perfected" (D&C 67:13).
>
> We need not be dismayed if our earnest efforts toward perfection now seem so arduous and endless. Perfection is pending. It can come in full only after the Resurrection and only through the Lord. It awaits all who love him and keep his commandments. It includes thrones, kingdoms, principalities, powers, and dominions. It is the end for which we are to endure. It is the eternal perfection that God has in store for each of us. ("Perfection Pending," p. 88.)

What a comforting yet inspiring thought it is to know that even the sinless Christ was not fully perfect—"complete," "whole," "finished"—until after His resurrection. He beckons me to come unto Him and partake of that same kind of perfection—that which only He can provide. It is not so much a command to be *perfect*—though it is that—as it is an invitation to "cast my burdens" upon Him and *become perfect*—resurrected, glorified, exalted—through Him. He is both the means of our finite perfection—our justification and cleansing from sin—and the end of our eternal perfection—"immortality and eternal life" (Moses 1:39). "I would that ye should be perfect even as I, or your Father who is in heaven is perfect" (3 Nephi 12:48) is our charge to continually partake of the atonement of Jesus Christ through faith, repentance, the ordinances of the gospel, and by being "steadfast and immovable, always abounding in good works"—not always perfect, but being good, trying hard, doing "all we can do"—that we may *become* "perfect in Christ" here and now and enjoy the ultimate perfection promised by King Benjamin:

> that Christ, the Lord God Omnipotent, may seal you his, that you may be brought to heaven, that ye may have everlasting salvation and eternal life, through the wisdom, and power, and justice, and mercy of him who created all things, in heaven and in earth, who is God above all. Amen. (Mosiah 5:15.)

And if it so be that the children of men keep the commandments of God he doth nourish them, and strengthen them, and provide means whereby they can accomplish the thing which he has commanded.
—1 NEPHI 17:3

CHAPTER 9

STRENGTHENED BY THE HAND OF GOD

During the time I served a full-time mission to the Denmark Copenhagen Mission, I was assigned to reopen for missionary work the island of Bornholm in the Baltic Sea. Missionaries had not labored there for many years. The small island is only about fifteen or twenty miles across and less than a hundred miles in circumference. There was a small branch of the Church located in the main city, and there were a few members scattered all around the island in various villages. My companion and I were responsible for the entire island, although bicycles were our main mode of transportation.

One day after meeting with a member in one of the outlying cities, we began our bike ride back to the main city for an appointment with an investigator. Although we had made that trip before, this time the bike ride seemed unbearably long. As we started our trek, a storm moved into the area. We encountered a very stiff, bitter-cold headwind. At first I just tried to tough it out, but soon my ears were aching and my head was throbbing from the freezing wind in my face. My legs were burning from the physical strain of riding against the wind. (This was in the days before the sophisticated multi-gear mountain bikes, so it took all the energy I had to just keep pedaling.)

To make matters worse, my junior companion discovered that the headwind wasn't so bad and the strain to his body not so intense if he rode close behind me—I was his windbreak. When I would turn around to see how he was doing because I felt I couldn't go on much further, he would be smiling and pedaling his bike almost effortlessly. Because he looked so fresh and unbothered by the winds, I did not want to let on that I was on the verge of collapse—a senior companion just can't let his junior get the best of him! So I did the only thing left for me to do. I prayed. I reminded Heavenly Father that we were on His errand, that we were going to an important appointment and we would be late if He didn't stop the wind.

I thought that sounded reasonable, but it didn't work. In fact, I think the winds gusted a little harder. So I tried another angle—I mustered all the faith I could and prayed even more fervently that the winds would subside. I reminded God that He had blessed us in remarkable ways in the past when we needed help and when we approached Him in faith. I even reminded Him of the scriptural passage that says something about faith as small as a mustard seed can move mountains, though I don't think I needed to remind Him about that. Still the wind persisted. When all else fails, try the action of last resort—beg! So I begged the Lord to please stop the wind—NOW! I pleaded with Him with all the energy of my soul, but still the wind blew and I was cold and my body ached.

Then something remarkable happened. No, the wind didn't stop blowing! I did, however, begin to become distracted. I began to notice the cold wind less and less, because I started thinking about some of my favorite stories from the Book of Mormon. As I thought about them, it was as if I was reliving them. I could almost visualize the events in my mind. It was

almost like I was part of the story. There were 2,000 stripling
warriors plus one. I was with Ammon as he protected the king's
flocks from the wicked rustlers at the waters of Sebus. I was on
top of the city walls with Samuel the Lamanite prophet. And I
was there when the 2500 saw and felt the resurrected Christ at
the temple in Bountiful. All of these events were so vivid to my
mind that it was almost like a vision.

I must have really enjoyed the "show," because before I was
even through thinking about my favorite stories we had arrived
at our destination. What happened to the wind? Nothing. It was
still blowing just as hard as ever. Had Heavenly Father heard and
answered my prayers? Absolutely. It just wasn't done in the manner for which I had prayed. There was nothing sensational or
dramatic, but the end result was still the same. He had manifested His love and concern for me, heard my heartfelt petitions,
and blessed me in a way that I had not expected. He took my
mind off my problems without taking my problems off me.

From this experience I learned a valuable lesson about how
the Lord answers our prayers and watches over us in times of
need. We may not always recognize what He is doing, but He is,
nonetheless, doing remarkable things in our lives. I have seen
this principle at work often in my life since that experience in
Denmark many years ago. In fact, each time I read the scriptures
I see examples of this principle taught. One of those timeless
Book of Mormon themes we see throughout that volume of
scripture is that God is "mindful of us, wanderers in a strange
land" and that "he numbereth his people, and his bowels of
mercy are over all the earth" (Alma 26:36–37). The Book of
Mormon teaches and testifies, both by precept and example, how
the Lord bestows upon the righteous the strength to bear their
burdens, protection from physical and spiritual harm, and an
endowment of power from on high.

STRENGTH TO BEAR ONE'S BURDENS

It is a natural tendency for us to ask the Lord to take away
our problems and pains when they are weighing us down,

whether those burdens be physical or emotional. Even the Apostle Paul spoke of a "thorn in the flesh" that burdened him and that he three times pleaded with the Lord to remove (see 2 Corinthians 12:7–10). But just as he discovered, we often come to learn that the burdens aren't necessarily lifted nor are the thorns in the flesh always comfortably and conveniently removed. The Lord does, however, promise us that He will be mindful of us, will answer our prayers, and will visit us in our afflictions, but there is a "catch" to that promise—it will be according to His will and His timetable.

The Book of Mormon provides us with a dramatic portrayal of how God keeps His promise. After Alma and his followers fled from King Noah and his wicked priests, they established the Church and prospered spiritually as they faithfully lived the gospel in the land of Helam. Their peace and comfort were shattered, however, when they were captured and enslaved by the Lamanites. They were ultimately subjected to the harsh rule of Amulon, formerly one of the wicked priests in King Noah's court. As slaves to the Lamanites, Alma's people were forced to be "beasts of burden." Weighed down by their physical burdens and their discouragement and heavy hearts, Alma's people cried to the Lord for relief from their afflictions.

> And it came to pass that so great were their afflictions that they began to cry mightily to God.
>
> And Amulon commanded them that they should stop their cries; and he put guards over them to watch them, that whosoever should be found calling upon God should be put to death.
>
> And Alma and his people did not raise their voices to the Lord their God, but did pour out their hearts to him; and he did know the thoughts of their hearts.
>
> And now it came to pass that the voice of the Lord came to them in their afflictions, saying: Lift up your heads and be of good comfort, for I know of the covenant which ye have made unto me; and I will covenant with my people and deliver them out of bondage.
>
> And I will also ease the burdens which are put upon your

shoulders, that even you cannot feel them upon your backs, even while you are in bondage; and this will I do that ye may stand as witnesses for me hereafter, and that ye may know of a surety that I, the Lord God, do visit my people in their afflictions.

And now it came to pass that the burdens which were laid upon Alma and his brethren were made light; yea, the Lord did strengthen them that they could bear up their burdens with ease, and they did submit cheerfully and with patience to all the will of the Lord. (Mosiah 24:10–15.)

Implicit in this testimony of God's faithfulness to His promise to "visit [His] people in their afflictions" is the message that He usually answers our prayers not by lifting the burdens and tribulations but rather by bolstering our capacity to endure them. Not too infrequently, and quite naturally, we may become discouraged that our problems persist despite prolonged prayerfulness. In these perplexing moments it becomes easy to let our faith waver and second-guess God's purposes. The truth of the matter may very well be, as evidenced in Alma's account, that the Lord often answers our prayers and provides us with comfort in a different manner than what we desire or expect. Kay Yow, coach of the 1988 U.S. Women's Olympic basketball team, tells how the Lord answered her prayers when she was diagnosed as having breast and lymphatic cancer: "My immediate tendency was to pray to God that this circumstance might change. But in my case it didn't happen. God chose to change me instead of my circumstance, and through the whole experience I have grown deeply. I'm a better person in a lot of ways." (*USA Today*, 22 October 1987, p. 10C.)

In addition to the account of Alma and his people, the Book of Mormon provides us with other profound illustrations of this principle. One of my favorites is the manner in which the Lord cared for Lehi and his family during their eight-year journey across the dangerous Arabian desert. "And we did travel and wade through much affliction in the wilderness," Nephi wrote, "and our women did bear children in the wilderness" (1 Nephi

17:1). Under these extremely difficult circumstances it would be quite understandable for fathers, mothers, and especially children to murmur and to feel forsaken by the Lord and terribly burdened by such difficulties. No doubt there were many heartfelt pleadings to the Lord. Yet God did not "beam them up" and mystically transport them to the promised land. He left them to make their own way through the heat and harshness of the desert—mile after mile, sand dune after sand dune, year after year.

On top of that, they were forbidden from using fire on their journey. There could be no bonfire to heat them in the bitter cold of desert nights. Their food could not be cooked over the campfire. They must eat their meat raw. Think of it—eating raw meat, bearing children in that environment, nursing babies with little nourishment, shivering in the desert cold at night and sweltering in the desert heat of day. How could God expect them to endure such hardships? Didn't He care about them? Didn't He answer their prayers? Absolutely! While we may view their burdensome circumstances as intolerable, and they certainly were difficult, Nephi described their conditions in a different light.

> And so great were the blessings of the Lord upon us, that while we did live upon raw meat in the wilderness, our women did give plenty of suck for their children, and were strong, yea, even like unto the men; and they began to bear their journeyings without murmurings.
>
> And thus we see that the commandments of God must be fulfilled. And it it so be that the children of men keep the commandments of God he doth nourish them, and strengthen them, and provide means whereby they can accomplish the thing which he has commanded them; wherefore, he did provide means for us while we did sojourn in the wilderness. (1 Nephi 17:2–3.)

God didn't take away their pains and discomforts. They were not blissfully wafted away on beds of ease. They were, however, strengthened beyond their natural powers of endurance.

Endurance of these tribulations certainly was not easy, but God made it, if not comfortable, at least possible. "We had suffered many afflictions and much difficulty," Nephi recalled, "yea, even so much that we cannot write them all." Yet, amidst all this, the goodness of God and His strengthening influence bore them up and, as Nephi declared, "we were exceedingly rejoiced when we came to the seashore." (1 Nephi 17:6.)

I certainly have never had to experience anything close to that kind of difficulty and deprivation. My suffering and sorrows have been relatively insignificant by comparison. There have, however, been many moments when burdens seemed extraordinarily heavy. Sometimes the burdens were in the form of heavy responsibilities or weighty decisions. Other times there were the challenges of child-rearing and the accompanying financial demands, emotional turmoil, and occasional heartaches. There have also been moments of discouragement and depression, sickness, and sadness. My "thorns in the flesh" may not be much different from or more difficult to bear than others, but they are mine—heavy burdens that have to be borne while I am yet mortal. I, like many others, on occasion have prayed, "Let this cup pass from me," only to later discover that although the cup couldn't pass by, I was nonetheless borne up, "stengthened by the hand of God" (Alma 2:28). How did we make it through those challenges? Sometimes there is no clear answer, but the end result is that we did. In retrospect, we often marvel at how the Lord gave us strength and skills, unrecognized by us at the time, to "bear up [our] burdens with ease."

While laboring among the Zoramites, Alma recognized his heavy burdens and prayed, "O Lord, wilt thou give me strength, that I might bear with mine infirmities" (Alma 31:30). His prayer was answered. He was given strength to meet his personal challenges and he was also endowed with a strengthening influence to bless the lives of those with whom he labored and taught. As a result, the humble and repentant Zoramites were also blessed and "strengthened by the hand of God" in many ways. Not all their burdens were lifted, not all suffering was eliminated—but the Lord "gave them strength, that they should suffer no manner of afflictions, save it were swallowed up in the joy of Christ" (Alma 31:38). So, too, can it be for us, even when the Lord does not see fit to take away our problems or lift from our shoulders all heavy burdens. He will strengthen us, lift our spirits, and fill our hearts with hope because of the atonement of Jesus Christ. There is no greater strength, no greater hope, no greater joy than that! His yoke is easy and His burden light. That is what gives us strength to carry on. "May God grant unto you that your burdens may be light, through the joy of his Son" (Alma 33:23).

PROTECTION FROM HARM

"Wherefore, [God] will preserve the righteous by his power," Nephi paraphrased from the prophet Isaiah. "Wherefore, the righteous need not fear" (1 Nephi 22:17). One of the timeless themes we see in the scriptures—both ancient and modern, both Bible and Book of Mormon—is that the Lord will protect and preserve those who love Him and keep His commandments. This preservation and protection is both physical and spiritual, seen and unseen. There are several examples contained in the Book of Mormon that dramatically illustrate how God fulfills His promise of protection. I have always loved the paintings of Book of Mormon scenes by the famous artist Arnold Friberg. Two of my favorites are Abinadi standing before King Noah and his wicked priests and Samuel the Lamanite prophet standing on the wall of the city prophesying about the coming of Christ. Each of these paintings, in my estimation, captures both the spirit of the scriptural account and the imagination of the observer.

The prophet Abinadi is portrayed as an elderly, frail, thin man bound by ropes or chains. Despite his weak appearance, he is portrayed with a strength that exudes confidence and seems to glow with inward power and light. As beautiful as Friberg's painting is, I am sure that it cannot completely portray the spiritual power the prophet possessed and the divine protection that encompassed him. This power and protection was both spiritual and physical. Spiritually, he was filled with the Spirit to the point that he confounded his accusers with his words and teachings (see Mosiah 12:16–19). Physically, they could not harm him until he had fulfilled his assignment and delivered the message God intended for them to hear. His words, accompanied by the condemning power of the Spirit—"which is quick and powerful, sharper than a two-edged sword"—exposed their false doctrines and wicked practices and cut them to the very core of their souls. Pained by the truth that the "wicked taketh to be hard," Noah sought to have Abinadi immediately killed. He discovered to his dismay that neither his kingly power nor the combined strength of his servants and subjects were greater than the unseen power that an aged and seemingly weak prophet possessed.

> And now when the king had heard these words, he said unto his priests: Away with this fellow, and slay him; for what have we to do with him, for he is mad.
>
> And they stood forth and attempted to lay their hands on him; but he withstood them, and said unto them:
>
> Touch me not, for God shall smite you if ye lay your hands upon me, for I have not delivered the message which the Lord sent me to deliver; neither have I told you that which ye requested that I should tell; therefore, God will not suffer that I shall be destroyed at this time.
>
> But I must fulfill the commandments wherewith God has commanded me; and because I have told you the truth ye are angry with me. And again, because I have spoken the word of God ye have judged me that I am mad.
>
> Now it came to pass after Abinadi had spoken these words that the people of king Noah durst not lay their hands on him, for the Spirit of the Lord was upon him; and his face shone with exceeding luster, even as Moses' did while in the mount of Sinai, while speaking with the Lord.
>
> And he spake with power and authority from God. (Mosiah 13:1–6.)

The second episode, portrayed so beautifully in Friberg's art, is Samuel standing atop the Nephite city wall. He, like Abinadi before him, was commissioned of the Lord to prophesy and warn. We don't see him glowing from the protective power of the Spirit, but he was, nonetheless, miraculously protected from harm and preserved to fulfill his mission. While I don't fully understand how Samuel was protected, the scriptural record is clear—the wicked could not harm this righteous man! Was he clothed in some sort of spiritual armor that repelled the arrows or stones? Did God cause an alteration in the law of physics so the arrows went astray? Or did He cause the unbelievers to have a temporary case of bad vision, so they couldn't take proper aim? Did He cause their arms to go weak and their bows to lose their spring? I don't know! But I do know that the Book of Mormon is true and that it states that Samuel was protected by the power of God.

> And now, it came to pass that there were many who heard the words of Samuel, the Lamanite, which he spake upon the walls of the city. And as many as believed on his word went forth and sought for Nephi; and when they had come forth and found him they confessed unto him their sins and denied not, desiring that they might be baptized unto the Lord.
>
> But as many as there were who did not believe in the words of Samuel were angry with him; and they cast stones at him upon the wall, and also many shot arrows at him as he stood upon the wall; but the Spirit of the Lord was with him, insomuch that they could not hit him with their stones neither with their arrows. (Helaman 16:1–2.)

These are but two of the many examples of miraculous protection and divine preservation that are recorded in the Book of Mormon. Alma and Amulek were protected from their enemies and miraculously delivered from prison, as the walls crumbled about them (see Alma 14:19–29). Similarly, Nephi and Lehi, sons of Helaman, were divinely delivered from prison with the help of heavenly ministrants. They were encircled by fire—a fire that did not consume them, but rather protected them (see Helaman 5:22–52). One inspiring story that young Latter-day

Saints read with interest is the account of the two thousand stripling warriors who, despite great hardships and many painful battle wounds, were likewise protected by the powers of heaven. Helaman recorded:

> And it came to pass that after the Lamanites had fled, I immediately gave orders that my men who had been wounded should be taken from among the dead, and caused that their wounds should be dressed.
>
> And it came to pass that there were two hundred, out of my two thousand and sixty, who had fainted because of the loss of blood; nevertheless, according to the goodness of God, and to our great astonishment, and also the joy of our whole army, there was not one soul of them who did perish; yea, and neither was there one soul among them who had not received many wounds.
>
> And now, their preservation was astonishing to our whole army, yea, that they should be spared while there were a thousand of our brethren who were slain. And we do justly ascribe it to the miraculous power of God, because of their exceeding faith in that which they had been taught to believe—that there was a just God, and whosoever did not doubt, that they should be preserved by his marvelous power. (Alma 57:24–26.)

But are these just stories? Of course not! Did they really happen? They surely did! Do these kinds of miracles still exist? Yes, indeed! "God has not ceased to be a God of miracles," Moroni declared (Mormon 9:15). Sometimes it is easier for us to believe in miraculous protective powers and divine intervention in ancient days than in our own. But if there are no miracles today it may be because, as Moroni taught, men "dwindle in unbelief, and depart from the right way, and know not the God in whom they should trust" (Mormon 9:20). Then what is it the Lord wants us to learn from these accounts of divine protection and preservation? Remember that the Book of Mormon prophets repeatedly remind us their words were written for us today, as voices from the dust. What is especially relevant to us and our challenges and circumstances by this theme of divine intervention?

We are living in the day and age when the Savior's words concerning the last days are being fulfilled right before our eyes. "Iniquity [does] abound, the love of men [does] wax cold" (Joseph Smith—Matthew 1:30), and "all things [are] in commotion; and surely, men's hearts [do] fail them; for fear [has] come upon all people" (D&C 88:91). Members of the Church are not immune from the incursions of the adversary into our communities, our neighborhoods, and even our own homes. We are witnessing, as the scriptures attest, that Satan "maketh war with the saints of God, and encompasseth them round about" (D&C 76:29). "We, of all men, should not be surprised to see wickedness increase—though we deplore it," President Ezra Taft Benson observed. "Nor should we be surprised to see a rising increase in divorces, family break-ups, moral problems, infidelity, unchastity, and every conceivable evil. The Savior said that iniquity would abound, and because of it the love of many will wax cold in the latter days." (*The Teachings of Ezra Taft Benson* [Salt Lake City: Bookcraft, 1988], p. 409.)

Perhaps there has never been a time when the message of protection from harm, both physical and spiritual, has been more needed than now. It would be easy to live in a state of constant fear for one's personal safety. It would be easy to fall prey to cynicism and hopelessness. For these reasons, this message was truly written for our day: God does still, as in times past, protect the righteous, preserving them from harm's way, and He provides the way of deliverance.

Now, I can almost hear someone saying: "Wait just one minute! Hold your horses! How can you make such claims? God doesn't always protect the righteous! The righteous suffer from the evils of the world and die at the hands of the wicked, too. How do you explain that?" Well, here goes.

The Book of Mormon does indeed testify of the miraculous power of God to protect and preserve the righteous. It does, however, also include examples of righteous men and women who had devoted their lives to God who were nonetheless killed or harmed by wicked men. Although Alma and Amulek were protected by the powers of heaven and miraculously liberated from prison, the believing men who accepted their message were stoned, and the women and children who likewise believed were burned alive at the hands of the enemies of the Church (see Alma chapter 14). Although the two thousand stripling warriors were preserved by the Lord, many converted Lamanites, known as Anti-Nephi-Lehies, were killed by other Lamanites because they would not break a covenant they had made not to take up arms against their brethren (see Alma chapter 24). The righteous suffered at the hands of the wicked bands of Gadianton. Even Mormon, righteous prophet of God, was killed by his enemies.

The scriptures, particularly the Book of Mormon, do not teach that the righteous will be isolated from all the consequences of evil or suffering in the world. The righteous as well as the wicked get sick and die, have hardships and heartaches, experience all kinds of pain and problems (see Matthew 5:45). Does this mean that God is not mindful of them or does not love them or protect them? Of course not! Because God safeguards the principle of agency and allows the laws of nature to operate in ways that fulfill His purposes, there will always be painful side effects of mortality. To intervene and provide a protective plastic bubble, so to speak, in which the faithful Saints could live free from any opposition, suffering, or death would be contrary to the very plan of salvation—"the great plan of happiness." Instead of protecting and preserving the righteous, it would actually inflict greater harm, both now and throughout eternity. Such an artificial life would smack of Lucifer's premortal efforts to "destroy the agency of man" (Moses 4:3). The Prophet Joseph Smith also explained that suffering and afflictions are an inherent and necessary part of life. Speaking of the prophesied trials and tribulations associated with the Second Coming, the Prophet wrote:

> I explained concerning the coming of the Son of Man; also that it is a false idea that the Saints will escape all the judgments, whilst the wicked suffer; for all flesh is subject to suffer, and "the righteous shall hardly escape;" still many of the Saints will escape, for the just shall live by faith; yet many of the righteous

shall fall a prey to disease, to pestilence, etc., by reason of the weakness of the flesh, and yet be saved in the Kingdom of God. So that it is an unhallowed principle to say that such and such have transgressed because they have been preyed upon by disease or death, for all flesh is subject to death." (*Teachings of the Prophet Joseph Smith*, sel. Joseph Fielding Smith [Salt Lake City: Deseret Book, 1938], pp. 162–63.)

There will be painful consequences of agency and the laws of nature that prevail in our mortal existence, but the Lord in His loving kindness has also promised compassionate compensation—all part of His promise of preservation and protection. This type of compensation is seen in Captain Moroni's epistle to Pahoran: "For the Lord suffereth the righteous to be slain that his justice and judgment may come upon the wicked; therefore ye need not suppose that the righteous are lost because they are slain; but behold, they do enter into the rest of the Lord their God" (Alma 60:13).

The Book of Mormon testifies of the spiritual preservation and protection that await the righteous. "O how great the goodness of our God," declared Jacob, "who prepareth a way for our escape from the grasp of this awful monster; yea, that monster, death and hell" (2 Nephi 9:10). We are promised protection from the adversary while yet in mortality and preservation of life until our life's mission is complete, if we are true to our covenants. Other glorious promises of redemption and preservation await the righteous. Though we may suffer in mortality, and though not all losses sustained in the course of life's adversities can be restored to us in this life, nor can all of our anguish be completely eliminated while we are yet in the flesh, the Lord has promised divine compensation. If we are faithful to our covenants, we will be beneficiaries of that eternal compensation that is infinitely more generous and just than any earthly remuneration. President Lorenzo Snow spoke of this divine compensation and of how faithful endurance in mortality will ultimately lead to even greater rewards in heaven:

I suppose I am talking to some who have had worry and trouble and heart burnings and persecution, and have at times been caused to think that they never expected to endure quite so much. But for everything you have suffered, for everything that has occurred to you which you thought an evil at that time, you will receive fourfold, and that suffering will have had a tendency to make you better and stronger and to feel that you have been blessed. When you look back over your experiences you will then see that you have advanced far ahead and have gone up several rounds of the ladder toward exaltation and glory. (*The Teachings of Lorenzo Snow*, comp. Clyde J. Williams [Salt Lake City: Bookcraft, 1984], p. 117.)

How grateful I am for the teachings of the Book of Mormon concerning the atonement of Jesus Christ. It is from those teachings that we learn that ultimately all losses can be restored, all suffering can cease, and all inequities and injustices can be rectified through the grace, love, and mercy of the Only Begotten. This is the epitome of that preservation promised to the faithful and spoken of by Book of Mormon prophets, as Nephi declared, "He will preserve the righteous by his power" (1 Nephi 22:17).

This promise, however, is not merely referring to our eternal reward. It isn't just about "deferred gratification"—promises that apply later, but not now. The Lord's promise of preservation applies to us *here and now* not just *hereafter*. Just as He protected and preserved faithful Saints in Book of Mormon times, He will do the same today. This promise of preservation and protection is realized in mortality in two ways: 1) through miraculous divine interventions and 2) as the natural consequence of living the gospel of Jesus Christ.

While we may not always see the miracles in our lives, they surround us continually, if we are faithful. We may not see angels ministering to us or have the walls of prisons dramatically fall down around us, or be encircled about by protective flames of fire, like we read about in the scriptures, but we can be and are often protected and blessed by unseen powers just as surely. If we will pause and ponder, we will recognize the many ways the

Lord's hand has protected us and guided us to safety throughout our lives. We may never know in mortality all of the ways that the promise of preservation and protection has been realized in our lives, but we can get a glimpse now and again of the ways whereby God has "disperse[d] the powers of darkness from before you, and cause[d] the heavens to shake for your good" (D&C 21:6). As Elder Dallin H. Oaks testified:

> I am grateful for the Book of Mormon promise to us of the last days that "the righteous need not fear," for the Lord "will preserve the righteous by his power" (1 Nephi 22:17). I am grateful for the protection promised to those who have kept their covenants and qualified for the blessings promised in sacred places. (In Conference Report, October 1992, p. 56.)

Just as Elder Oaks stated, protection comes in miraculous ways, but also by virtue of keeping the covenants one has made. Righteousness may entitle us to the ministering of angels or some dramatic preservation, but it also gives a real, though natural, protection. Being obedient to the commandments of God keeps me protected from many of the temptations of the world. That creates a shield that protects from the "fiery darts of the adversary." By being where we should be and by doing what we should do we are protected from the "fiery darts" because we are out of the devil's range—we are on the Lord's side of the line. That is safety in itself.

Keeping the commandments protects us in other ways as well. It gives us increased spiritual strength to resist temptation; and of course the more obedient we are the more worthy we are to receive the guidance and companionship of the Holy Ghost. The Holy Spirit can protect us by leading us away from places, people, and circumstances that may cause us harm, both physical and spiritual. Righteousness not only provides protection against and preservation from evil, which is a sure defense against the adversary, but also provides us with power from on high to assist us in our own challenges, responsibilities, and callings. That, too, is a sure promise to the faithful.

ENDOWED WITH POWER FROM ON HIGH

Not only does the Lord promise strength and protection to the righteous, but He promises them power. When I think of *strength*, I usually think of physical energy and capacity—"muscle power," something that comes from within, from being in great condition and shape, by working out and taking vitamins and nutritional supplements. In contrast, when I think of *power*, though both words are closely related, I think of electricity—a power that comes from an external source that surpasses anything the human body can produce by itself. I am impressed with the strength of bodybuilders and weight lifters, but I am in awe of lightning. I believe both strength and power are gifts from God, but often one gift comes from *within* while the other God bestows *upon*.

For example, I see the prophet Nephi as a man of extraordinary strength, physical and spiritual. He was strong and able to endure hardships, not only because of his large physical stature but also because of the inner strength that came from his faith in God and obedience to the commandments. Yet when he needed something beyond just his strength he was given a remarkable power, a power that mere mortals do not possess. He was endowed with something supernatural, something miraculous— an actual "power from on high." Praying and keeping the commandments helps condition us so that we have spiritual strength, but periodically as needed the Lord allows us to tap into a spiritual power substation, if you will. Let's look at Nephi as an example of this principle.

Despite Nephi's spiritual and physical strength, his inspiration, and his profound teachings, his own brothers opposed him and persecuted him. They murmured and complained about everything, but especially about the command to build a ship. How could Nephi build a ship? They mocked him openly when he explained that he was given the plans and the means to do so from God. When they refused to help, he exhorted them by teaching them and bearing testimony. He reminded them of the goodness of God and called them to repentance, but it was the "exclamation point" of his sermon that grabbed their attention and demonstrated the power of God.

> My soul is rent with anguish because of you, and my heart is pained; I fear lest ye shall be cast off forever. Behold, I am full of the Spirit of God, insomuch that my frame has no strength.
>
> And now it came to pass that when I had spoken these words they were angry with me, and were desirous to throw me into the depths of the sea; and as they came forth to lay their hands upon me I spake unto them, saying: In the name of the Almighty God, I command you that ye touch me not, for I am filled with the power of God, even unto the consuming of my flesh; and whoso shall lay his hands upon me shall wither even as a dried reed; and he shall be as naught before the power of God, for God shall smite him. . . .
>
> And it came to pass that I, Nephi, said many things unto my brethren, insomuch that they were confounded and could not contend against me; neither durst they lay their hands upon me nor touch me with their fingers, even for the space of many days. Now they durst not do this lest they should wither before me, so powerful was the Spirit of God; and thus it had wrought upon them.
>
> And it came to pass that the Lord said unto me: Stretch forth thine hand again unto thy brethren, and they shall not wither before thee, but I will shock them, saith the Lord, and this will I do, that they may know that I am the Lord their God.
>
> And it came to pass that I stretched forth my hand unto my brethren, and they did not wither before me; but the Lord did shake them, even according to the word which he had spoken. (1 Nephi 17:47–48, 52–54.)

I love this story. I have always wanted to do it, but never had that power—or at least, God never inspired me to use His power in that way. We don't always see the power of God manifest in this way, through "spiritual shock therapy," but we see the endowment of God's power on His servants in many other ways. It may not seem as dramatic as Nephi giving his murmuring brothers an "electrical kick in the pants," but the power of God is all around us—and if we keep our covenants, we are endowed with it as well. That is why aged prophets even today can "run rings around" men and women half their age and perform miraculous works and declare mighty words that touch hearts with a power as real as electricity. Although mountains may not be literally moved today, there is power attending the work of modern prophets and Apostles that moves men and organizations and brings ideas into reality as monumental as moving mountains. It is this endowment of power that causes unlearned and unsophisticated young elders and sisters to preach the gospel with power and authority so that even the high and mighty of the world can feel the Spirit as surely as if they put their finger in an electrical outlet. It is this literal power that casts out devils, heals the sick, and raises the dead even in this day and age.

I love the phrase that Nephi used to contrast mortal strength with God's power. "I am full of the Spirit of God," he declared, "insomuch that my frame has no strength." God's power is greater than any man or earthly enterprise. We have that kind of power at our fingertips. If we are faithful and obedient we, too, can be filled with the Spirit of God, thus having claim upon whatever power we may need to further the work of God as He sees fit—even to the "shocking" of others, if necessary. But ordinarily, the power of God is manifest quietly by ordinary men and women that do and say extraordinary things because they are endowed with power. It may be manifest through seemingly simple acts of service, like Ammon protecting the king's flocks from marauding rustlers (see Alma chapters 17–18). Yet such power-enhanced service leads to great influence in the lives of others.

We can have that same kind of influence and power. We may not even recognize the power that is within us until we lose the Spirit through wickedness. Then that loss will be recognized as a major "power outage." In contrast to the stripling warriors of Helaman's army who were miraculously preserved and endowed with great power because of their righteousness, the wicked Nephites "had become weak, like unto their brethren, the Lamanites." Mormon recorded: "The Spirit of the Lord did no more preserve them; yea, it had withdrawn from them because the Spirit of the Lord doth not dwell in unholy temples. . . . Thus had they become weak, because of their transgression." (Helaman 4:24, 26.) Righteous men and women who live the gospel, keep the covenants, and trust in the Lord may appear as ordinary people doing ordinary things, but they are not—they are endowed with a power that is anything but ordinary. They are not like anyone else. While the wicked and worldly walk by the flickering of their puny candles, the righteous can be filled with light "until the perfect day" (see D&C 50:24).

We can have that kind of spiritual strength to help bear our burdens today. The same divine powers of protection and preservation that we see manifest in the Book of Mormon are afforded the faithful today. That is one of the great themes of the Book of Mormon—as a message of hope for our day. No matter what we face in life, no matter how difficult our own unique challenges and circumstances may be, we need not give up, give in, or lose hope. For we have the promise that if we remain "true and steadfast" we have at our disposal a "secret weapon"—a sure defense, the means whereby any problem can be solved and any enemy defeated—the infinite power of God. No wonder Ammon, who had experienced this power many times in life, gloried in the blessing of being "stengthened by the hand of God."

> I do not boast in my own strength, nor in my own wisdom; but behold, my joy is full, yea, my heart is brim with joy, and I will rejoice in my God.
>
> Yea, I know that I am nothing; as to my strength I am weak; therefore I will not boast of myself, but I will boast of my God, for in his strength I can do all things. (Alma 26:11–12.)

If ye have not charity, ye are nothing, for charity never faileth.
Wherefore, cleave unto charity, which is the greatest of all, for
all things must fail—but charity is the pure love of Christ,
and it endureth forever; and whoso is found possessed of it
at the last day, it shall be well with him.
—MORONI 7:46–47

CHAPTER 10

"CHARITY NEVER FAILETH"

The word *charity* **means different things to different people.** Some definitions are more positive than others. It can mean an act of good will or benevolence. Often it is used in connection with some form of voluntary contribution of money or service to an individual or institution. "All proceeds go to charity," the announcement may declare. A person who may go to a "charity ball" is going to be donating money at the function with the hopes that the monies will be used for the benefit of those who are in need. Unfortunately, in our day, the word *charity* can also take on a slightly negative connotation. "I don't want to be a 'charity case,'" I heard some people say when as their bishop I offered to help them in their need. "Charity case" was spoken with derision—implying freeloading or being viewed with pity and seen as one who is "down and out." In this context, *charity* is seen as *welfare,* and that word, unfortunately, has fallen from grace in many circles and has much negative baggage attached to it—often undeservedly so. In each of these cases the definition or connotation may be correct but incomplete. Charity means so much more.

In the King James version of the New Testament, we read Paul's words concerning charity:

> Though I speak with the tongues of men and of angels, and have not charity, I am become as sounding brass, or a tinkling cymbal.
>
> And though I have the gift of prophecy, and understand all mysteries, and all knowledge; and though I have all faith, so that I could remove mountains, and have not charity, I am nothing.
>
> And though I bestow all my goods to feed the poor, and though I give my body to be burned and have not charity, it profiteth me nothing.
>
> Charity suffereth long, and is kind; charity envieth not; charity vaunteth not itself, is not puffed up.
>
> Doth not behave itself unseemly, seeketh not her own, is not easily provoked, thinketh no evil;
>
> Rejoiceth not in iniquity, but rejoiceth in the truth;
>
> Beareth all things, believeth all things, hopeth all things, endureth all things.
>
> Charity never faileth. (1 Corinthians 13:1–8.)

It is clear from his own words that Paul thought of charity as much more than giving to the poor or doing good to others. To Paul, charity was even more important than religious worship and most spiritual gifts. For this reason, many New Testament translations don't use the word *charity*. Instead it is translated as *love*. Yet, even that word is insufficient.

Love can likewise mean different things to different people at different times and within different contexts. Love is affection and devotion, but it is also much more. Love can be a feeling of good will and compassion, but that is not all. I love chocolate, but I don't serve it—it serves me. I love to garden, but that is different than the love I have for my children. I love sports. I love my job. I love a good meal. I would love a new car. But each of these kinds of "love" pale in comparison to the love I have for my wife. Yet even in the context of love for my wife, there are different meanings and varying levels. To use the word *charity* in place of the word *love* in each of those things would not necessarily fit.

The ancient Greeks had different words to define the various kinds or levels of love. *Philia* might be used to denote a close friendship with many people—often friends of the same gender. *Storge* would be used to describe the kind of affection and closeness that exists in a family—parents' love and attachment to children and children's devotion to and love for parents. *Eros* denotes romantic, passionate, even sexual love between a husband and a wife. It is an exclusive love. Each of these words have powerful meanings, each affecting some aspect of love. Yet none of them would wholly qualify as *charity*, as defined in the scriptures. Charity is love and sometimes love is charity, but what Paul is speaking of far surpasses benevolence, friendship, affection, devotion, or passion. It is "love plus." The Greek word from which Paul's term charity was translated is *agape*. It expresses a love that is freely bestowed on another without condition or expectation of return. Often *agape* is mercifully given to one who is undeserving of it or would be unappealing for the other kinds of love—friendship, deep affection, or romantic passion. It is a pure and undefiled love that encompasses and surpasses all other love. No wonder it is used to describe God's love. It is far greater than any mortal kind of love or devotion. It is a divine love—a perfect love.

The Book of Mormon not only reflects this interpretation but also expounds and expands upon it. The "love plus" that Paul spoke of is defined by Mormon as "the pure love of Christ" (Moroni 7:47)—the *sine qua non* of the gospel—that which is not only the greatest but that which gives life and meaning to all other principles.

If a man be meek and lowly in heart, and confesses by the power of the Holy Ghost that Jesus is the Christ, he must needs have charity; for if he have not charity he is nothing; wherefore he must needs have charity. . . .

Wherefore, my beloved brethren, if ye have not charity, ye are nothing, for charity never faileth. Wherefore, cleave unto charity, which is the greatest of all, for all things must fail—

But charity is the pure love of Christ, and it endureth forever; and whoso is found possessed of it at the last day, it shall be well with him.

Wherefore, my beloved brethren, pray unto the Father with all the energy of heart, that ye may be filled with this love, which he hath bestowed upon all who are true followers of his Son, Jesus Christ; that ye may become the sons of God; that when he shall appear we shall be like him, for we shall see him as he is; that we may have this hope; that we may be purified even as he is pure. Amen. (Moroni 7:44–48.)

Not only does the Book of Mormon define what charity is, "the pure love of Christ," but also it declares what it does to us and for us. We also learn how and in what manner this "pure love of Christ" emanates outward, blessing others, healing wounded hearts and souls, lifting the lonely and the downtrodden, affecting institutions as well as individuals, elevating all of humanity. Charity, in this scriptural sense, is much more than giving to the poor, serving others, loving our neighbors, or forgiving our enemies. Though it envelops all those, charity—which never fails and is the greatest of all attributes—is the perfect love of Christ *for us*, a perfect love in our hearts *for Christ*, resulting in a Christlike love and compassion *for our fellowmen*. Each is essential. There is no "pure love of Christ" with one missing. Charity is not only *divine* love, but also *directional* love—it leads in a certain direction and directs one's actions toward God and others. The "pure love of Christ" for each of us is that charity which is the greatest of all loves. Only when our hearts are filled with that love can we begin to experience perfect love for God and our fellowmen. While we may do good works and even love and serve our neighbors, until Christ's love for us transforms our souls and permeates our lives we do not have charity. In the final equation, without Christ's love in us we are nothing. That perfect and divine love will lead us to all others.

CHRIST'S PERFECT LOVE FOR MANKIND

Both the Apostle Paul and the prophet Mormon declared that charity endures forever and can never fail. Whether I like it or not, whether or not I am willing to admit it, my love can fail. My service can be limited and ineffective. But Christ's love is boundless and eternal. I can fail Him, and often do, but He never fails me. Nephi described the love of God—both the Father who gave His Only Begotten Son (see John 3:16) and the Son who willingly laid down His life for mankind "for he loveth the world" (see 2 Nephi 26:24)—as "most desirable above all things" and "most joyous to the soul" (1 Nephi 11:22–23). Charity is often spoken of in the same context as faith and hope. Yet each of these is firmly attached to the atonement of Jesus Christ. A person can have a belief in something else, hope for a brighter day or winning the sweepstakes, and even possess general goodwill for mankind. Yet these attitudes and attributes, as noble as they may be, have no saving power in the eternal sense. On the other hand, true faith, hope, and charity are spiritual imperatives that can only be found in Christ, rooted completely in His atoning sacrifice (see Ether 12:27–28). This is true charity—that perfect love that never fails and can, does, and will save. As Moroni declared in an inspired prayer of praise and worship:

> O Lord, thy righteous will be done, for I know that thou workest unto the children of men according to their faith. . . .
>
> And again, I remember that thou hast said that thou hast loved the world, even unto the laying down of thy life for the world, that thou mightest take it again to prepare a place for the children of men.
>
> And now I know that this love which thou hast had for the children of men is charity; wherefore, except men shall have charity they cannot inherit that place which thou hast prepared in the mansions of thy Father. (Ether 12:29, 33–34.)

When Mormon admonished his people and us today to "pray unto the Father with all the energy of heart, that ye may be filled with this love" (Moroni 7:48), he wasn't just asking us to pray that we would love our neighbors more, render more service and be filled with more Christlike compassion (even though we should do that as well). He was commanding us to pray that we might more fully experience the fruits of the Atonement in our personal lives, that we might be forgiven of our sins, transformed into "new creatures in Christ," and filled with His perfect love for us. That is "true charity"—the only pure and perfect love that never fails, without which we are indeed, both physically and spiritually, nothing. "*True* charity has been known only once," Elder Jeffrey R. Holland wrote. "It is shown perfectly and purely in Christ's unfailing, ultimate, and atoning love for us."

The greater definition of "the pure love of Christ," however, is not what we as Christians try but largely fail to demonstrate toward others but rather what Christ totally succeeded in demonstrating toward us. . . . It is as demonstrated in Christ that "charity never faileth." It is that charity—his pure love for us—without which we would be nothing, hopeless, of all men and women most miserable. Truly, those found possessed of the blessings of his love at the last day—the Atonement, the Resurrection, eternal life, eternal promise—surely it shall be well with them.

This does not in any way minimize the commandment that we are to try to acquire this kind of love for one another. . . . We should try to be more constant and unfailing, more longsuffering and kind, less envious and puffed up in our relationships with others. As Christ lived so should we live, and as Christ loved so should we love. But the "*pure* love of Christ" Mormon spoke of is precisely that—Christ's love. With that divine gift, that redeeming bestowal, we have everything; without it we have nothing and ultimately are nothing, except in the end "devils [and] angels to a devil."

Life has its share of fears and failures. Sometimes things fall short. Sometimes people fail us, or economies or businesses or governments fail us. But one thing in time or eternity does *not* fail us—the pure love of Christ. . . .

Thus, the miracle of Christ's charity both saves and changes us. His atoning love saves us from death and hell as well as from carnal, sensual, and devilish behavior. That redeeming love also transforms the soul, lifting it above fallen standards to something far more noble, far more holy. Wherefore, we must "cleave unto charity"—Christ's pure love of us and our determined effort toward pure love of him and all others—for without it we are nothing, and our plan for eternal happiness is utterly wasted. Without the redeeming love of Christ in our lives, all other qualities—even virtuous qualities and exemplary good works—fall short of salvation and joy. (*Christ and the New Covenant* [Salt Lake City: Deseret Book, 1997], pp. 336–37.)

Charity is the "redeeming love" of which Alma speaks (see Alma 5:26; 26:13). This "pure love of Christ" opens the door for the reception of other blessings and fruits of the "great plan of happiness" (see Alma 13:28–29; Moroni 8:25–26). If we desire to be filled with charity, we must do more than just love our neighbor, work on the welfare farm, and take a meal to a sick member of the ward. We must avail ourselves of the *full* plan of redemption. This saving love of Christ comes to us as we exercise faith in His holy name, repent of our sins, submit to the ordinances of the gospel, receive the Holy Ghost, and endure in righteous obedience to the end of our lives. "If ye keep my commandments ye shall abide in my love," the Savior taught His disciples (John 15:10). Without these elements, our love for and service to others may be "charitable acts" but not charity—the pure love of Christ. When I have experienced "true charity"—the sanctifying power of the Atonement—in my own heart, it has unfailingly led me and given purpose to my love for God and others. It is His perfect love, not my own, that enables me to love and serve Him as I must. It is His charity, not any feelings of fondness or devotion to duty that I may possess, that empowers my love and compassion for others and sanctifies my service in their behalf. Without this charity—left on our own merits and mortal love—our feeble efforts fail and fall short.

God loved us, so he sent his Son,
Christ Jesus, the atoning One,
To show us by the path he trod
The one and only way to God.

He came as man, though Son of God,
And bowed himself beneath the rod.
He died in holy innocence,
A broken law to recompense.

Oh, love effulgent, love divine!
What debt of gratitude is mine
That in his off'ring I have part
And hold a place within his heart.

In word and deed he doth require
My will to his, like son to sire,
Be made to bend, and I, as son,
Learn conduct from the Holy One.

(Edward P. Kimball, *Hymns*, no. 187.)

OUR PERFECT LOVE FOR CHRIST

"Herein is love," the Apostle John wrote, "not that we loved God, but that he loved us, and sent his Son to be the propitiation for our sins" (1 John 4:10). "We love him, because he first loved us" (1 John 4:19). When my life is filled with charity, Christ's pure love for me, when I have felt the cleansing power of His atonement, not only am I overcome with profound awe and appreciation, but also my love for Him is intensified. His pure love for me is both motivational and invitational. "I have loved thee with an everlasting love," the Messiah declared, "therefore with lovingkindness have I drawn thee" (Jeremiah 31:3). The word *draw* means "invite," "urge," or "motivate." Christ's charity, His loving-kindness, draws from me love and devotion. His love invites me to love and serve Him even more. The more love I feel *from* Him the more I am motivated to give *to* Him. It becomes much easier to live the first, great commandment—"Thou shalt love the Lord thy God with all thy heart, might, mind and strength"—when I am filled with charity. "If ye love me, keep my commandments," Jesus taught His disciples (John 14:15). Perhaps it could also be said, "When you are filled with charity, Christ's perfect love, you will keep His commandments, because you love Him so much." Elder David B. Haight illustrated the directional nature of divine love. "If we could feel or were sensitive even in the slightest to the matchless love of our Savior and his willingness to suffer for our individual sins, we would cease procrastination and 'clean the slate,' and repent of all our transgressions" (in Conference Report, April 1988, p. 26).

All of us can think of times in our lives when someone really cared about us and loved us with a perfect and unconditional love. It not only brought peace and a sense of acceptance and well-being to our hearts, but it also motivated us to reciprocate that love by doing and being what that person desired of us. Their love for us brought love for them and that love invariably led to showing our love through actions. "Nothing is so much calculated to lead people to forsake sin as to take them by the hand, and watch over them with tenderness," the Prophet Joseph Smith declared. "When persons manifest the least kindness and love to me, O what power it has over my mind, while the opposite course has a tendency to harrow up all the harsh feelings and depress the human mind." (*History of the Church* 5:23–24.) If fallible and finite mortal love—even the "least kindness and love"—can do that to us, what transforming power is found in "the pure love of Christ." Charity evokes perfect love for God. When we feel that kind of love, other essential attitudes and actions will inevitably follow. The following experience illustrates how charity can be a powerfully motivating force for obedience and righteousness.

I remember when I first earned my license to drive. I was

about sixteen, as I recall. I'd been driving off and on for three years (scary thought, isn't it?). My father had been with me most of the time during my learning experiences, calmly sitting alongside me in the front seat, giving me tips, helping me know what to do. My mother usually wasn't in on those excursions because she spent more of her time biting her nails (and screaming) than she did advising. My father was a little more easygoing. Loud noises and screeching brakes didn't bother him nearly as much. My grandfather was the best of all. When I would drive his car, I would hit things . . . *Boom!* He'd say stuff like, "Just keep on going, Bud. I can buy more fenders, but I can't buy more grandsons. You're learning." What a great old gentleman. After three years of all that nonsense, I finally earned my license.

I'll never forget the day I came in, flashed my newly acquired permit, and said, "Dad, look!" He goes, "Whoa! Look at this. You got your license. Good for you!" Holding the keys to his car, he tossed them in my direction and smiled, "Tell you what, son . . . you can have the car for two hours, all on your own." Only four words, but how wonderful: "All on your own."

I thanked him, danced out to the garage, opened the car door, and shoved the key into the ignition. My pulse rate must have shot up to 180 as I backed out of the driveway and roared off. While cruising along "all on my own," I began to think wild stuff—like, *This car can probably do 100 miles an hour. I could go to Galveston and back twice in two hours if I averaged 100 miles an hour. I can fly down the Gulf Freeway and even run a few lights. After all, nobody's here to say "Don't!"* We're talking dangerous, crazy thoughts! But you know what? I didn't do any of them. I don't believe I drove above the speed limit. In fact, I distinctly remember turning into the driveway early . . . didn't even stay away the full two hours. Amazing, huh? I had my dad's car all to myself with a full gas tank in a context of total privacy and freedom, but I didn't go crazy. Why? My relationship with my dad and my granddad was so strong that I couldn't, even though I had a license and nobody was in the car to restrain me. Over a period of time there had developed a sense of trust, a deep love relationship that held me in restraint. (Charles R. Swindoll, *The Grace Awakening* [Dallas: Word Publishing, 1990], pp. 47–48.)

Righteousness is not obtained out of guilt, embarrassment, humiliation, or fear. While these attitudes may induce a temporary change, it is only through the pure love of Christ that enduring change and spiritual transformation are obtained. "And see that ye have faith, hope, and charity," declared Alma, "and then ye will always abound in good works" (Alma 7:24). That is the directional nature of this divine love. I pray to be filled with charity—to experience more fully in my life the soul-changing power of the Atonement, to be "born again" and filled with the Spirit so that I can love the Lord more fully and more perfectly. When filled with that kind of pure love *from* God and *for* God I will want to obey. I will want to repent. I will want to serve. I will want to submit. All because of charity—the pure love of Christ.

"Charity is a total submission to the Savior's will," Elder Vaughn J. Featherstone wrote. "It is total commitment of the soul."

When the Holy Ghost pervades every particle of our being, we are filled with awe and respect for all God's creations. . . .

And if we have such marvelous respect for God's creation, shall we not stand in absolute wonder at a man, a woman, or a child? Charity may cause us to detest what they do, but we can never cease to strive with them. We can look to their faults and be patient and forgiving because charity suffereth long and is kind. . . .

Charity means to put on our beautiful garments to become saviors on Mount Zion, and to walk in paths of service normally obscured from our sight by shades of less worthy things. It means that we make ourselves totally available for service, that we realize we were born to serve our fellowmen, that we remember that we are God's agents to do his work. (*Charity Never Faileth* [Salt Lake City: Deseret Book, 1980], pp. 5–6.)

PERFECT LOVE FOR OUR FELLOWMEN

The prophet Nephi exemplifies how charity—Christ's perfect love for us as manifest in the Atonement and our perfect love for Him as manifest through our faith and righteousness—naturally reaches out beyond ourselves to others. This kind of charity is much more than merely being nice, doing good for others, forgiving our enemies, or rendering compassionate service. It is a love that results in those byproducts because our hearts are filled with love for others *because* we have experienced Christ's perfect love in our own lives. "The Lord God hath given a commandment that all men should have charity, which charity is love," Nephi wrote. "And except they should have charity they were nothing." (2 Nephi 26:30.)

He then explained that if our hearts are filled with charity— if we have experienced a mighty change of heart through the atonement of Christ, if we have felt to sing the song of "redeeming love"—our hearts will be likewise filled with Christlike love for others. This is why "charity never faileth." It is not just my love and compassion that is extended outward to others. It is Christ's love that fills me so full that it *must* spill over to others. In this manner, charity is both directional and sequential. I am loved perfectly by God. My heart is softened and my soul transformed. I love God and desire to serve Him. When I am filled with charity I not only experience God's perfect love for me, but also I begin to understand and experience His divine love for others. My love for others then naturally flows from that.

Nephi further expounded on this sequence and direction when he explained that when we are "relying wholly upon the merits of him who is mighty to save" we "must press forward with a steadfastness in Christ, having a perfect brightness of hope, and a love of God and of all men" (see 2 Nephi 31:19-20). Nephi not only taught this process, he experienced it as well. Later in his discourse he declared: "I have charity for my people" (2 Nephi 33:7) and "I have charity for the Jew" (vs. 8) and finally, "I also have charity for the Gentiles" (vs. 9). His charity

for all mankind was not just mortal goodwill or even a more spiritual feeling of brotherhood, but rather pure love resulting from
the charity he had experienced in his own life. "I glory in my
Jesus," he testified, "for he hath redeemed my soul from hell" (2
Nephi 33:6). That "redeeming love" led to his charity toward
others.

King Benjamin likewise taught that charity toward others
(and all that it entails) comes as a natural byproduct of being
spiritually "reborn" through the Atonement and by possessing
the Spirit of the Lord. After his profound discourse on the atonement of Christ (Mosiah chapter 3), he taught his people that if
they and we "have tasted of his love, and have received a remission of [our] sins, which causeth such exceeding great joy in
[our] souls" (Mosiah 4:11) then certain actions and attitudes
will naturally follow. We often view this portion of his discourse
as his exhortation to give to the poor, to be kind to others and
live peaceably together. That certainly is not a bad exhortation
and we should all do those things. In reality, however, King Benjamin is giving what I characterize as an "if/then declaration"—
if certain things are done and/or experienced *then* certain other
things will naturally follow. *If* we are filled with charity—pure
love from God and for God—*then* "ye will not have a mind to
injure one another, but to live peaceably, and to render to every
man according to that which is his due."

> And also, ye yourselves will succor those that stand in need
> of your succor; ye will administer of your substance unto him
> that standeth in need; and ye will not suffer that the beggar
> putteth up his petition to you in vain, and turn him out to per-
> ish. . . .
>
> For behold, are we not all beggars? Do we not all depend
> upon the same Being, even God, for all the substance which we
> have, for both food and raiment, and for gold, and for silver,
> and for all the riches which we have of every kind?
>
> And behold, even at this time, ye have been calling on his
> name, and begging for a remission of your sins. And has he suf-
> fered that ye have begged in vain? Nay; he has poured out his

Spirit upon you, and has caused that your hearts should be filled with joy, and has caused that your mouths should be stopped that ye could not find utterance, so exceedingly great was your joy.

And now, if God, who has created you, on whom you are dependent for your lives and for all that ye have and are, doth grant unto you whatsoever ye ask that is right, in faith, believing that ye shall receive, O then, how ye ought to impart of the substance that ye have one to another. (Mosiah 4:12–13, 16, 19–21.)

At the Last Supper the Savior gave a "new commandment" to His disciples—"That ye love one another; as I have loved you, that ye also love one another" (John 13:34). There are a few very significant words and phrases in that passage. One is "as I have loved you." We often think of that phrase in terms of loving Christ *like* He loved us. While I certainly need to strive with all my heart and soul to be more Christlike in my love and service to God and my fellowmen, there is no way on earth that I can ever really love God or anyone else with the kind of love that only a God can give—at least not in this lifetime. Therefore, I think this passage is saying something else. "As I have loved you," could mean "Inasmuch as I have loved you" or "Because I love you." Then the next word "that" seems to be another spiritually significant word—a word that bespeaks direction and sequence. "I have loved you," the Savior seems to be saying, "*in order* that you will love others." Because of His love for me, my heart has greater capacity to love others in some small measure, the way He loves me. Charity—"the pure love of Christ"— makes my heart larger. Left to my own efforts and emotions, I could never love and serve others that way. His *agape*—charity or God's love—makes it possible for me to experience and exhibit godly love toward others.

After Enos received a forgiveness of his sins and experienced the "peace that surpasses all understanding" through the Atonement, his next inclination was concern, compassion, and prayers on behalf of others. His soul reached out not only to his brethren, the Nephites, but also to his enemies, the Lamanites. His heart was filled with charity toward them, because his heart was filled with charity from God (see Enos 1:1–17). Similarly, Alma spent his entire life loving, serving, strengthening, teaching, and even forgiving others, because he had experienced "exquisite joy" and his life had been filled with a "marvelous light" through the spiritual rebirth that comes with repentance and forgiveness. Because Alma had tasted of charity—the "pure love of Christ"—in his own life he desired others to experience that love in their own lives.

> Yea, and from that time even until now, I have labored without ceasing, that I might bring souls unto repentance; that I might bring them to taste of the exceeding joy of which I did taste; that they might also be born of God and be filled with the Holy Ghost. . . .
>
> For because the word which he has imparted unto me, behold, many have been born of God, and have tasted as I have tasted, and have seen eye to eye as I have seen. (Alma 36:24, 26.)

The Book of Mormon repeatedly teaches and illustrates this important principle—that *charity begets charity.* Although they had been "the very vilest of sinners" (see Mosiah 28:4) the sons of King Mosiah experienced "the pure love of Christ"— "redeeming love"—when they repented of their sins, exercised faith in the Lord Jesus Christ, and sought to live the gospel. Their hearts were filled with charity—perfect love from Christ and perfect love for Christ, but that love naturally emanated beyond self. "They were desirous that salvation should be declared to every creature," the scriptures record, "for they could not bear that any human soul should perish; yea, even the very thoughts that any soul should endure endless torment did cause them to quake and tremble" (Mosiah 28:3). Their desires to serve among the hardened and bloodthirsty Lamanites was no "service project." It was not intended to be merely an act of restitution or "paying their debt to society." It was prompted out of genuine love, godly love, born out of hearts filled to over-flowing with the "pure love of Christ." Because God loved them so deeply, so divinely, they absolutely could not contain their love for their fellowmen.

The pure love of Christ in my heart not only transforms my life but also opens my eyes and heart to others. Because He loved me with such a pure and perfect love and has extended to me such great mercy and compassion, I begin to see others in the light of His love, viewing them as He views them. One example in particular illustrates how charity allows us to see the divine in others and how our love and service of others is directly linked to our love of God. In an address to officers at the annual Relief Society general conference in October 1969, Elder Bruce R. McConkie read from the journal of his father, Oscar W. McConkie, the following story about Oscar's widowed mother, Emma Somerville McConkie:

> Mother was president of the Moab Relief Society. J___ B___ [a nonmember who opposed the Church] had married a Mormon girl. They had several children; now they had a new baby. They were very poor and Mother was going day by day to care for the child and to take them baskets of food, etc. Mother herself was ill, and more than once was hardly able to get home after doing the work at the J___ B___ home.
>
> One day she returned home especially tired and weary. She slept in her chair. She dreamed she was bathing a baby which she discovered was the Christ Child. She thought, Oh, what a great honor to thus serve the very Christ! As she held the baby in her lap, she was all but overcome. She thought, who else has actually held the Christ Child? Unspeakable joy filled her whole being. She was aflame with the glory of the Lord. It seemed that the very marrow in her bones would melt. Her joy was so great it awakened her. As she awoke, these words were spoken to her, "Inasmuch as ye have done it unto one of the least of these my brethren, ye have done it unto me." (Quoted in "Charity Which Never Faileth," *The Relief Society Magazine*, March 1970, p. 169.)

This kind of charity is also circular. When I am filled with Christ's love I begin to view others with the kind of love He has for them and I can see Christ in them. Yet when I serve my fellowmen, even without feelings of love of them, my love for the Savior increases. I feel more keenly His love for me which, in turn, makes my serving and loving others even more significant. Charity is a circle—God's love, my love for God, and godly love for others. The two great commandments are thus completely intertwined. You can't live one without the other, because charity, "the pure love of Christ," is at the very heart of each. Elder Neal A. Maxwell noted this relationship:

> We, more than others, should not only carry jumper and tow cables in our cars but in our hearts by which means we can send the needed boost or charge of encouragement or the added momentum to mortal neighbors. . . . Service keeps us from forgetting the Lord our God, because being among and serving our brothers and sisters remind us that Father is ever there and is pleased when we serve, for while the recipients of our service are our neighbors—they are His children. ("When the Heat of the Sun Cometh," unpublished address delivered at young adult fireside, Salt Lake Tabernacle, 20 May 1979.)

So what does all this mean? So what is it that Lehi and Nephi, Alma and Amulek, Mormon and Moroni want us to know about charity? I believe the answer to those questions is to be found in the very purpose of the Book of Mormon—testifying to the world that Jesus is the Christ. Charity is Christ's love, not mine. The "pure love of Christ" is shown in His "infinite and eternal atonement"—that supreme act of love—the one and only true manifestion of charity in its purest sense. Charity changes me. Charity changes my heart. Charity fills me with unspeakable love, awe, and adoration for my Heavenly Father and His Only Begotten. Charity invites me, instructs me, enables me, and empowers me to fulfill the "new commandment"—that I love others with Godly love, *because* Christ loves me.

Charity is indeed a spiritual gift that is obtained through

desire, faith and prayer. But it cannot be bestowed independent of or separate from the blessings of the Atonement. The Father bestows it upon those who have experienced a "mighty change" and have "felt to sing the song of redeeming love"—"bestowed upon all who are true followers of his Son, Jesus Christ" (Moroni 7:48). We can and must more fully live the Golden Rule. We can and must render greater service and extend more mercy and compassion upon others. We can and must be kind and patient and forgiving. But most of all, as the Book of Mormon teaches us, we must be filled with and cleave to that one thing which "never faileth"—the pure love of Christ. If I want more charity, I must love Him more, serve Him more, pray more, more fully keep His commandments. That is how we "cleave unto charity"—by cleaving unto Christ and continually pressing forward with steadfastness in Him and His love for us. When we are filled with the love of God—that love which is most joyous to the soul and most desirable above all things—we, as Lehi experienced with his own family, will desire that others also partake (see 1 Nephi 8:10–12). "It is the love that prompted the suffering and sacrifice of Christ's atonement. It is the highest pinnacle the human soul can reach and the deepest expression of the human heart," President Howard W. Hunter testifed. "Charity encompasses all other godly virtues. It distinguishes both the beginning and the end of the plan of salvation. When all else fails, charity—Christ's love—will not fail. It is the greatest of all divine attributes." (*The Teachings of Howard W. Hunter*, ed. Clyde J. Williams [Salt Lake City: Bookcraft, 1997], p. 99.) Though I may do many great things and help many people of my own accord, I am nothing without Him, without His pure love, without His atoning sacrifice. Love, kindness, forgiveness, patience, and service are important, but charity is imperative! Charity is the crowning virtue of the spiritual life and the vessel of our ultimate perfection and peace. In the Doctrine and Covenants the Lord concludes a lengthy list of counsel and commandments to the Saints with this simple yet profound admonition and assurance: "Above all things, clothe yourselves with the bond of charity, as with a mantle, which is the bond of perfectness and peace" (D&C 88:125).

Charity never faileth, endless fount of love,
Springing pure and perfect from pristine realms above;
Love that asks no merit, no promise or requite,
Love that kindles faith and hope, virtue, strength, and light.

Charity granteth power, charity bringeth peace,
Love that casteth out all fear and sweetly breathes release;
Frees from chains of hatred, confusion, vengeance, strife.
Charity—the mantle soft that cloaks the pains of life.

Charity reigns supernal, exceeding faith and hope.
Pure love endows the humblest life with height and depth
    and scope.
For though I speak with angels and pious heights obtain,
If these stem not from charity, then empty is my gain.

Charity seeks the stranger with coarse or foreign ways,
The neighbors, friends, and loved ones who may try my
    patient days;
The enemy and derelict, for more like Christ I'll be
When compassion swells my bosom unconditionally.

Charity, priceless gift of God for followers of Christ,
Aim of ceaseless, reaching prayer and selfhood sacrificed;
If I am in his image when he appears above
'Twill be the face of charity, for God, himself, is love.

—Wendy C. Top

And now, O man,
remember, and perish not.
—MOSIAH 4:30

CHAPTER 11

REMEMBER

I am reminded of a cute story about an elderly couple that were having problems remembering things. Unfortunately, this phenomenon is not exclusive to senior citizens. When I am wandering around the parking lots on the BYU campus trying to remember where I parked my car, I may not think this anecdote is so funny, but it is something to which we can all relate.

The older couple were each having problems with their short-term memory. Concerned that something serious might be wrong, they decided to go to the doctor for his evaluation. After a complete check-up, the doctor assured them that there was nothing seriously wrong with them and that their memory loss was a normal part of growing older. "You may want to write notes to yourself so you don't forget important things," the doctor suggested. Relieved that they were not afflicted with Alzheimers or some other serious malady, the couple thanked the doctor and returned home.

Later that evening while they were watching television, the elderly husband got up from his easy chair to leave the family room. "Where are you going?" his wife asked.

"To the kitchen," he responded.

"While you are there will you get me a bowl of ice cream?" she asked, and then jokingly added, "Don't you think you should write that down so you don't forget?"

Laughingly he responded, "No, I think I can remember that."

A moment later she called out to him, "I want some strawberrries on top of the ice cream. Can you remember that or do you need to write a note to yourself?"

"No," he said, "I'll put strawberries on your ice cream."

After a few more minutes passed, she said, "I want some whipped cream on it as well. Can you remember that or do you need to write it down?"

This time his response reflected irritation that her verbal jabs about written reminders were no longer a loving joke, but rather were offered with serious intent. "I don't need to write it down," he declared. "My memory is just fine."

About twenty minutes later he emerged from the kitchen and presented to his wife a plate of bacon and scrambled eggs. "I knew it," she protested. "I knew if you didn't write it down you would forget something. You forgot my toast!"

While we may laugh about being absentminded or losing our memory, it certainly is a serious subject. All of us dread to some degree not being able to remember something important. Remembering is critical to our existence. A person who can't remember appointments, names, places, and important things that must be done is in a world of hurt both personally and professionally. Remembering, however, is more than just a mental or cognitive process. It involves doing as well as thinking; actions as well as memory.

For example, as a bishop I counseled with a young couple who were having marital problems. The wife was irritated that her husband was so insensitive and thoughtless. "He never remembers my birthday or our anniversary or anything," she stated. "He forgets to kiss me when he leaves for work and doesn't remember to tell me he loves me."

"I remember your birthday and our anniversary," he protested. "I just don't do anything about it." Bingo! He had identified the very problem with his own admission. It was not his memory that hurt his wife so much. It was his behavior—his unwillingness to act upon his memory.

That is the way the word *remember* or *remembrance* is used in the scriptures, particularly the Book of Mormon. The word *hearken* or *hear* in the scriptures means more than just an auditory process and involves more than the ears—it means to "hear and obey." So, too, does *remember*. Remembrance, the way the Lord intends and describes it in holy writ, requires much more than just the mind. It requires the person's whole heart, soul, and life.

The words *remember* and *remembrance* are used scores of times in the Book of Mormon—in fact, nearly one hundred times. While there are many different contexts for its usage, the vast majority emphasize some form of righteous actions or endeavors that is to accompany the mental act of remembering. "Remember the words of thy dying father," Lehi pleaded with his family (see 2 Nephi 3:25). His exhortation to *remember* his words was really a plea to *do* the things he had taught them—to have faith in the Lord Jesus Christ, repent of their sins, and obey the commandments of God. Similarly, Nephi exhorted his brothers to *"remember to keep [God's] commandments always in all things"* (1 Nephi 15:25; emphasis added).

I love that phrase—"remember to keep." Nephi didn't want them to merely know the commandments in their heads, but rather to have them in their hearts and to follow them in their lives. It wouldn't do them much good just to mentally recall the commandments, as if recalling trivial facts or minute details. Saving remembrance is found in obedience, in doing and being, not in just recalling.

Intertwined with historical events and doctrinal teachings, we find this timeless theme throughout the pages of the Book of Mormon. The prophets, who wrote for our day, desired that we would *remember* certain specific things so that we would do, act, and become in order that we might be saved by the grace of God; for it appears that this godly form of remembrance is directly linked to our salvation. As a phrase in a familiar song of yesteryear declares, "And if you remember, then follow." To follow the Lord in faith and obedience we must be brought to a divine remembrance of 1) the awfulness of sin, 2) the goodness of God, 3) the covenants of the fathers, 4) our duties to God and fellowmen, and, most important, 5) the atoning sacrifice of the Lord Jesus Christ. The Book of Mormon is vital in bringing these things to our remembrance.

REMEMBER THE AWFULNESS OF SIN

"Remember the awfulness in transgressing against that Holy God," Jacob declared to his brethren, "and also the awfulness of yielding to the enticings of that cunning one. Remember, to be carnally-minded is death, and to be spiritually-minded is life eternal" (2 Nephi 9:39). Remembering our sins and the accompanying pains is an essential part of the repentance process. There can be no discipline—no shaping the soul into a Saint—without a good spiritual memory. I have always found it interesting that when Corianton strayed from the strait and narrow path and committed serious transgressions, Alma, his father, did not pat him on the head and say, "It's okay. Forget about it!" No, quite the opposite. "Let your sins trouble you," he said to his son. Remembering was to serve an important purpose. To eliminate or minimize that process would be to short-circuit the cleansing power of repentance.

Alma knew firsthand the redemptive power of remembering the awfulness of sin. "I was harrowed up by the memory of my many sins," he explained regarding his own miraculous transformation. Those memories as painful as they were—causing him to be racked with "inexpressible horror" and desire to "become extinct both soul and body"—led him to reach out for the only help that could cleanse and heal him, the power of the Atonement. (See Alma 36:14–15.) No wonder King Benjamin declared unto his people: "I pray that ye should awake to a remembrance of the awful situation of those that have fallen into transgression" (Mosiah 2:40). The prophet Jacob, likewise, told the wicked Nephite husbands and fathers to "remember your own filthiness. . . . Remember your children, how that ye have grieved their hearts because of the example that ye have set before them." (Jacob 3:9–10.) Remembering our sinful state before the Lord, in the truest sense of the word, is not merely a mental exercise in recalling our long list of sins, but rather a spiritual yearning, a reaching out for help—like a drowning man desperately reaching out for a saving hand. While we should not unnecessarily dwell on sins repented of, we should always be in remembrance of our sinful nature and our total dependence upon the cleansing blood of Christ for a forgiveness of our sins and a changing of our sinful natures.

The Book of Mormon teaches another important aspect of remembering the awfulness of sin. I have often heard people teach that once a person has truly repented he will not remember any of his sins. But Alma remembered his sinful past in graphic detail a generation later as he recounted to his son the events of his conversion. At some levels it is good that we remember our sins (see Alma 5:18). Remembering should lead to doing. Remembering our sins not only should lead us to repentance, but even thereafter it should also serve as a spiritual safeguard against once more falling into the traps of temptation.

The human mind and body have their own way of remembering past pains and self-induced sicknesses. Those memories serve as a protective warning system. If I am shocked with a painful surge of electricity when I accidently or purposely stick my screwdriver into a live electrical socket, I will remember that next time! If I remember the painful burn of touching a hot pan on the stove I'll be more careful (or at least I should be) next time I am cooking something. It works much the same way spiritually. If all memory of sin and suffering was taken away with repentance, we would more easily fall prey to Satan's lies and deceptions. Even with a remembrance of the awfulness of sin, I still stumble, but at least the Lord lovingly warns me with painful memories. Remembering is a merciful gift of God. We need not resist or recoil from a memory of our sins. While we need not dwell on them or browbeat ourselves mercilessly, we can use that remembrance to our advantage. We can obtain protection for our lives through a remembrance of the awfulness of transgression and find peace to our souls through the forgiveness Christ offers us. "Let us remember him," Jacob declared, "and lay aside our sins, and not hang down our heads" (2 Nephi 10:20).

REMEMBER THE GOODNESS OF GOD

There are many parallels between the various books of scripture and even Church history. One of those parallels is the repetition of the history of God's dealings with His children. There is often a concerted effort on the part of the prophets to bring to the people's remembrance the miraculous means whereby the Lord has preserved them, delivered them from their enemies, and prospered them in their lands. Why? Cetainly not because they needed to cram for a final exam in the "History of God's Covenant People" course. Remembering the goodness of God is a recognition of the hand of the Lord in our lives. Such recognition leads to gratitude. Gratitude leads to love. Love—genuine love—always leads to service and obedience. "If [we] have come to a knowledge [or we could say *remembrance*] of the goodness of God, and his matchless power, and his wisdom, and his patience, and his long-suffering towards the children of men; and also, the atonement which has been prepared from the foundation of the world," we would, as King Benjamin reminded his people, recognize that we "should put [our] trust in the Lord, and should be diligent in keeping his commandments, and continue in the faith even unto the end of [our lives]" (Mosiah 4:6).

Several years ago as my wife and I were on a Sunday afternoon walk, we stopped in a city park and sat on a bench and *remembered* the many ways in which the Lord had blessed our lives. This was not just romantic nostalgia or a casual stroll down "Memory Lane." It may have commenced as that, but we soon realized that something remarkable was taking place in our souls. With each recounting of small miracles we had experienced in our lives, with each testimony of answered prayers, with each stated recognition of blessings received, our gratitude to God swelled and our love for the Lord increased. We were both so overcome with emotion and an accompanying witness of the

Spirit that we could not speak. Yet even in silence, there was communication. In fact, more was said between us and more was spoken to our hearts and souls than words could convey.

This exercise in remembering the goodness of God in our own lives yielded something far greater than merely fond memories. We were blessed with unspeakable gratitude which in turn inspired us to demonstrate our love and appreciation with lives of service and faithfulness. I better understood why King Benjamin exhorted his people to "always retain in remembrance, the greatness of God, and your own nothingness, and his goodness and long-suffering towards you" (Mosiah 4:11). For in retaining that remembrance of God we experience, as Benjamin described, important "fruits"—humility, increased desire to pray daily and walk "steadfastly in the faith." Remembering, not just recalling, God's goodness causes us to rejoice and "be filled with the love of God." This love and gratitude, born of divine remembrance, always leads to a retaining a remission of our sins, growing in the "knowledge of the glory of him that created [us]," and love and compassion for our fellowmen (see Mosiah 4:11–12). Remembering the goodness of God and our total dependence upon Him helps us view life in proper perspective—even from an eternal perspective that allows us to "have great views of that which is to come" (Mosiah 5:3).

REMEMBER YOUR COVENANTS

There are numerous references in the Book of Mormon concerning the remembrance of covenants. The interesting thing about these references, however, is that virtually all of them speak of God remembering His covenants with the ancient patriarchs—remembering His covenants with the house of Israel (see 1 Nephi 15:18; 19:15; 2 Nephi 29:1, 14; 3 Nephi 16:5, 11–12; Mormon 5:20; 9:37; Ether 4:15; 13:11). Why do the prophets in the Book of Mormon repeatedly stress God's remembrance of His covenants with us rather than continually urging us to remember our covenants with Him? Perhaps the answer is that the more we realize *how* God remembers His covenants, the more we will be instructed and inspired as to *how* we must always remember our covenants.

To our Heavenly Father, remembering covenants is not merely a mental process. I can't imagine the Almighty being like the husband I described earlier, who remembered, but did nothing. "Oh, yeah, I remember that I made that promise. So what?" God doesn't work that way. When He remembers He fulfills. His words are sure. He means what He says. When He promises, He delivers. That is what remembering covenants really means.

Closely akin to the word *remember*—in fact, stemming from the same root—is the word *reminder*. It is something that helps us remember. Lovingly the Lord has given to us reminders of our covenants, so that we will remember and fulfill them. The scriptures not only teach us what the covenants are, but also remind us how we are to fulfill them. The "final exam" in the course of life will not ask us to list our baptismal covenants. It will not be enough to merely memorize Alma's words:

> And now, as ye are desirous to come into the fold of God, and to be called his people, and are willing to bear one another's burdens, that they may be light;
>
> Yea, and are willing to mourn with those that mourn; yea, and comfort those that stand in need of comfort, and stand as witnesses of God at all times and in all things, and in all places that ye may be in, even until death, that ye may be redeemed of God, and be numbered with those of the first resurrection, that ye may have eternal life—
>
> Now I say unto you, if this be the desire of your hearts, what have ye against being baptized in the name of the Lord, as a witness before him that ye have entered into a covenant with him, that ye will serve him and keep his commandments, that he may pour out his Spirit more abundantly upon you? (Mosiah 18:8–10.)

Remembering our covenants is not just a response to an "essay question" but rather a daily, living experience. God lovingly gives us reminders and helps along the way. There are daily and weekly tangible, physical reminders of our covenants. These reminders don't just jog the memory but also prod the person to "remember and keep" sacred covenants.

As we think of how God remembers His covenants with us, we can rest assured that He keeps His word. There is no question about that. The only question is, will we keep ours? Will we remember our covenants? He offers us reminders, repentance, and renewal. In the end, however, remembrance of our covenants depends on keeping them, not just recalling, reciting, or even renewing them.

REMEMBRANCE OF DUTY

Closely related to a remembrance of covenants is the remembering of one's duty to God and others. As the presiding high priest of the Nephite church, Alma went among the people who had drifted into inactivity and had fallen into iniquity preaching the gospel and bearing testimony of truth. The scriptures record that he did "preach the word of God unto them, *to stir them up in remembrance of their duty*, and that he might pull down, by the word of God, all the pride and craftiness and all the contentions which were among his people, seeing no way that he might reclaim them save it were in bearing down in pure testimony against them" (Alma 4:19, emphasis added; see also Alma 7:22). In addition to the "power of the word" and "bearing down in pure testimony," the Lord uses other things to remind us of our spiritual duties. Abinadi explained to King Noah and his wicked priests that the ancient law of Moses, with all its rituals, performances, and carnal commandments, "which they were to observe strictly from day to day," was "to keep them in remembrance of God and their duty towards him" (Mosiah 13:30). Even trials and tribulations, the prophets remind us, are given and allowed in our lives, just as they were in the lives of the Book of Mormon peoples, "to stir them [and us] up in remembrance of their duty" (Mosiah 1:17).

In our day, the Lord has declared: "Wherefore, now let every man learn his duty, and to act in the office in which he is appointed, in all diligence. He that is slothful shall not be counted worthy to stand, and he that learns not his duty and shows himself not approved shall not be counted worthy to stand." (D&C 107:99–100.) Learning our duties precedes remembering them. To remind us of our duties we have the scriptures, handbooks, instruction, and all kinds of training materials. The Doctrine and Covenants not only defines in great detail the duties of each of the offices of the priesthood but also discusses specific duties of other officers in the kingdom of God. Each of these is important and we should certainly "remember and keep" those duties by being faithful in our callings, but the Book of Mormon's reference to "remembrance of duty" seems to imply something deeper—a duty even more paramount, more eternally significant. Our duty to God, which we are to hold in "sacred remembrance," is as Alma declared, to "walk blameless before him, that ye may walk after the holy order of God. . . ."

> And now I would that ye should be humble, and be sub- missive and gentle; easy to be entreated; full of patience and long-suffering; being temperate in all things; being diligent in keeping the commandments of God at all times; asking for whatsoever things ye stand in need, both spiritual and temporal; always returning thanks unto God for whatsoever things ye do receive.
>
> And see that ye have faith, hope, and charity, and then ye will always abound in good works. (Alma 7:22–24.)

"Remember your duty" is not merely a call for knowing what the handbooks say or understanding how to be an effective administrator in the Church. Being a good home teacher, a car- ing Relief Society president, or an efficient priesthood quorum leader—these are important duties to "remember and keep." We can and should learn those duties by study, prayer, and practice. Some may view going to the temple or doing genealogical research as "remembering" a duty. Yes, those are important and rewarding tasks—duties, if you will. But fulfilling an assignment or completing a task, however important it may be, is not always the same as doing one's duty to God. If we are to "remember" our duty in the truest sense of the word we must be more concerned about our "walk and talk" each day—each moment of our lives—than just on Sundays, at homemaking meeting or activity night, while serving on a welfare project, or in conducting interviews. For the divine duty God asks us to "remember and keep" is far beyond just faithfully fulfilling our callings and completing assignments. The duty, however, that is most important, that which we should always remember, has no official handbook, except the scriptures.

> *The duty of the members after they are received by baptism.* . . .
> And the members shall manifest before the church, and also before the elders, by a godly walk and conversation, that they are worthy of it, that there may be works and faith agreeable to the holy scriptures—walking in holiness before the Lord. (D&C 20:68–69.)

"ALWAYS REMEMBER HIM"

One of the most important reminders God has given us is the sacrament of the Lord's Supper. "And this shall ye do in remembrance of my body [and blood]," the Savior taught His disciples in both the Old and New World. That sacred ordinance was to be, as He declared, "a testimony unto the Father that ye do always remember me. And if ye do always remember me ye shall have my Spirit to be with you." (See 3 Nephi 18:7, 11.) This sacramental remembrance gives us a weekly reminder of what matters most in life and eternity. It is the Savior's loving invitation, not only to remember His sacrifice but also to be renewed by it and rejuvenated by the promise of His Spirit. Each week as we partake of the sacrament we covenant to "always remember him." Like the other forms of spiritual remembering that have been addressed here, remembering Christ involves more than mentally recounting His life, teachings, and sacrifice during the quiet moments of the administration of the sacrament. It must also include taking inventory of our lives. When we "remember him" we ask ourselves, How am I doing in my quest to be more like the Master? Have I fallen short this week? What can I do better during the coming days? Not only do we renew our covenant to keep the commandments, but also, as we partake of the symbols of Christ's flesh and blood, we can commune with God and petition Him for strength and direction in our lives. "Try to remember . . . and if you remember, then follow." Always remembering Christ is a catalyst for following Him. Remembering what He did for me and how he lived His life prods me forward in love to walk more closely in His footsteps. Remembering Him is covenanting—covenanting that I will keep trying to become more Christlike no matter how wide the gap may seem between the Ideal and myself—covenanting to strive to be a little better tomorrow than I was today—covenanting to be more kind, compassionate, loving, and forgiving. Remembering Him is earnestly praying for and diligently seeking after more holiness in our lives. No wonder President Howard W. Hunter urged us to "remember [Christ] more often than we remember him" (see Conference Report, April 1994, pp. 83–84). For if we truly remember Him, always keeping Him in sacred remembrance, we will not suffer from a spiritual loss of memory. Remembering is following Him. Remembering is loving Him. Remembering is keeping His commandments. Always remembering Him will inevitably lead me to a remembrance of everything else of eternal import.

"REMEMBER THE NEW COVENANT"

As Moroni closed the Nephite record with his final testimony of the gospel and of the truthfulness of the words that he and his father, Mormon, had included in the Book of Mormon, he declared:

> And I exhort you to remember these things; for the time speedily cometh that ye shall know that I lie not, for ye shall see

me at the bar of God; and the Lord God will say unto you: Did I not declare my words unto you, which were written by this man, like as one crying from the dead, yea, even as one speaking out of the dust?

I declare these things unto the fulfilling of the prophecies. And, behold, they shall proceed forth out of the mouth of the everlasting God; and his word shall hiss forth from generation to generation.

And God shall show unto you, that that which I have written is true. (Moroni 10:27–29.)

Moroni's exhortation "remember these things" clearly is referring to the Book of Mormon. Remembrance of the Book of Mormon, like all divine remembering, involves more than merely reading, pondering upon, and praying about. Since 1830 we as Latter-day Saints have "remembered" the Book of Mormon and proclaimed its truth to the world. Yet the Lord declared in 1832, and President Benson reaffirmed in our day, that "vanity and unbelief have brought the whole church under condemnation" (D&C 84:55). The resulting spiritual darkness comes, then and now, "because you have treated lightly the things you have received" (D&C 84:54). The darkness is dispelled and the condemnation is lifted only by heeding Moroni's final exhortation— "remember these things" (see D&C 84:56–62). The Lord emphasized anew that remembering requires more than mental exertion. "Remember the new covenant, even the Book of Mormon . . . ," he declared, "not only to say, but to do according to that which I have written" (D&C 84:57).

A relevant message of the Book of Mormon that we must never forget is that we must always remember. Remembering the "new covenant"—the Book of Mormon—requires more than reading and learning; it requires doing and becoming. Only by our remembering through living does this remarkable book, "Another Testament of Jesus Christ," have power to transform lives. It is not just its words, however profound and powerful they are, that allows a person, as the Prophet Joseph declared, to draw nearer to God than by reading any other book. The promised nearness to God and the spiritual illumination that disperses darkness in minds and hearts come to us, just as the Prophet promised, "by abiding by its precepts."

The Book of Mormon will change your life.
It will fortify you against the evils of our day.
It will bring a spirituality into your life that no
other book will. It will be the most important
book you will read.
—PRESIDENT EZRA TAFT BENSON

CHAPTER 12

THE REMARKABLE BOOK THAT CHANGES LIVES

When Jacob Hamblin first heard the restored gospel in 1842, he recalled, it "so fired up my mind, that I at once determined to be baptized, and that too, if necessary, at the sacrifice of the friendship of my kindred and every earthly tie."

The evening after the Elder had preached I went in search of him, and found him quite late at night. I told him my purpose, and requested him to give me a "Mormon Bible." He handed me the Old and New Testament.

I said, "I thought you had a new Bible." He then explained about the coming forth of the Book of Mormon, and handed me a copy of it.

The impressions I received at that time cannot be forgotten. The spirit rested upon me and bore testimony of its truth, and I felt like opening my mouth and declaring it to be a revelation from God.

On the 3rd of March, 1842, as soon as it was light in the morning, I started for a pool of water where I had arranged to meet with the Elder, to attend to the ordinance of baptism. On the way, the thought of the sacrifice I was making [by going against my family's wishes] . . . caused my resolution to waver.

As my pace slackened, some person appeared to come from above, who, I thought, was my grandfather. He seemed to say to me, "Go on, my son; your heart cannot conceive, neither has it entered into your mind to imagine the blessings that are in store for you, if you go on and continue in this work."

I lagged no more, but hurried to the pool, where I was baptized by Elder Lyman Stoddard. (In *Stories from the Early Saints: Converted by the Book of Mormon*, ed. Susan Easton Black [Salt Lake City: Bookcraft, 1992], pp. 41, 42.)

What is it about this remarkable book, the Book of Mormon, that caused Jacob Hamblin and thousands of early Saints to forsake comforts, possessions, reputations, and even friends and family to follow a young prophet? What is so remarkable about this book that it has so profoundly transformed the lives of millions who have read it? Why does it continue to draw men and women from "every nation, kindred, tongue, and people" (Alma 37:4) to The Church of Jesus Christ of Latter-day Saints?

Many books have influenced the course of history or inspired popular followings or movements, but their failings and limitations are eventually recognized and their influence is limited, sporadic, or temporary. In contrast, the Book of Mormon is today "flooding the earth" (see Ezra Taft Benson, "Flooding the Earth with the Book of Mormon," *Ensign*, November 1988, p. 67). In a magazine survey reported in the United States in 1991, for example, the Book of Mormon was eighth on a list of books readers said had been most influential in their lives (see "Our Best Books," *Parade*, 29 December 1991, p. 20). The number of those who bear witness of its truthfulness and alter their lives accordingly is multiplying exponentially across the world. "Like the mustard seed, [it] becomes the greatest of all herbs," taught the Prophet Joseph Smith. "And it is truth, and it has sprouted and come forth out of the earth, and righteousness begins to look down from heaven, and God is sending down His powers, gifts and angels, to lodge in the branches thereof." (*Teachings of the Prophet Joseph Smith*, sel. Joseph Fielding Smith [Salt Lake City: Deseret Book, 1976], p. 98.) What is the "secret" of its phenomenal worldwide recognition and its acceptance? What is the source of its power to produce life-changing transformations and enduring spiritual effects of countless individuals?

Undoubtedly there are myriad answers to this question, some of them personal to individual recipients of the book's soul-satisfying, eternal truth. Generally speaking, however, there are at least four aspects of this singular book that make it more remarkable than any other book on earth:

- Its sacred origins and the divine manner in which it came forth.
- The profound depth, breadth, and clarity of its doctrines.
- Its unassailable role as the "keystone of our religion."
- Its confirming witness of the Atonement and the Resurrection of Christ.

SACRED ORIGINS

A few years back, I had the opportunity to spend several days with some Baptist ministers at an evangelical college in another part of the country. During our time together we had many spirited discussions about theology. We talked about just about everything. Many of their arguments against "Mormonism" and their depiction of us as "non-Christian" I had heard a million times before. There was one thing, however, that one of the pastors said that I had never encountered before in any of my precious discussions with religious leaders of other denominations. As we were talking about the Book of Mormon, its origins, its stated purposes, its contents, and its unique doctrinal contributions, one of the Baptist ministers stated, "I have no real problem with what your Book of Mormon contains. In fact, I really like its teachings and its testimony of Christ. My problem is with how you say it came about. All that talk about angels, visions, gold plates, etc.—that is the problem!"

To say I was surprised by his comment would be a gross understatement. We had previously heard all kinds of criticisms of the Book of Mormon and the Prophet Joseph Smith, ranging from such things as how the book had been manufactured out of his vivid imagination to how he had been completely deceived by the devil—that the Book of Mormon and all of Joseph's revelations and teachings had originated "in the depths of hell." How is it possible to accept the teachings and reject the origin of that foundational book? You can't have it both ways—you cannot accept its message but deny the miracle of its coming forth.

Truly, the Book of Mormon is nothing less than a miracle of God upon the earth—"a marvelous work and a wonder." There was nothing ordinary in its genesis. It was engraved upon golden plates by ancient prophets. It was divinely preserved in the earth until an angel of God gave the record to Joseph Smith, who translated its antiquated and obscure engravings by the power of God and later declared it to be "the most correct of any book on earth" (*History of the Church* 4:461; see also introduction to the Book of Mormon). Some, like the evangelical pastors with whom I shared several days, scoff at the Prophet Joseph's account of ancient gold plates, heavenly messengers, and divinely aided translation, characterizing it as outrageous and unbelievable. Yet how else but with divine help could a barely literate, inexperienced young farm boy in his early twenties have translated such a record and have 5,000 copies of the first edition published, with most of the work occurring in the space of but only a few months?

Were the account of the origin of the Book of Mormon and the narrative of the book itself fabricated stories, they would surely have been disproved long ago. Yet the Book of Mormon withstands all attempts to disprove it or to lessen its inspiring effect on the people who gain a testimony of it. Why? Because it is true, and the story of its remarkable origin is true!

God did not, however, expect people to believe the words of Joseph Smith alone. The Lord Himself bore witness of the book's divine origin and sent others to so testify as well (see D&C 20:8–13). Though the Three Witnesses of the Book of Mormon each left the Church at some point (two eventually returned), they nevertheless stood by their testimony that they had indeed been shown the gold plates by an angel from God and had heard the Lord's voice out of heaven command them to bear witness of the truthfulness of the book. Amidst the persecution in Jackson County, Missouri, David Whitmer was accosted by an angry mob in 1833. Placing a loaded rifle next to Whitmer's chest, one of the mobsters told David that if he did not deny his testimony of the Book of Mormon he would be killed. If he would recant his testimony and repudiate the Book of Mormon, not only would his life be spared but the mob would allow him to retain his property and remain in the county. Much to the amazement of the mob, David Whitmer refused their offer, and raised his hands to the crowd and again declared his testimony of the divine origin of the Book of Mormon and its truthfulness. Even near the end of his life, after he had left the Church and when many expected him to recant his earlier testimony, he repeatedly reaffirmed that he had seen an angel of God, felt the gold plates with his own hands, and had heard with his own ears the voice of God declaring the truthfulness of that record. He often told his critics that he had not been deluded, nor was his experience a hallucination. "I saw with these eyes and I heard with these ears! I know whereof I speak." Regarding those who doubted his testimony he stated, "They will know someday that my testimony was true." (Cited in Milton V. Backman, Jr., *Eyewitness Accounts of the Restoration* [Salt Lake City: Deseret Book, 1986], pp. 135–40.)

Even Emma Smith, the Prophet's wife, eventually became estranged from the Church after it moved west, but she bore powerful testimony to the end of her life of the miraculous translation of the book and its divine authenticity. She noted that at the time the Book of Mormon was translated her young husband "could neither write nor dictate a coherent and well-worded letter; let alone dictating [composing] a book like the Book of Mormon" (as quoted in Joseph Smith III, "Last Testimony of

Sister Emma," *The Saints' Advocate*, October 1879, p. 51). Since that time, millions of others have borne witness of the book's spiritual nature, which touches their lives, and of the assurance of the Holy Ghost that the unusual, even extraordinary, account of its origin is indeed true.

Bishop LeGrand Richards recalled: "I heard Brother [Charles A.] Callis once say that when Joseph Smith received the plates he got down on his knees before the Lord, and said, 'O, God, what will the world say?' And the voice of God came to him, 'Fear not, I will cause the earth to testify of the truth of these things.'" (In Conference Report, October 1946, p. 125.) We see the Lord's promise being fulfilled almost daily. Ongoing scholarly study of the Book of Mormon continues to reveal the book's consistencies and bear witness of its veracity. Both external evidences, such as archeological discoveries, and internal evidences, such as linguistic, cultural, and doctrinal analyses, continue to testify of the book's own claim—that it has come to us through power from on high "by inspiration, and is confirmed to others by the ministering of angels, and is declared unto the world by them" (D&C 20:10).

No one on earth, regardless of how educated, has been able to produce such a remarkably consistent, intricate, and influential book. Dr. Hugh Nibley, one of the most renowned LDS scholars in the world, once proposed a test for any who would claim that the Book of Mormon is fictional narrative born of an overactive imagination of Joseph Smith. Focusing on the account of Lehi's journey from Jerusalem through the Arabian desert to the shore of an ocean, as recorded in 1 Nephi, he suggests that the skeptic

> sit down to write a history of life, let us say, in Tibet in the middle of the eleventh century A.D. Let him construct his story wholly on the basis of what he happens to know right now about Tibet in the eleventh century—that will fairly represent what was known about ancient Arabia in 1830, i.e., that there was such a place and that it was very mysterious and romantic. . . . But there will be other obstacles, for in your chronicle of old

Tibet we must insist that you scrupulously observe a number of annoying conditions: (1) you must never make any absurd, impossible or contradictory statement; (2) when you are finished, you must make no changes in the text—the first edition must stand forever; (3) you must give out that your "smooth narrative" is not fiction but true, nay, sacred history; (4) you must invite the ablest orientalists to examine the text with care, and strive diligently to see that your book gets into the hands of all those most eager and most competent to expose every flaw in it. The "author" of the Book of Mormon observes all these terrifying rules most scrupulously. (*Lehi in the Desert/The World of the Jaredites/There Were Jaredites*, vol. 5 of *The Collected Works of Hugh Nibley* [Salt Lake City: Deseret Book and F.A.R.M.S., 1988], p. 119.)

Every individual who seriously considers the Book of Mormon must confront the extraordinary account of its origins. No one has yet found a truthful or even sensible argument that could expose it as a fictional work of man. There simply is no other explanation—the Book of Mormon came from God.

DEPTH, BREADTH, AND CLARITY OF DOCTRINE

The Book of Mormon offers ample internal evidence of its divine origins. It is truly a "marvelous work and a wonder" because of the remarkable consistency of its history, characters, and cultural details, but, more important, because of the brilliant light it sheds on the basic doctrines of the gospel and the plan of salvation. Some of these "plain and precious" doctrines are missing or only superficially treated in the Bible (see 1 Nephi 13:34). We would probably not even realize that they are superficially treated if it weren't for the Book of Mormon. We would struggle on with the limited understanding, confusion, and uncertainty that sometimes beset those who rely solely on the Bible for doctrine.

The Prophet Joseph Smith was informed that this sacred volume of scripture "contains a record of a fallen people, and the fulness of the gospel of Jesus Christ to the Gentiles and to the Jews also" (D&C 20:9; see also Joseph Smith—History 1:34). Although the Book of Mormon does not contain all gospel teachings or practices of The Church of Jesus Christ of Latter-day Saints, it clearly and unmistakably proclaims again and again the fulness of the gospel—the saving power of the atonement of Jesus Christ and of the fundamental principles and ordinances that will enable every person who espouses them to return to the presence of God. A thoughtful reading of the book makes clear what is required in order to "come unto Christ, and be perfected in him" (Moroni 10:32). Yet it is much, much more than a gospel principles and practices manual. Within its pages, prophet after prophet testifies of the profoundness of the Creation, the Fall, and the Atonement of Jesus Christ—"the three pillars of eternity," as Elder Bruce R. McConkie called them (see *A New Witness for the Articles of Faith* [Salt Lake City: Deseret Book, 1985], p. 81). These prophetic testimonies open to our view an eternal destiny described with more clarity than that found in the Bible.

Other important principles and ordinances of the gospel are clarified as well. The book's teachings on faith, repentance, baptism, enduring to the end, the sacrament, the gift of the Holy Ghost, the plan of salvation, the universal resurrection, and the judgment of God are doctrinal diamonds. Elder Bruce R. McConkie challenged those who would question the breadth and depth of the Book of Mormon's doctrinal teachings:

> Let every person make a list of from one hundred to two hundred doctrinal subjects, making a conscious effort to cover the whole field of gospel knowledge. . . .
>
> Then write each subject on a blank piece of paper. Divide the paper into two columns; at the top of one, write "Book of Mormon," and at the top of the other, "Bible."
>
> Then start with the first verse and phrase of the Book of Mormon, and continuing verse by verse and thought by thought, put the substance of each verse under its proper heading. Find the same doctrine in the Old and New Testaments, and place it in the parallel columns.

Ponder the truths you learn, and it will not be long before you know that Lehi and Jacob excel Paul in teaching the Atonement; that Alma's sermons on faith and on being born again surpass anything in the Bible; that Nephi makes a better exposition of the scattering and gathering of Israel than do Isaiah, Jeremiah, and Ezekiel combined; that Mormon's words about faith, hope, and charity have a clarity, a breadth, and a power of expression that even Paul did not attain; and so on and so on. ("What Think Ye of the Book of Mormon?" *Ensign*, November 1983, p. 73.)

Conversely, one might make a list of the doctrinal misunderstanding and shortness of sight that would plague us without the Book of Mormon. We need not look far to see the confusion over the path to salvation that has resulted in Christianity because many plain and precious truths of the gospel were lost from the Bible (see 1 Nephi 13:19–29). As William W. Phelps, an early convert to the Church, testified: "The book of Mormon, is just what it was when it first came forth—a revelation from the Lord. The knowledge it contains is desirable; the doctrine it teaches is from the blessed Savior; its precepts are good; its principles righteous; its judgments just; its style simple, and its language plain: so that a way-faring man, though a fool, need not err therein." ("Letter No. 10," *Latter Day Saints' Messenger and Advocate*, September 1835, p. 178.)

"KEYSTONE OF OUR RELIGION"

Today there are many people in the world who express admiration for the Church's teachings and its influence on its members. They appreciate the Church's emphasis on family issues and even sometimes adopt some of our programs and activities for use in their own churches or organizations. Yet these same people are usually very troubled over the Book of Mormon—feeling they could never believe in a book based on what they see as spurious claims as to angels, gold plates, and mystical translation powers. Nevertheless, the Prophet Joseph

Smith testified that the Book of Mormon is not simply one aspect of our faith, but the very "keystone of our religion"— the stone that holds together and strengthens the overarching system of beliefs. The doctrines, teachings, and virtues of our faith rise and fall with that one book. If it is false, all else is false; a corrupt tree cannot bring forth good fruit (see Matthew 7:18). "Take away the Book of Mormon and the revelations, and where is our religion? We have none," the Prophet Joseph declared. (*History of the Church* 2:52.)

One could not logically embrace the ethics and Christian sociality and virtues of a church that is based on an outrageous lie and contrived doctrines. Enemies understand that the doctrines and practices of the Latter-day Saints are based upon the unique nature—its origin and its teachings—of the Book of Mormon. "This is why they go to such great lengths to try to disprove the Book of Mormon," said President Ezra Taft Benson, "for if it can be discredited, the Prophet Joseph Smith goes with it. So does our claim to priesthood keys, and revelation, and the restored Church. But in like manner, if the Book of Mormon be true—and millions have now testified that they have the witness of the Spirit that it is indeed true—then one must accept the claims of the Restoration and all that accompanies it." (*A Witness and a Warning* [Salt Lake City: Deseret Book, 1988], p. 19.)

Indeed, this witness borne by the millions who have received it is another affirmation that the Book of Mormon is the keystone of our faith. The very strength and essence of the Church stems from individual, as well as institutional, testimony of that book. This testimony binds us together like the stonemason's keystone, which can hold together an entire arch without cement or mortar. A very literal endowment of strength comes into one's life by reading, pondering, and praying about the Book of Mormon. Correspondingly, the more power the Book of Mormon infuses into the lives of individual members of the Church, the greater power it suffuses into the Church as a whole. This is the ongoing miracle of that divine book. We can never outgrow it. It continues to define us as a people collectively and as followers of Christ individually. The Book of Mormon is truly "the keystone of our religion" when it comes to our doctrines, our testimony of the Restoration, and our witness of the divinity of Jesus Christ and the reality of His resurrection (see Ezra Taft Benson, "The Book of Mormon—Keystone of Our Religion," *Ensign*, November 1986, pp. 4–7).

WITNESS OF THE DIVINITY OF JESUS CHRIST AND THE TRUTHFULNESS OF THE BIBLE

The Book of Mormon: Another Testament of Jesus Christ, is perhaps more important now than ever before as atheists, scoffers, secularly oriented historians, and even so-called Christian scholars and religionists attempt systematically to discredit the events of the Bible and dismantle the divinity of Christ. Some self-professed Bible scholars, for example, quibble with accounts of the Resurrection. A major news magazine recently reported:

> Of the dozens of recent books denying the resurrection stories, many are written by liberal scholars who think the time has come to replace the "cultic" Jesus of Christian worship with the "real" Jesus unearthed by academic research. Theirs is not disinterested historical investigation but scholarship with a frankly missionary purpose: by reconstructing the life of Jesus they hope to show that belief in the bodily resurrection of Jesus is a burden to the Christian faith and deflects attention from his role as social reformer. (Kenneth L. Woodward, "Rethinking the Resurrection," *Newsweek*, 8 April 1996, p. 62.)

Along these same lines, a major cable network recently broadcast a documentary entitled, "From Jesus to Christ." The primary thrust of the program was to show that virtually all of what we have recorded in the New Testament, especially the accounts of miracles, did not come from Jesus, but many, many years later as Christian disciples created the "myth" of Jesus as the divine Son of God. This "Jesus Seminar" of scholars suggests that Jesus never declared Himself divine, but rather, later disciples created the story of His divinity, His miracles, and His ultimate resurrection.

Unfortunately, the skepticism of these so-called scholars seems also to plague much of the clergy and membership of mainline Christian denominations who profess a belief in the Bible. Because of their doubts regarding the "miraculous" of the Christ story many have made their religion more of a socioethical movement than a literal means to eternal salvation. And even many conservative Christians—those who claim belief in the inerrancy and historicity of the Bible—are unsure. A survey conducted by an evangelical Christian organization, the Barna Research Group, found that "30 percent of 'born again' Christians do not believe that Jesus 'came back to physical life after he was crucified'" (Woodward, "Rethinking the Resurrection," p. 62). I read in an academic journal a few years ago an article by a fairly prominent Catholic priest who postulated that the account of Jesus' resurrection was not to be taken literally, but rather should be viewed as nothing more than a psychological near-death experience.

There seem to be precious few (relatively speaking) willing to declare the divinity of Jesus Christ and the authenticity of the biblical record. The Book of Mormon bears testimony with absolute certainty that Jesus was and is the Messiah, the literal Son of the Almighty God, who took our sins upon Him, broke the bands of death, and lives as a resurrected, glorified Being in the heavenly realm. While some scholars question the biblical testimony of these realities, there is no room for argument when it comes to the Book of Mormon's declaration—Jesus is the very Christ! Not only does the Book of Mormon stand as a powerful second witness of the Resurrection of Jesus Christ, but it also bears witness of the biblical record—as modern revelation declares: "proving to the world that the holy scriptures [the Bible] are true, and that God does inspire men and call them to his holy work in this age and generation, as well as in generations of old" (D&C 20:11). As one new convert to the Church discovered, belief in the Bible can be renewed and strengthened through study and acceptance of the Book of Mormon.

For me the experience [of gaining a testimony of the Book of Mormon] was exhilarating because I was able to bring my intellect to bear without reservation, and the book stood up to it. It is hard to express how exciting it was to be able to work with a religious document one could trust and be fed by. The previous model I had from the Bible was a group of embarrassed scholars and teachers trying to explain what was myth and what was symbolic truth in the Bible. I am and will remain eternally grateful to those people who wrote that record so that we might have the benefit of it. And as the Book of Mormon predicted, my confidence in it spread to a new confidence and trust in the Bible. Thus one book gave me two. (Dustin H. Heuston, in *Converted to Christ Through the Book of Mormon*, ed. Eugene England [Salt Lake City: Deseret Book, 1989], p. 108.)

How ironic it is that many uninformed critics speak of Latter-day Saints as non-Christian, often claiming our belief in the Book of Mormon as evidence. The Book of Mormon unquestionably praises our Savior and clearly sets Him forth as what He is—literally "the Son of God, the Father of heaven and earth, the Creator of all things from the beginning" (Mosiah 3:8). He came to earth, miraculously born of a divine Father and a mortal mother. He not only taught those things attributed to Him by the great writers of the Gospels in the Old World, but, as the Book of Mormon testifies, He taught many of them again in the New World. Not only did his great miracles and healings actually happen in the Holy Land, but many were repeated in the Americas. While hundreds witnessed His resurrected body in the Old World, thousands bore record of it on the American continent (see 3 Nephi 17:25).

Though many Christians today may be uncertain about who and what Jesus of Nazareth really is, the Book of Mormon leaves not a shade of doubt that He has "ascended into heaven, having the bowels of mercy; being filled with compassion towards the children of men; standing betwixt them and justice; having broken the bands of death, taken upon himself their iniquity and their transgressions, having redeemed them, and satisfied the demands of justice" (Mosiah 15:9). His arms are open to us. He invites us to partake of His salvation—if we will but repent and come unto Him. This is the essential message and witness of the Book of Mormon—truly another testament of the divinity of Jesus Christ.

The very title page declares that the Book of Mormon was written for the "convincing of the Jew and Gentile that JESUS is the CHRIST, the ETERNAL GOD, manifesting himself unto all nations." The book's pages are replete with expositions and explanations about the Savior's merciful plan of salvation. Its pages are filled with testimonies and grateful declarations that He is indeed the Son of God, the only name and means under heaven "whereby salvation can come unto the children of men" (Mosiah 3:17). Those who are touched by these remarkable testimonies in the Book of Mormon can then add their witness to that of Nephi: "We talk of Christ, we rejoice in Christ, we preach of Christ, we prophesy of Christ . . . , that our children may know to what source [we] may look for a remission of [our] sins" (2 Nephi 25:26).

There are many modern-day pioneers whose lives have been dramatically transformed by the power of the Book of Mormon—by its inspiring examples, its doctrines, and most of all, its testimony of the Son of God. When these people's lives have been so powerfully affected by that remarkable book, they are willing to sacrifice whatever is necessary to abide by its teachings. One such member, representative of thousands of others who could be cited, is Paull Hobom Shin. Because of the great example of an American soldier he met during the Korean War, the young Korean was doggedly determined to discover what made this Latter-day Saint military man so different from the other American GIs he had encountered. The Korean youth suspected the difference had something to do with the book his soldier friend was always reading. This LDS American soldier had given this young Korean an English copy of that book that he was always reading—the Book of Mormon. "Despite the fact that I could not read English," Paull recalled, "I admired [the soldier] so much I determined to read the book at all costs."

I took a quick ABC lesson from a fellow Korean, purchased an English-Korean dictionary, and started to read. I would read one word in the Book of Mormon, then I would refer to the dictionary for the meaning. I would write each word and its meaning down in a notebook. When I finished one sentence, I would try to translate the meaning with my own comprehension. At that time, we were not allowed light in the combat zone, so each night, even in sweltering heat of the Korean summer, I would cover myself with a blanket to block out the light and read the Book of Mormon with a flashlight. It took me seven months to read the book once completely through.

When I finished that first time, I did not really understand what I had read. Mostly I had only connected with the continual war stories. I asked [the soldier] how he had found the meaning of life in a book of unending war stories. He replied that perhaps I had missed the real point of the book and had better read it again! Because I could feel its importance to him, and I wanted to be like [him], during the next three years I read the book five times, trying to penetrate its depth with my limited language and life experience. Each time I read I understood at a different, deeper level. Finally, the fifth time, I caught the vision of Christ's mission and His love for all people. (In *Converted to Christ Through the Book of Mormon*, p. 71.)

The Book of Mormon is indeed a most remarkable volume because of its divine origin, its sacred and profound teachings, and its direct testimony of the Savior. But there is a power associated with the book that is greater than the sum of all these things, a witness that leaves its mark indelibly on the souls of all who will read it and ask to know its truth "with a sincere heart, with real intent, having faith in Christ" (Moroni 10:4). That power is the witness of the Holy Ghost that the book is true. That power not only convinces and converts, but transforms lives. Throughout the world millions of Latter-day Saints are living testimonies of that transforming power. Like modern pioneers, they boldly testify in word and deed, by their expressions of faith and their examples of righteousness. Their voices and lives bear witness—along with the Prophet Joseph Smith, the Three Witnesses, Jacob Hamblin, thousands upon thousands who have spent their lives in the cause of righteousness, including our modern prophets and Apostles—of the truthfulness of this most remarkable book of books, the Book of Mormon. The influence felt by their testimonies continues to touch hearts and motivate men and women around the world to put Moroni's promise to the test, which in turn leads them to the spiritual transformation the Book of Mormon offers.

One such is my friend, Joel Temple, president of the Wilmington Delaware Stake. This good man, who prior to his call as stake president served as the stake patriarch and had previously served as a bishop, has been able to raise his family under the influence of the gospel of Jesus Christ, to introduce the gospel to many others, and has influenced thousands through his service in the kingdom, all because of the transforming power of the Book of Mormon. I am inspired by his testimony and his example. "When the missionaries came to our door I had been looking for something stable in life for quite awhile," President Temple recalled. "But I could not find the comfort I was looking for in the writings of the world's great philosophers or in the teachings of other religions."

> So I was sort of happy to sit with these young men and listen to their story and perhaps debate philosophy or religion with them and see what would happen. I remember telling them as soon as they came in, "Now, we're not interested in the Church at all, and don't intend to change our religion (even though we didn't really have a religion), but you are welcome to come and we'd like to hear what you have to say." And with that I sat down in my chair and lit up a cigar, took a sip of scotch and water, and blew a cloud of smoke in their direction. As they taught us the first discussion, I knew what the answers were that they were looking for, but I would say things like, "I know what the answer should be, but I don't believe in prophets" or "I don't believe in angels or that sort of thing." They were frustrated with me, to say the least.
>
> After a week or two of that, my wife, Mary Jane, looked over some of the pamphlets and the Book of Mormon that the

Elders left with us. "You should really read some of this," she said, holding up the Book of Mormon. "No, no thank you," I replied. But at the next missionary discussion when Elder Duerden, a brand new "greenie," bore his testimony of the truthfulness of what we were being taught, I knew he really believed what he was saying. And I knew he was not trying to "pull the wool over my eyes." Therefore, I decided to look at the Book of Mormon and give it a chance.

I had a long weekend off from work, so I went up into one of the upper rooms of our house to be alone and to begin reading the Book of Mormon—reading mainly to find errors and prove that it wasn't true. But as I went through the book, I was impressed with the way the words sounded and that there was a certain spirit in it. I had a difficult time with some of the parts of First and Second Nephi. When I hit the Isaiah chapters, it was like hitting a sand bar, so I sort of leaped through those chapters and got to different parts. As I came to Second Nephi chapter 3—Joseph's prophecies about a latter-day prophet named Joseph who would also be named after his father, I thought to myself, "Well, I've got him now! Nobody would be stupid enough to put that kind of nonsense in a book except a fraud and fake." But I continued to read. Alma chapter 32 made a lot of sense to me. I began to "experiment upon the word," as Alma called it. I began to pray about the Book of Mormon. I read and prayed and read some more and prayed some more. Over a period of three or four days I read continually and prayed more than I had in the last ten years of my life. I was deeply moved by the writings of Moroni. My heart was especially touched by the 27th verse of the 10th chapter of Moroni where he describes us standing before the bar of God, who says to us, "Did I not declare my words unto you which were written by this man?" The thought occurred to me very strongly at that time—What if this book is really true? Do I want to be standing before the bar of God and realize that I had missed my opportunity to become a member of the only true and living church upon the earth? Therefore, I prayed more earnestly and received a witness that I should become a member of the Church and that the Book of Mormon was true—a reality which had to be dealt with. I continued reading and praying for many hours—into the wee hours of the early morning. As I left my study to go back to the bedroom, I fell and broke the banister of the stairs. I was so weak from my experience that I just lay there on the floor. My worried wife came rushing out of the bedroom to see what had happened and saw me lying in a heap on the floor. "Honey, the Book of Mormon is true!" I said to her. "I'm going to join the Church."

A day or two later when the missionaries came to see us, I met them at the door and said, "I want to be baptized." You can imagine the amazement and bewilderment over this guy who had been blowing smoke in their faces only a week before now asking to be baptized. I was so filled with the Spirit that I wanted to be baptized right at that moment. I felt they should fill up the font and baptize me right then and there. I didn't want to wait another moment.

"But Brother Temple, You have got to be interviewed and we have to teach you about the other commandments," the missionaries told me.

When we arrived at the church for my baptism a few days later and while I was getting dressed in my baptismal clothes, the missionaries were worried that I wasn't ready. "We haven't taught you about tithing yet," one of the Elders said.

"I don't care about that!" I responded.

"But its ten percent of your income," he said.

And I responded with, "It doesn't matter how much it is. The Book of Mormon is true and this is the Lord's Church and I'm going to join it!" So that is the way it was and I was baptized. . . .

The Book of Mormon is the word of God. I am certain of that—emotionally, intellectually, and most of all, spiritually. The spirit of that book is the most powerful voice and witness for Christ that exists on earth today. (Excerpt from oral history transcript, taped on 5 April 1997, Salt Lake City, Utah; in possession of author.)

Although I haven't had a singular spiritual experience that dramatically confirmed to my soul the truthfulness of the Book of Mormon like President Temple or Paull Hobom Shin or Parley P. Pratt or numerous others, I do, nonetheless, know with all my heart of its divinity. I have read that remarkable book scores of times. Each time my testimony is reaffirmed, my understanding of the gospel enlarged, and my desire to live its principles intensified. The Spirit of the Lord has confirmed to me again and again that the Book of Mormon was written for our day—written for me. I add my witness to those who have gone before— the Book of Mormon is truly the word of God, the "keystone of our religion," the book that can change lives for the better more than any other book on earth. I testify that I know that God lives and that His Only Begotten Son is Jesus Christ, who lived, died, was resurrected, and lives today. I bear witness that Joseph Smith was truly a prophet of God—the Prophet of the dispensation of the fulness of times. He was empowered from on high to bring forth the Book of Mormon and the restoration of the gospel in its fulness. There is no doubt in my mind that he established the kingdom of God on earth today—"the only true and living Church upon the face of the earth"—The Church of Jesus Christ of Latter-day Saints. How grateful I am for that knowledge and the assurance I have in my mind and in my heart that we are led by living prophets today. All of these things I know of a surety *because I know the Book of Mormon is true!* My life has been enriched, blessed, directed—transformed by the "power of the word."

To any who may doubt the Book of Mormon's veracity, may I invite you to do as was said to those ancient disciples who doubted that Jesus could be the Messiah—"Come and see." If you will feast upon the words of Christ contained in this remarkable book, you will not only come to know in your head and heart of its truthfulness, but your life will be changed forever. That is a promise!

Without reservation I promise you that if you will prayerfully read the Book of Mormon, regardless of how many times you previously have read it, there will come into your hearts an added measure of the Spirit of the Lord. There will come a

strengthened resolution to walk in obedience to his commandments, and there will come a stronger testimony of the living
reality of the Son of God. (Gordon B. Hinckley, "The Power
of the Book of Mormon," *Ensign*, June 1988, p. 6.)

INDEX